Babies and Bosses: Reconciling Work and Family Life

Canada, Finland, Sweden
and the United Kingdom

Volume 4

OECD

ORGANISATION FOR ECONOMIC CO-OPERATION AND DEVELOPMENT

ORGANISATION FOR ECONOMIC CO-OPERATION AND DEVELOPMENT

The OECD is a unique forum where the governments of 30 democracies work together to address the economic, social and environmental challenges of globalisation. The OECD is also at the forefront of efforts to understand and to help governments respond to new developments and concerns, such as corporate governance, the information economy and the challenges of an ageing population. The Organisation provides a setting where governments can compare policy experiences, seek answers to common problems, identify good practice and work to co-ordinate domestic and international policies.

The OECD member countries are: Australia, Austria, Belgium, Canada, the Czech Republic, Denmark, Finland, France, Germany, Greece, Hungary, Iceland, Ireland, Italy, Japan, Korea, Luxembourg, Mexico, the Netherlands, New Zealand, Norway, Poland, Portugal, the Slovak Republic, Spain, Sweden, Switzerland, Turkey, the United Kingdom and the United States. The Commission of the European Communities takes part in the work of the OECD.

OECD Publishing disseminates widely the results of the Organisation's statistics gathering and research on economic, social and environmental issues, as well as the conventions, guidelines and standards agreed by its members.

This work is published on the responsibility of the Secretary-General of the OECD. The opinions expressed and arguments employed herein do not necessarily reflect the official views of the Organisation or of the governments of its member countries.

Publié en français sous le titre :
Bébés et employeurs : Comment réconcilier travail et vie de famille
Canada, Finlande, Suède et Royaume-Uni – Volume 4

Foreword

The reconciliation of work and family life directly involves two goals that are important both to individuals and societies: the ability to participate fully in the labour market, generating income but also seeking fulfilment in one of the most important social activities of modern life, and to provide the best for one's own children, giving them the care and nurturing they need. These aspirations need not be mutually exclusive.

Family-friendly policies help parents, and potential parents, to match their care commitments for young children with their preferred labour market outcomes. Family-friendly policies including improved access to affordable and quality childcare, arrangements to take leave to care for children, flexibility in workplace arrangements, financial incentives to work, and, employment support for jobless parents, provide a key to better employment opportunities for families with young children. As such, family-friendly policies help both fathers and mothers to simultaneously increase the living standards of the family, fulfil individual aspirations to have both a career and a family, and give their children the care and support they need.

This fourth OECD review of the reconciliation of work and family life analyses how the existing mix of policies, including tax/benefit policies, childcare policy and employment and workplace practices, contributes to different parental labour market outcomes and and other societal outcomes in Canada, in particular the province of Québec, Finland, Sweden, and the United Kingdom. The review is based on visits to the four countries that took place in March, April and May 2004, and the analysis concerns the situation at that time. The report was prepared by Willem Adema (Project Manager), Anaïs Loizillon, Elina Pylkkänen, and Olivier Thevenon, assisted by Maxime Ladaique (Statistician), and Elma Lopes, under the overall supervision of the Head of the Social Policy Division, Mark Pearson.

Table of Contents

List of Charts

ISBN 92-64-00928-0
Babies and Bosses: Reconciling Work and Family Life
Canada, Finland, Sweden and the United Kingdom
© OECD 2005

Chapter 1

Main Findings and Policy Recommendations

This chapter presents the main findings and policy recommendations of the review of work and family reconciliation policies in Canada, in particular the province of Québec, Finland, Sweden and the United Kingdom. After introducing the key issues under review, the first chapter presents a list of policy recommendations for individual countries and jurisdictions. The chapter summarises key labour market outcomes and succinctly captures how workplace practices, childcare policy and tax/benefit policy affect the behaviour of parents who are trying to find their preferred balance of work and family commitments.

1.1. Introduction to the review of work and reconciliation policies

Many people manage to achieve their preferred work-family balance. However, there are many others who find it very difficult. Some people therefore do not have children or not as many as otherwise desired, while some parents have the number of children they desire, but by taking time out to provide personal care to their children risk compromising their career. As long as there are people who are somehow constrained in their work-family balance, the result may be both too few babies and too little employment or that the charge they take on has a long-term effect on the well-being of the family.

Among parents, there are those who have enough resources to be able to afford to choose the work-family balance of their liking. In line with their preferences, some parents choose to work full-time and buy formal childcare for their children, while other parents prefer to provide full-time personal care to their children, at least until school-age, regardless of the employment opportunities open to them. Many parents are, however, constrained in their choices. Some working parents would like to reduce hours at work to spend more time with their children but either cannot afford this or workplace practices do not allow them to. Yet other parents, who are at home, would like to be in paid work, or work more hours to generate more family income, but cannot because they have limited access to affordable childcare for sufficient hours, or have difficulties resuming their careers after childbirth. The issue is critical for children as both poverty and a lack of personal attention can significantly harm child development. Finding a good work-family balance thus enhances child development and helps parents to realise their labour market and family aspirations. Furthermore, a better reconciliation of work and family life reduces stress and health risks, thereby strengthening parent-child and parent-parent relationships.

Public policy in all countries aims to enhance well-being of both parents and children, and therefore strives to increase choice for parents in finding their preferred work and family outcomes by reducing barriers to both parenting (e.g. through time-related support) and employment (e.g. through childcare support). However, governments have many other reasons to invest in family-friendly policies (Box 1.1), and policy has to strike a balance between different objectives, including enhancing equity between different income groups, family types, and men and women; promoting child development;

Box 1.1. **What are family-friendly policies?**

Family-friendly policies are those policies that facilitate the reconciliation of work and family life by ensuring the adequacy of family resources, enhance child development, facilitate parental choice about work and care, and promote gender equality in employment opportunities. Family-friendly policies include improved access to affordable and quality childcare, financial support to children, arrangements that allow working parents to take leave to care for children, and flexible workplace practices that allow a better reconciliation of work and care commitments. They also include financial incentives to work for families with children and, employment support for jobless parents.

For the purpose of the review, "work" is defined to encompass all *paid* work (employment and self-employment), while "families" and "reconciliation" policies are defined as follows:

Families: "Each household of one or more adults living together with, and taking responsibility for the care and rearing of one or more children".

Reconciliation policies: "All those measures that extend both family resources (income, services and time for parenting) and parental labour market attachment".

underpinning economic growth and ensuring future labour supply; and, supporting the financial sustainability of social protection systems. Although these objectives often reinforce each other, there can be some tension between them, which complicates policy development. For example, a short period of paid parental leave allows parents to earn and care simultaneously, without it harming employment and future earnings. By contrast, prolonged periods out of work facilitate providing personal care for children, but put at risk family resources and, thus, child development, as well as parents' ability to achieve their labour market potential and personal well-being.

The need for policy change also depends on existing societal outcomes. If these are unacceptable, for example, in terms of the number of children living in poverty, then policy may wish to stimulate more parents to be in paid work. Or, if current use of parental leave arrangements is unsatisfactory from a gender equity perspective, policy might consider introducing periods for exclusive use by fathers.

Given the importance of these different objectives and given as well the wide-ranging potential consequences of work-life conflict, it is not surprising that many countries have made considerable investments in family-friendly polices. Others are starting to do so, overcoming more traditional policy reflexes that caution against direct intervention in family matters and industrial relations. This *Babies and Bosses* review brings together two groups of such countries: Finland and Sweden who started to invest in family – friendly policies in the late 1960s/early 1970s, and Canada (and in particular the province of Québec) and the United Kingdom where widespread public work-family reconciliation support is a much more recent feature.

At first sight, parental labour market outcomes in the four countries do not seem to reflect these different histories in policy development. All four labour markets are doing well in generating female employment: at least three out of four women in the age-group 25-54 are in employment. On closer inspection, female and maternal labour outcomes are very different in terms of if, where, and under what conditions women and mothers work. In particular, there are substantial cross-country differences in regular maternal working hours. Full-time jobs are the norm in Canada, Finland and Sweden, whereas part-time jobs are very common in the United Kingdom. The nature of employment contracts differ and are often of a temporary nature in Sweden, and in particular in Finland. The duration of the periods of income support during leave after childbirth also varies considerably, being particularly long in Finland.

This chapter starts by presenting policy recommendations for individual countries and jurisdictions building on existing family-friendly policy measures. There are fewer such recommendations for Sweden and Finland than for Canada and the United Kingdom (Box 1.2). This should be no surprise: Sweden and Finland introduced many family policies before Canada and the United Kingdom, and have long embraced the ideal of having a continuum of supports for parents until children are in their teens. The model involves flexible use of paid parental leave entitlements: affordable high quality childcare and extensive out-of-school hours care in Sweden, and entitlements to reduce working hours for parents with young children. The main negative consequence of having such a general approach is expense (as reflected in high tax-to-GDP ratios). The model is not directly "exportable" to other OECD countries unless they embrace similarly high spending (OECD, 2002, 2003, and 2004).

The remainder of this chapter summarises the main findings of the review. Chapter 2 outlines the socio-economic context in the four countries under review, while Chapter 3 presents parental labour market outcomes and trends. The subsequent three chapters try to relate the differences in parental family and labour market outcomes to differences in childcare policy (Chapter 4), tax/benefit policies (Chapter 5), and time-related employment supports for working parents (Chapter 6).

Box 1.2. **Family-friendly policy recommendations for Canada, Finland, Sweden and the United Kingdom**

Canada (with a particular focus on the province of Québec)

Increase government childcare support (including out-of-school-hours care services) to ensure that a broader group of Canadians have access to affordable good quality childcare. Ideally, funding should follow parental choices, and use could be made of a mixture of financing tools. Recognizing the current absence of a pan-Canadian childcare system, direct subsidies should be made towards capital investment, providers in deprived and/or scarcely populated areas, or concerning the provision of services to children with special needs. In addition, earmarked support (or vouchers) could be awarded to parents in order to improve: efficiency through competition; and, choice in terms of providers and types of care, including out-of-school-hours care. Further, in order for a voucher system to contribute to quality care provision, vouchers should be linked to licensed providers only. Through income-testing and (partial) linkage of entitlements to working hours, employment objectives can be pursued while scarce resources are targeted at those most in need.

In contrast to the rest of Canada, parents who wish to use childcare in the province of Québec already have access to public childcare support. However, low-income families cannot always access the CAD 7 per day childcare places. Extension of childcare capacity is underway: it should be priority to ensure access to childcare facilities for all low-income families who wish to use it.

To reduce long-term and intergenerational benefit dependency and child poverty, extend employment supports (financial incentives to work, case management, work-experience places, training, and childcare) for sole parents on social assistance support in the province of Québec, while retaining the current work-test for clients with children. Current caseloads of social assistance clients per case manager are too high for employment counseling to be effective and should be reduced initially to around 1 staff member to 100 to 125 clients.

Federal and provincial governments can enhance the family-friendly nature of workplaces, for example, through the introduction of subsidies to employers for participating in assessment processes that give enterprises advice on family-friendly measures tailored to workplace needs. Ensure long-term commitment of enterprises to family-friendly policies through regular re-assessment of workplace practices.

To give employers due notice on the return of their employees, consider increasing the notice period for those on parental leave to approximately two months.

> Box 1.2. **Family-friendly policy recommendations for Canada, Finland, Sweden and the United Kingdom** (cont.)
>
> **Finland**
>
> The simultaneous provision of a childcare guarantee and Home Care Allowance payments to parents who do not use municipal childcare support, increases choice to parents with children not yet 3 years of age. However, given the level (some municipalities provide additional payments) and duration of payments, it is no surprise that many parents of very young children, usually mothers, are not in paid work. This reduces female earnings profiles and hampers the pursuit of gender equity objectives. Moreover, the system of Home Care Allowances holds back labour supply growth, while projections point to emerging labour supply concerns. For these reasons, policy should consider reform options limiting benefit payments and/or duration.
>
> To contribute to the long-term financial viability of the childcare system, maintain where possible, the role of family day-care services as such services are less costly than centre-based care services.
>
> Explore opportunities to extend out-of-school-hours care entitlements to children aged 9-10.
>
> To encourage part-time work, reform the current partial care payments for parents with children up to school age into a part-time work entitlement of two years, and use current funding to finance benefit payments during this period.
>
> **Sweden**
>
> To contribute to the long-term financial viability of the childcare system, maintain where possible, the role of family day-care services, as such services are less costly than centre-based care services.
>
> Take measures aimed at reducing the differences in the use of parental leave between men and women by, for example, granting a bonus to parents who equally share parental leave entitlements, increasing the duration of leave periods that are non-transferable between the parents, and/or increasing information to both parents about fathers' rights to parental leave.
>
> To give employers due notice on the return of their employees, consider increasing the notice period for parents on parental leave to approximately two months.

1.2. Key work and family outcomes

This review of work and family reconciliation policies brings together four countries with an above-average record in terms of female employment rates and relatively small gender employment gaps. For prime-age workers (age 25-54) in 2003, female employment rates were highest at 82% in Sweden,

Box 1.2. **Family-friendly policy recommendations for Canada, Finland, Sweden and the United Kingdom** *(cont.)*

United Kingdom

Ensure that integrated family support, including childcare delivered through children's centres, is accessible to all low-income families, and further increase public support on childcare, including reviewing, and when required, increasing the generosity of the childcare element of the Working Tax Credit so as to help more working low-income families buy quality childcare.

In line with government commitments, extend free nursery school services (*e.g.* to three hours per day) to reduce the cost of work to all parents, and ensure with local authorities that nursery schools are better integrated with different sources of care, *e.g.* day-care, playgroups, etc, on a local basis. Extend investment in out-of-school-hours care as planned, also by exploring options to make better use of existing education facilities for the provision of such care.

To reduce the risk of long-term benefit dependency and poverty among sole parents and their children a comprehensive strategy of active and early interventions in labour market re-integration is needed. To build such a system takes time, and the UK support strategy of mandatory Work Focussed Interviews (WFI), the New Deal for Lone Parents (NDLP), and integrated employment and benefit support (Jobcentre Plus) is still being rolled-out. Once employment and childcare support is available on a comprehensive basis, it would be reasonable to oblige sole parents on income support to make use of it. Further down the line, some form of compulsory work-related activity, beyond the Work Focused Interview, could be introduced.

Ensure more flexible delivery of childcare support through the Working Tax Credit for parents moving between jobs or when parents have been forced to reduce working hours to below 16 hours per week.

Extend existing initiatives that provide workplaces with tailored advice on family-friendly policy both in duration and the number of participating firms to build long-term enterprise commitment to family-friendly policies through regular re-assessment of a greater number of workplaces.

Give parents greater choice in their return-to-work decision, by allowing greater flexibility in taking leave payments, *e.g.* allow a parent to return to work after four months, possibly on a part-time basis, without loss of the overall entitlement. In line with announced plans, reform "maternity leave" into "parental leave" and give fathers the opportunity to share in the use of entitlements. This need not require additional spending.

For employees who extend maternity leave to 12 months, increase the notice period to approximately two months.

and were at 79%, 76% and 74% in Finland, Canada and the United Kingdom, respectively: well above the OECD average of 64%. The gender employment gap for prime-age workers is highest at 13% in the United Kingdom, followed by 10% in Canada, and only 3-4% in Finland and Sweden; in all four countries the gap is well below the OECD average of 23%.

These high prime-age female employment rates mask cross-country differences in labour market trends. Private service sector growth facilitated expansion of female employment since 1980 in both Canada and the United Kingdom. By contrast, the economic crisis that hit Finland and Sweden in the early 1990s led to a decline in female employment rates by about 12 percentage points, and rates in both countries have not recovered yet to their 1990 levels.

There are also considerable differences in the nature of maternal employment outcomes, in particular for mothers with young children. At 80%, employment rates for mothers with a child aged less than 3 are very high in Sweden, but this also reflects the long leave periods during which they are counted as employed, but are not in fact working. By contrast, not all British and Canadian mothers have access to long leave entitlements, and may not use them fully because of limited income support. Mothers in Finland with a child of the same age face strong financial incentives to provide personal care on a full-time basis (see below).

In 2003, more than 50% of all Swedish female employees work in the public sector and this was 40%, 32%, and 25% in Finland, the United Kingdom, and Canada, respectively. The crisis of the early 1990s, stringent employment-protection legislation and costs considerations have contributed to a greater use of temporary employment contracts for younger workers by local governments (who are responsible for health, education, social services, etc.) particularly, in Finland, where 44% of all female employees in their twenties have a temporary contract.

Women generally get paid less per hour than men, and although gender wage gaps are decreasing in Canada and the United Kingdom, they have not narrowed since the 1980s in Finland and Sweden. At *low earnings* levels, the gender wage gap is only 8% in Finland and Sweden, but at *high earnings* levels, gender wage gaps are above the OECD average (16%) in all four countries: about 19% in Canada and Sweden and 23-24% in Finland and the United Kingdom (Chapter 3). The large earnings gap at higher earnings levels, and the failure of gender wage gaps in Finland and Sweden to narrow over time, illustrates how difficult it seems for many women in these two countries to climb the career ladder. Gender wage gaps persist because of relatively precarious labour force status of women, and because mothers rather than fathers reduce working hours (or withdraw from the labour force) after childbirth.

Dual-earners in couple families are the norm in all four countries (Table 1.1). In Sweden, in 84% of couple families, both parents are in paid work, compared with two-thirds of all couple families in Finland, Canada and the United Kingdom. In 92% of dual-earner couples in Finland, both parents work full-time, and this pattern is also relatively high (75%) among working couples

Table 1.1. **Key indicators on employment, birth rates and public policy support**

	Canada	Province of Québec	Finland	Sweden	United Kingdom
Employment rate (2003)	72.1	69.9	67.4	74.3	72.9
Maternal employment rate (children age 0-3)[a]	58.7	61.1	52.1	71.9	49.2
of which part-time	30.4	23.1	..	37.0	61.6
Employment status of both parents (% of couples with children)[b]					
Both in full-time employment	44.6	48.2	58.9	39.4	28.3
One parent in full-time employment with the partner in part-time employment	19.2	15.5	5.0	39.1	36.3
One parent in employment	27.1	27.0	31.2	13.0	27.2
No parent in employment	6.1	6.4	4.8	2.9	5.6
Total fertility rate (2002)	1.52	1.46	1.72	1.65	1.64
Maximum duration of paid leave allocated to mother around childbirth (weeks)	50	–	156	60	26
Childcare coverage (0-2 year olds)[c]	15.2	34%	25%	65%	26%
Public spending on childcare (% of GDP)[d]	0.2%	0.8%	1.1%	2.0%	0.4%
Public spending on leave payments (% of GDP)[e]	0.24%	0.28%	0.62%	0.81%	0.11%
Public spending on child allowances (% of GDP)[f]	0.69%	..	1.02%	0.93%	0.90%

.. Not available.
– Not applicable.
a) For definitions, see notes to Table Box . Data for both rows concerns 2001 for Canada and Québec; 2002 for Finland and 2003 for Sweden and the United Kingdom. For Finland, part-time employment rate for all women is relatively low at 15%.
b) FT: Working full-time, at least 30 hours per week. PT: working part-time, less than 30 hours per week, except for Sweden where PT is less than 35 hours per week. Years of data: Canada and Québec, 2001; Finland and Sweden, 2002; United Kingdom, 2003.
c) Estimate for 0 to 6 year olds from Friendly, M., J. Beach and M. Turiano (2003), *Early Childhood Education and Care in Canada 2001*, Childcare Resource and Research Unit, University of Toronto, Toronto. Childcare coverage is for 1 to 2 year olds in Sweden. Figure for the United Kingdom concerns England; coverage in Scotland is 27%.
d) For national and provincial definitions, see notes to Table 4.4. Data is from 2001 for Sweden; 2002 for the province of Québec and Finland; and 2003 for the United Kingdom.
e) For national and provincial definitions, see notes to Table 6.1. Data is from 2001 for Sweden; 2002 for Canada, the province of Québec and Finland; and 2003 for the United Kingdom.
f) Child allowances in 2001 include: Child tax benefit in Canada, child allowances in Finland and Sweden, and child benefit in the United Kingdom.
Source: National authorities for data except where noted otherwise. For population, United Nations (2003), *World Population Prospects: The 2002 Revisions*, New York, *www.un.org/esa/population/unpop.htm*, and Statistics Canada for Québec 2001 census. For fertility rates, Eurostat, Demographic data, NewCronos database 2000 and Statistics Canada for Canada and the province of Québec.

in the province of Québec. By contrast, the most common type of working couple in the United Kingdom is the so-called "one-and-a-half-earner couple family", with mothers working part-time. In Sweden too, many mothers work less than 35 hours per week until their children enter primary school (Table 1.1). At almost 6% of all couple families, Sweden has the highest incidence of couples in which both partners work less than 35 hours per week. Sweden also has the best record in generating high employment rates among sole parents, 82% in 2002, with employment rates in Canada and Finland about 10 percentage points lower (but with more sole parents working full-time). Just over 54% of British sole parents are in paid work (half of them part-time). The change in employment outcomes among sole parents in the province of Québec has been most significant: an increase from 47% in 1981 to 68% in 2001.

Total Fertility Rates (TFR) are around 1.7 children per mother in Finland, Sweden and the United Kingdom, and 1.5 in Canada (1.4 in Québec). TFRs appear most volatile in Sweden where they fell from replacement level in 1990 to 1.5 in the late 1990s, before increasing again. In part these trends are explained by general economic developments: birth rates are higher when economic prospects are good. TFRs are also under pressure because family formation is often being deferred, until parents have completed more years of education and they are more securely established in their careers, which has become an issue in Sweden, and particularly Finland with the increase of temporary employment among young women (see above). A continuous model of employment and family support, as exists in Sweden, probably helps to sustain birth rates, and Swedish fertility rates hold up well in international comparison. Available evidence for Sweden on individual fertility decisions shows that combining a career with motherhood are not widely regarded as mutually exclusive activities: the proportion of childless women in Sweden with a university degree is low at 15%, compared with 25% for Finland (directly comparable information is not available for Canada and the United Kingdom).

With declining marriage rates and increasing divorce rates the incidence of sole-parent families has increased in all four countries. Fewer marriages are taking place than in the past particularly in the province of Québec and Sweden, where an estimated 32% and 47% of the population gets married (Chapter 2). The ratio of divorces to marriages in 2001 was highest in Sweden (59 out of 100 marriages), and 23% of Swedish children live in sole-parent families (this is 21-22% in Canada, the province of Québec and the United Kingdom) compared with 17% in Finland. In Finland and Sweden, the mean age of first marriage is about one year above the mean age of first childbirth, while in Canada and the United Kingdom women generally first marry and then have children. In the province of Québec, where the incidence of marriage is relatively low, 58% of all births are to unwed mothers. Teenage motherhood is relatively rare in the province of Québec, Finland and Sweden where this concerns about 12, 11 and 7 births per 1 000 births while teenage fertility is about two and three times as high in Canada as a whole and the United Kingdom respectively.

1.3. The family-friendly policy stance

Social and family policies have recently had a strong employment focus in all four countries, even though the individual policy approaches are very different. In Finland and Sweden, social policy objectives are pursued through a universal welfare system, which supports all throughout the life course, while in Canada and the United Kingdom social policy has traditionally been more targeted at low-income groups. These differences in approach are reflected in cross – country differences in public social spending which is highest at 29% of GDP in Sweden, and amounts to 25%, 22%, and 18% in Finland, the United Kingdom and Canada, respectively, and mirrored in a high tax burden in Sweden at 50% of GDP compared to 46% in Finland, and 38% in Canada and the United Kingdom. The design and scope of social and family policies thus differ greatly across the four countries, and so does the likelihood that parents choose one work and family reconciliation solution over another, even though the avowed policy objective in all four countries is to support parents so they have a real choice in their work and care decisions.

Both Finland and Sweden have relatively homogenous populations: they are cohesive and equitable societies, where policy development closely involves employers and unions who are also involved in social protection delivery (unionisation rates are over 70%, and collective agreements cover around 90% of employees). The pursuit of gender and other equity objectives has played an important role in policy development, and there is a strong local government tradition, in whose ability to deliver social services there is a high degree of trust. This contributes to the willingness among the populace to sustain the high tax burdens in both countries.

Despite some significant differences, both Finnish and Swedish policy models provide *a continuum of support* to parents with children. From childbirth through to primary school, policy supports parents on a continuous basis, so that they can both engage in full-time work *and* spend time with their children. Paid parental-leave periods allow parents to look after their children during the first phase of childhood, while subsidised childcare and, in particular in Sweden, out-of-school-hours care facilitate full-time employment until children enter their teens. Parents in Sweden also have the option to reduce working hours by 25% and/or take parental leave in patches until the child is 8 years of age. In both countries, policies aim to create an environment in which parents can realistically plan combining their care and career commitments without interruption.

Family-formation issues are still widely considered as beyond the scope of public concern in the United Kingdom. However, great political significance is attached to tackling child poverty, and enhancing child development. Other policy objectives such as promoting female employment and gender equity, for example, are seen as instrumental in achieving this aim, but they are not the principal objectives of policy. Very substantial childcare subsidies have been put in place since 1997 to reduce barriers to work for mothers, while at the same time income-tested tax credits for children have been expanded to address poverty more directly. These efforts have been complemented by the *Sure Start* programme initiating the development of family services (including childcare) in relatively deprived areas, and the Working Tax Credit includes childcare assistance for working low-income families (see below). A free early education offer in nursery schools for 3 and 4 year olds (for 2.5 hours per day) is aimed at *all* children to strengthen child development, but also to reduce the cost of childcare to all parents.

The general pattern of Canadian social policy has also evolved from a narrow focus on low-income families to encompass broad parental employment and child development concerns. Responsibility for family policy is shared between the federal and provincial/territorial governments. Historically, the federal government has tended to focus on income support measures, while provinces and territories have the primary responsibility of providing welfare assistance to families and in designing and delivering a broad range of programmes and services, including family services. There is thus a considerable variety of policy objectives and the nature of support programmes across the country. Federal policy plays a key role through co-financing of provincial social and family support programmes via the Canadian Social Transfer, while the introduction of the national Child Care Tax Benefit (CCTB) improved the income position of families. The recently extended paid parental leave entitlement is available through the federal Employment Insurance programme; as from 1 January 2006, residents in Québec will have access to maternity and parental leave benefits under the Québec parental insurance programme. Working with the provinces/territories and building on the existing 2000 Early Childhood Development Agreement and the 2003 Multilateral Framework on Early Learning and Childcare the Government of Canada is also taking a leadership role in the development of childcare capacity and improving access among Canadians: federal authorities are planning to spend additional funding of CAD 5 billion over the next five years.

In contrast to some other provinces, family and childcare policy development in Québec has a strong focus on both supporting working parents and child development. Since 1997, an extensive network of subsidised childcare places has been developed, emulating to some extent the Scandinavian family-support policy models. However, as in the rest of Canada and the United Kingdom, concerns about public budgets and tax burdens limit the scope for public family-friendly policy support.

1.4. Childcare policy

Female employment growth preceded the development of public childcare support in all four countries. Initially, female employment growth relies on care by relatives, neighbours and friends, but as they are increasingly likely to be in work themselves, that source of care dries up. Female employment rates were around 55% in Sweden and 60% in Finland in the late 1960s, when formal childcare development was initiated (early 1970s in Finland), which helped female employment rates to reach 80 to 90% in the late 1980s. In Canada and the United Kingdom, female employment rates of around 55-60% were reached in the late 1980s and are currently just above 65%.

Both in the province of Québec and the UK public spending on childcare has more than doubled since the late 1990s to 0.8% GDP in the province of Québec, and 0.4% of GDP in the United Kingdom. The long-established municipal childcare systems in Nordic countries are more costly: 1.1% of GDP in Finland and 2% of GDP in Sweden. Public childcare support reduces barriers to employment, but also serves other policy objectives as promoting gender equity and child development. The different stages of policy development contribute to national debates emphasising different aspects of childcare policy: the listing below reflects these different flavours, but is not mutually exclusive, as, for example, quality issues play a role in all four countries.

Improving quality in Sweden: During its expansion the Swedish childcare system evolved from a "care to facilitate parents working" system to an "early education and care system", in which childcare services, known as pre-schools in Sweden, have become an integral part of the education system with its own curriculum. The ongoing childcare debate focuses on further improvement of the already high level of quality and "professionalisation" of childcare workers. Given the large public subsidy towards childcare costs, it is difficult to improve efficiency in use of the system through price signals: *e.g.* introducing a fee structure by the hour of use (as exists in half of the municipalities) makes little difference to the overall parental contribution, and thus has a limited impact on marginal childcare use decisions. Maintaining, where possible, the role of less costly family day-care could contribute to the long-run financial sustainability of system and provide a wider variety of options for parents to choose from.

Balancing choice objectives with concerns on labour supply, gender equity and family resources in Finland. Finland is the only country under review where parents of all young children up to school age have guaranteed access to a subsidised childcare place (even at night if work schedules so require). At the same time, parents who do not use these day-care facilities are entitled to a Home Care Allowance payment. Including both a childcare guarantee (taking away a major barrier to employment) and payments to parents of young children (addressing barriers to providing full-time personal care) increases choice to parents.

However, the current system tilts the balance between the options towards mothers choosing to stay at home. The existing Home Care Allowance payments generate very strong financial disincentives to engage in paid work, particularly when, as for about a quarter of all recipients, municipalities make additional payments to parents who do not use formal childcare. With central government covering 30% of spending on both the Home Care Allowance and a childcare place, and the former costing less than half of the latter, municipalities have a very strong incentive to discourage parents with young children from using childcare. This explains why most of the larger municipalities (including Helsinki) provide additional incentives to parents not to use childcare by paying an *additional* municipal "home care payment": in Helsinki this is worth about EUR 2 600 per annum. The strong financial incentives embodied in the system of Home Care allowances (see below) result in only just over half of the Finish mothers of very young children being in employment (compared to over 70% in Sweden) and a proportion of 2-year olds in formal childcare of around 44% in Finland, compared to 85% in Sweden. These outcomes raise gender equity concerns, while demographic trends point to a need to increase female labour supply: the system of Home Care Allowances needs to be reformed to address these challenges.

Building childcare in Canada. In many Canadian provinces public childcare support is limited and childcare coverage is patchy. In addition to federal/ provincial/territorial initiatives as the Early Childhood Development Agreement and the Multilateral Framework on Early Learning and Child Care, a further increase in federal spending on childcare has been announced to come into effect from 2005/06 onwards (see above). Ideally, funding follows parental choice and use could be made of a mix of financing tools. For example, there could be direct subsidies to providers towards capital investment, providers in deprived and/or scarcely populated areas or those who provide services to children with special needs. In addition, earmarked childcare (and out-of-school-hours care) support could also be directly awarded to parents. The certainty that public childcare support is available to parents helps attract private providers into the market. Funding parents does not favour one provider over another, improves efficiency in delivery through competition and gives parents more choice in type of care and provider. However, such funding should be strictly tied to providers adhering to pre-set quality standards (*e.g.* rules on the number of certified staff among personnel, staff-to-child ratios, but also on parental involvement in childcare provision, etc.). Demand-side support for childcare can be made income-tested to achieve an equitable allocation of public resources, and, when linked to working hours, to pursue employment policy objectives.

Compared to the rest of Canada, childcare policy in the province of Québec is much more developed: 40% of Canadian childcare capacity is in this province, while Québec's very young children account for only 22% of the Canadian total. Policy in Québec opted to develop childcare capacity through increasing subsidised places (often provided by NGOs) charging flat-rate fees, CAD 7 per day since January 2004. In this system of subsidised places, public funding covers more than 80% of the childcare costs. However, access to such subsidised childcare places is not universal, and they are allocated on a "first-come, first-serve" basis. As parents in relatively rich households seem to be either more assertive and/or have better access to information, their children are much more likely to use a subsidised place than children in poorer income groups. For parents without access to a subsidised place, there is a federal tax credit and a refundable provincial tax credit. However, for low and medium income families such support is often not worth as much as a subsidised childcare place (Chapter 5). Ongoing efforts are underway to extend childcare capacity in Québec; it should be priority to ensure access to childcare for all those low-income families who wish to use it.

Expanding childcare in the United Kingdom. Since the 1997/98 launch of the National Childcare Strategy, UK policy has increased public support for childcare through a combination of means. Providers have been encouraged to increase supply of childcare facilities through direct subsidies and seed funding of private providers in disadvantaged areas (which too often close down after start-up funds run out, as business plans were based on unrealistic expectations about demand or over-optimistic cost assumptions). Earmarked childcare support for working parents is provided through the tax system. The *Sure Start* initiative is a centrepiece of UK anti-poverty policy with its aim of improving the health and well-being of families and children; it is targeted at the most disadvantaged parts of England (the Scottish approach is slightly different, Chapter 4). However, subsequent reforms have brought together responsibility for childcare and early-years services in England under a broad "Sure Start" umbrella, and subsequently "Children's Centre" programmes, initiating the development of expanded and integrated family support services, including childcare, with the aim for all parents and children to have access to one of the 3 500 centres in 2010 (HM Treasury, 2004). Working with their partners through "Children's Trusts", local authorities will be responsible

;uring there is sufficient local childcare provision, building on their ᴄurrent responsibility to ensure delivery of the free early education offer in nursery schools for all 3 and 4-year-olds of 12.5 hours per week for 33 weeks per year.

Because the "free early education offer" in the United Kingdom only covers two and a half hours per day (though it will be gradually extended to 15 hours per week for 38 weeks per annum), parents often have to supplement such care with informal and/or market care. This contributes to the widely-reported phenomenon of parents having complicated work-life schedules, as they arrange to transport children from one source of care to another, a particular burden when care and schooling hours differ among siblings. There may well be parents who decide that the organisational challenges involved are such that it is not worth the hassle to try and find (full-time) employment, until their children are at least in the same primary school. This underscores the importance of childcare facilities being more conveniently located. The UK government aims to guarantee all parents of 3 and 4 year olds childcare linked to the early education offer that will be available all year round from 8 a.m. to 6 p.m. (Chapter 4).

The need for an expansion in childcare provision in the United Kingdom is based on a belief that lack of affordable childcare is a constraint on taking paid work. Recent UK policy reform extended financial support from 180 000 working low and middle-income households in 2002 to some 317 000 families by April 2004. However, because support is available to those in work only, it is cut almost immediately when parents in the household no longer work 16 hours per week, e.g. in case of job loss. For low-income families, the childcare element in the Working Tax Credit (WTC) covers up to 70% of the childcare costs (to be extended to 80% in 2006, Chapter 5), which nevertheless can imply significant out-of-pocket expense where low-income families face high childcare costs. This contributes to many such families continuing to use cheap informal care arrangements.

Surveys also report that location and reputation of providers, the quality of their facilities and the suitability of hours are important factors in determining the limited use of formal childcare. Parents need to be provided with more information on the range of childcare services available in their area. Children's Information Services do fulfil this particular function. Quality assurance systems need to be more broadly applied to give parents confidence to use the system, as only 40% of providers are currently accredited to quality assurance schemes. A new regulatory framework and inspection regime is to be in place in 2008, while reform of the qualification structure of childcare workers is being undertaken to raise workforce-quality, while local childminders and home-based care workers will increasingly be able to access quality support services provided by local Children's Centres. In the past, many British parents cared for children themselves or used informal care because the formal care system was widely regarded as expensive or did not have a good reputation. Policy is increasing access to and affordability and quality of formal childcare and past attitudes towards using formal childcare will change, but not overnight.

Out-of-school-hours care services (OSH) provided at school-facilities or elsewhere are key in helping parents combine their family and (full-time) work commitments when children get older. The absence of such services contributes to the existence of so-called "latch-key kids". There is evidence that such children are at greater risk of behavioural problems. OSH-care services are relatively cheap: for example, costs per child amount to one-third of the cost in day-care in Sweden.

The comprehensive Swedish family-friendly policy model involves OSH-care which covers about 80% of all 6, 7 and 8 years olds, while the Québécois system is estimated to serve about 80% of existing demand. The key to success for both systems has been the integration of the management of these services with that of primary schools. In Finland, municipalities are revitalising OSH-care services for 7 and 8-year-olds at school, after cutbacks in the early 1990s, while in the UK out-of-school-hours-care (OSH-care) has only recently emerged as a new policy priority. By 2010, UK policy aims to provide all parents of 5-11 year olds to have access to OSH-care services from 8 a.m. to 6 p.m., either at school or elsewhere with supervised transfer arrangements.

1.5. Giving parents the opportunity to engage in paid work

Average tax rates on family income equivalent to 133% of average earnings* are highest in Finland and Sweden at just below 30%, and lowest at about 20% in the United Kingdom and the province of Québec (where the degree of progressivity in income taxation is highest). At first sight, work thus seems to pay for all parents, but in fact this can vary with the age of child, replacement income support, spousal earnings and/or household status, and especially in the United Kingdom, hours of work and access to subsidised or informal childcare.

Finnish policy offers parents with a child not yet 3 years old a choice (see above): they can either exercise their right to affordable municipal day-care or receive a payment for not using this service, and, generally, provide parental care on a full-time basis. Parents with a very young child in Helsinki who do not use municipal day-care will receive transfers worth about

---

* "Average earnings" refer to the annual earnings of an employee in the manufacturing sector. In 2004, these were USD 34 358 per annum (CAD 41 574) in Canada, USD 29 966 (EUR 29 779) in Finland, USD 26 313 (SEK 254 544) in Sweden and USD 33 210 (GBP 21 359) in the United Kingdom.

EUR 520 per month (parents who do not use childcare do not have to pay childcare fees which saves about EUR 120 per month), equivalent to 35% of net average income. The associated income effect leads about two-thirds of mothers with very young children to stay at home until the child turns 3 years of age. Policy reduces effective female labour supply, which is at odds with the avowed policy objective to raise the female employment rate to 70% by 2010.

In view of widespread childcare support, work generally pays for second earners in couple families in Finland (for parents with children at least 3 years of age), Sweden (upon expiry of paid leave) and the province of Québec. On average, parental fees in Sweden amount to about 11% of childcare costs (down from 19% in 2001; maximum fees were introduced in 2002) compared with about 16% in Finland and 19% in the province of Québec; by contrast, estimates of the average parental share in childcare costs in the United Kingdom range from 45 to 75%.

Parents with access to subsidised childcare in Finland, Sweden and the province of Québec have therefore very strong financial incentives to choose to be in paid work. Parents in Canada can claim a deduction from income for childcare expenses through the federal tax system, but without additional support from provincial authorities (as in Québec) work often pays far less. Because of their general mobility and the vastness of the country, Canadians are likely to be far removed from their family networks, and informal care may be difficult to arrange. Nearly 40% of full-time dual-earner couples with children in Canada are organised such that parents work and care in shifts.

The policy approach towards sole parents in Finland and Sweden is the same as for any other parent: parents who are no longer entitled to parental leave are work – tested for benefit receipt. Most provincial authorities in Canada require sole parents on income support to look for work as from an early age (varying from six months to six years) of their youngest child: in the province of Québec, sole parents on income support are exempt from job-search until their youngest child is 5. The United Kingdom is the only country in this review without a work-test in the income support system for sole parents, and it is no coincidence that it has a much lower employment rate among this group (see above). UK policy has started gently to push sole parents into getting back to work. Tax credits to make work attractive have had a significant impact and contributed to the increase of sole parent employment rates from 45% in 1997 to 54% in 2004 (Chapter 5). Mandatory interviews for sole parents on income support have been introduced, and job search and childcare assistance is made available through the New Deal for Lone Parents, that is based on voluntary participation.

It is in the long term interest of sole parent families to engage in paid work, as this is the most effective way of reducing family poverty and so help child development. Reducing the risk of long-term benefit dependency and poverty among sole parents and their children requires active and early interventions in labour market re-integration. Such a strategy involves investment in employment supports (e.g. intensive case-management, training programmes, work-experience placements, job-search assistance and childcare support), and the UK version of such a system including the mandatory Work-Focussed Interviews, the New Deal for Lone Parents and fully integrated benefit and employment support services through Jobcentre Plus, is being rolled out. When comprehensive employment and childcare supports are available for all sole parents on income support, then it seems justified to oblige these clients to take advantage of the opportunities open to them. Further down the line, some form of compulsory work-related activity in the United Kingdom, beyond the Work-Focused Interview, could be introduced. Abolishing administrative sanctioning as is being considered in the province of Québec (where there are few new clients), is not advisable, as it sends the wrong policy signal to new clients, and may be taken to mean a limited commitment to employment support on the part of public authorities. Indeed, for many of the existing (long-term) income support clients, in both the United Kingdom and the province of Québec, additional medium-term investment in skills upgrading is necessary before a work-test can be meaningfully applied.

1.6. Making workplaces more attractive to parents

Collective agreements cover about 90% of the employees in Finland and Sweden. Working parents in Canada and the United Kingdom rely to a much greater extent on support made available in individual workplaces. UK policy has moved, however, since the late 1990s, and now encourages greater partnership among unions and employers. In Canada, a review of the federal labour code is underway, and this opportunity should be used to encourage greater workplace family-friendliness.

The design of time-related support measures for parents around childbirth differs markedly in the countries under review. In Finland and Sweden, employment-protected leave with relatively high replacement rates (in Finland particularly so during the first 10 months of combined maternity and parental leave) is an integral part of the family-friendly policy model that provides support from birth until young adolescence. By contrast, in Canada and the United Kingdom, income support during leave is relatively limited in amount and duration (legislation and reimbursement procedures for employers also seem unnecessarily complicated in the United Kingdom, Chapter 6).

Mothers in paid work in Finland and Canada (also in the province of Québec) are most likely to work full time, around 38 to 40 hours. Helped by a right to reduce working hours until children go to school, almost half the mothers in Swedish dual-earner couple families work less than 35 hours per week, while mothers in the United Kingdom are most likely to work part-time, i.e. less than 30 hours per week. Finnish parents are entitled to reduce their working hours until their children enter third grade (age 9) in school, but this option is hardly used, although there is small payment for parents who do so, until their child turns 3 or during the first two years in school. Indeed, part-time employment options are the most frequently offered and used form of family-friendly workplace flexibility measures in all countries in this review except Finland. Rather than reducing hours, British men work long hours, and almost one-third of fathers work more than 48 hours a week, although the incidence of long hours has declined somewhat since 1998, when working time regulations were introduced that included an opt-out clause for long working hours. Nevertheless, the long-hours culture in the United Kingdom raises concerns about the time that fathers are able to spend with their children.

Flexible work schedules are much more likely to be used in Canada (especially among men) than in the United Kingdom. Other forms of flexible working arrangements (e.g., teleworking, compressed hours, temporarily reducing hours)remain quite rare in the United Kingdom, but a quarter of very large British workplaces (mostly in the public sector) offer term-time employment options to workers (Chapter 6). As noted above, parents in almost 40% of the full-time dual-earner couples in Canada often use atypical hours to synchronise their full-time work and care commitments. Atypical hours are also quite common in the United Kingdom, where a quarter of mothers work until between 5.30 p.m. to 8.30 p.m. several times per week, while night-shift work is twice as common in Finland and the United Kingdom than in Sweden.

There is a "business case" for family-friendly workplace support. Such support serves to motivate and retain the existing workforce and/or attract new staff, reduces workplace stress and enhances worker satisfaction and productivity. Companies that have introduced family-friendly measures have experienced significant reductions in staff turnover, recruitment and training costs, absenteeism, and have increased the likelihood that mothers return to work upon expiry of maternity leave (one firm reports an increase of 35%). However, hard evidence for this business case is difficult to find, as it is not easy to identify separately the exact effect of, say, introducing flexible work-hours schedules on worker performance and/or profits.

Directive legislation is not always effective in flexible labour markets with considerable resistance from small and medium-sized firms to any public intervention that increases labour costs. One way to overcome such opposition is to financially-support "consultancy" initiatives that provide tailored advice to companies, as happens in the United Kingdom. However, for such initiatives to be effective, they should include re-assessment after a year or so, to ensure long-term enterprise commitment. In addition, in 2003 British parents with children under age 6 were granted the legislated *right to request* flexible working hours (which includes reduced working hours). The burden of proof lies with the employer. Case law has yet to establish "how strong" the right to flexible working hours in the United Kingdom really is.

1.7. Promoting gender equity in employment opportunities

In all four countries, women spend more time providing care for children than men; they overwhelmingly take more parental leave then men, and they are most likely to reduce working hours after childbirth. Since husbands, on average, earn more than their spouses, they contribute most to family income: in Sweden, differences in male and female contributions to household income are smallest at about one-third of average male earnings.

Compared to Canada and the United Kingdom, there is a strong emphasis on gender equity concerns in policy development in both Finland and Sweden. On the other hand, women in Sweden and particularly Finland find it increasingly hard to find employment security before establishing a family. As discussed above, Finnish policy financially supports parents with very young children who do not use childcare, and this contributes to almost 50% of Finnish mothers with very young children not being in employment. Employers are understandably reluctant to hire someone who may take a leave of absence for three years. The long leave periods in Sweden also contribute to mothers being absent from work for about 2.5 years if leaves for two siblings are taken sequentially. This is unlikely to help career prospects. Swedish firms are all required to have gender equity plans, but they do not seem to be actively pursued, nor do they contribute to Swedish women getting through to management jobs. Canadian women seem to be doing somewhat better: women hold 38% of management jobs in Canada compared with 30-33% in Finland, Sweden and the United Kingdom. Compared to their Finnish and Swedish counterparts, Canadian women are less likely to be on leave, work in public and/or female-dominated sectors and be in non-managerial occupations and, compared to mothers in Sweden and especially the United Kingdom, they work full-time.

In order to reduce the penalty on women for taking leave, Finnish and Swedish policies try to get more fathers to take more parental leave by reserving some generously-paid weeks of leave exclusively for their use. These policies have had some little success as, for example, in Sweden the fathers' share of total parental leave days taken increased from 11% in 1994 to 17% in 2003. However, even this does not reflect a fundamental behavioural change, as mothers almost exclusively take long periods of leave; fathers generally take a few weeks around summer and Christmas holidays. Suggestions to increasing public income support during leave are also based on the argument that this increased generosity will increase the likelihood that fathers take leave. However, this reform is more likely to further increase the effective duration of leave among women, which may be counterproductive. Paternal attitudes are not the only issue, as mothers frequently seem reluctant to give up leave to their partner. A Swedish government committee is reviewing different aspects of the parental leave system, including considering different options to achieve a more gender equitable use of parental leave. In many countries, the debate about a more equal sharing of the care burden during the early months, has yet to start in earnest.

ISBN 92-64-00928-0
Babies and Bosses: Reconciling Work and Family Life
Canada, Finland, Sweden and the United Kingdom
© OECD 2005

Chapter 2

The Socio-economic Environment

Economic and demographic conditions are key factors in explaining policy action and reaction with regard to family/work reconciliation. This chapter looks at three areas that set the scene (and also the limits) for national policy developments: the macroeconomic environment; the demographic environment; and the policy setting in which work-family reconciliation policy development unfolds. The chapter illustrates that such circumstances differ markedly in Canada and the province of Québec, Finland, Sweden and the United Kingdom.

Economic conditions have a major effect on parental labour market outcomes and family-friendly policy development. Buoyant economies make it more likely that workers can find employment at their preferred hours, while the chances of employers offering family-friendly workplace measures in time of labour market slack are relatively limited. Demographic trends may add to future labour supply concerns, challenge the nature of existing social protection systems and, more generally, change the shape of future societies. This chapter illustrates the relevant differences between Canada and the province of Québec, Finland, Sweden and the United Kingdom in three key areas: macro-economic trends, the demographic context and the general social policy background.

2.1. The macro-economic context

Canada, Finland, Sweden and the United Kingdom are among the wealthiest countries in the OECD area. GDP per capita is well above OECD average and is highest in Canada at about 20% higher than the average (Table 2.1). The province of Québec contributes to about 21% of Canada's GDP. Employment rates exceed the OECD average in all four countries under review largely because of high female labour force participation, which in Finland and Sweden is concentrated in the sizeable public sector (Chapter 3).

The scope for public policy intervention appears to be largest in Sweden where general government outlays (broadly mirrored by government receipts) amount to almost 60% of GDP: this proportion is 50% in Finland and approximately 40% in Canada and the United Kingdom.[1] In 2003, the general government balance was in surplus in all four countries except the United Kingdom, where the deficit was projected to increase slightly with additional spending plans (OECD, 2004) including those on childcare (Chapter 4) and maternity leave (Chapter 6).

Thus far in the 21st century, economic growth in the four countries has been at least on par with the average for the OECD area. The Canadian economy, in line with the US experience,[2] and the UK economy, generated the highest average GDP growth rate of almost 2.5% per annum. As a result, British and Canadian labour market performances have been relatively strong, leading to employment rates of just over 72% in both countries, about 2 percentage points below the employment rate in Sweden and 5 percentage points above that in Finland (Table 2.1).[3] In fact, since 2000, the Canadian

Table 2.1. **Four wealthy OECD countries under review**
Main economic indicators, and selected annual growth rates, latest available year

	GDP	GDP per capita	GDP (real) Annual average growth rate	Average wage USD PPPs	Employment		Standardised unemployment rate (%)	Consumer prices (%)	General government outlays	General government receipts
	Million USD PPP	USD PPP			Percentage of working population	Annual average growth rate			Percentage of GDP	
	2002	2002	2000-2004[a]	2002	2003	2000-2004[a]	2003	2003	2003	2003
Canada	951 929	30 303	2.4	28 726	72.1	1.8	7.6	2.8	40.1	41.3
Province of Québec	198 355	26 640	2.4	..	69.9	2.0	9.2	2.5	..	..
Finland	137 713	26 478	1.9	23 419	67.6	0.3	9.0	1.3	50.6	52.7
Sweden	242 840	27 209	1.8	23 798	74.3	0.3	5.6	1.9	58.2	58.7
United Kingdom	1 656 383	27 976	2.3	25 595[a]	72.4	0.8	5.0	1.4	42.6	39.3
OECD	955 738	25 808	2.1	22 990	74.7	0.7	7.1	..	40.7	37.0

.. Not available.

PPP: Purchasing power parities.

a) 2003 instead of 2004 in the province of Québec.

Source: OECD analytical database; OECD (2004), *Main Economic Indicators*; Statistics Canada, CANSIM database.

economy appeared to be most successful in translating economic growth into employment gains.

Both in Canada and the United Kingdom, economic expansion facilitated steady female employment growth since the beginning of the 1990s (Chapter 3). By contrast, Sweden and particularly Finland went through a profound economic recession during the first part of the 1990s (Chart 2.1), which led to an employment shake-out from which both labour markets have not yet fully recovered (Chapter 3). As a result, the unemployment rate in Finland (9.0%)[4] was still well above OECD average in 2003 (Table 2.1). Unemployment rates are the lowest in Sweden (5.6%)[5] and the United Kingdom (5.0%), while Canada's unemployment rate at over 7% remains relatively high with a significant seasonal component (OECD, 2004b). The economic downturn in the early 1990s also changed the nature of employment relationships in Sweden, and particularly Finland: employers increasingly seek to enhance workforce flexibility by making greater use of fixed-term employment contracts (see below and Chapter 3).

Chart 2.1. **The economic downturn in the beginning of 1990s was particularly severe in Finland**

GDP in volume, 1990 to 2003, index 1990 = 100

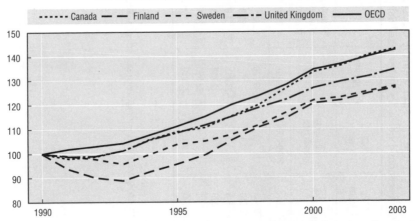

Source: OECD (2004), Economic Outlook, Vol. 2004/1, No. 75, June, OECD, Paris (www.oecd.org/eco/economic_outlook).

Concerns regarding labour productivity exist in all four countries (OECD, 2004d). Key drivers in this area are investment, competition and skills (OECD, 2003a). Compared to the other countries, the UK scores well in terms of deregulation and competition, but less so in terms of business and government sector investment (OECD, 2004e). In terms of skills, Finland seems well placed to face the future: when it comes to reading literacy, mathematics and science, Finland's 15 year-old students outperform their counterparts in other OECD countries (OECD, 2004b).

2.1.1. Income distribution and poverty

Countries with a strong egalitarian tradition, such as Finland and Sweden, have narrower income distributions than Canada and the United Kingdom (Chart 2.2).[6] Market incomes (earnings, self-employment income and capital earnings) are the main determinant of disparities in the income distribution. The relationship between employment growth and income disparity trends is not simple: income inequality seems to have increased with employment growth in all four countries since the mid-1990s, but this relationship does not always hold (as, for example, illustrated by the Canadian and Swedish experiences from the mid-1970s to mid-1980s).

Chart 2.2. **Income inequalities increased in all four countries since the mid-1990s**

Income inequality as measured by Gini coefficients,[a] mid-1970s, mid-1980s, mid-1990s and 2000

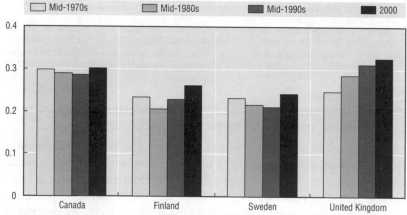

a) The income concept used is that of disposable household income, adjusted for household size (e = 0.5). Gini coefficient is a statistical measure that has a value of "0" if every person in the economy has the same amount of income, and "1" if one person had all the income, and everybody else had no income at all.

Source: Förster, M. and M. Mira d'Ercole (2005), "Income Distribution and Poverty in OECD Countries in the Second Half of the 1990s", Social, Employment and Migration Working Paper, No. 22, OECD, Paris.

In 2000, poverty rates, measured with respect to a threshold of 50% median income, were about half as high in Sweden and Finland at around 5% to 6% as in Canada and the United Kingdom (Chart 2.3). Recent trends, however, have narrowed the gap, as poverty rates in Finland and Sweden increased by about 1.5 percentage points during the second part of the 1990s,

Chart 2.3. **Poverty rates among jobless sole parent families are high, particularly in Canada**[a]

Poverty rates for the population, all households with children and sole parent families, 2000

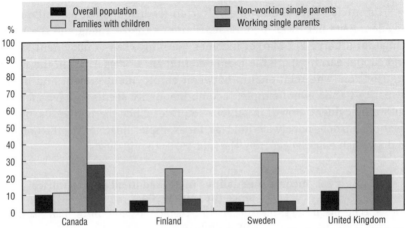

a) The income measure for relative poverty used here is 50% of the median "equivalised" disposable income of all individuals, where household disposable income is equivalised using the square root of household size. Date sources are: Canada, Survey of labour and Income Dynamics; Finland, Finnish Income Distribution Survey; Sweden, Income Distribution Survey; and the UK, Family Expenditure Survey. For full detail see Förster and Mira d'Ercole (2005), Annex I and Annex II.

Source: Förster, M. and M. Mira d'Ercole (2005), "Income Distribution and Poverty in OECD Countries in the Second Half of the 1990s", Social, Employment and Migration Working Paper, No. 22, OECD, Paris.

compared to increases of 0.8 and 0.5 percentage points in Canada and the United Kingdom, respectively (Förster and Mira d'Ercole, 2005)

Compared to households without children, families in Canada and the United Kingdom are more likely to live in poverty, while the opposite holds true in Finland and Sweden (Chart 2.3). In 2000, child poverty rates in Canada and the United Kingdom were quite close to the OECD average of one in eight children living in poverty (Förster and Mira d'Ercole, 2005). By contrast, the incidence of child poverty is particularly low in Finland and Sweden: child poverty rates were around 4% in 2000 (Chart 2.3). The poverty risk is high for children living in sole parent families where the parent is not engaged in paid work and the high proportion of sole parent households exacerbates the issue in the United Kingdom (see below).

Reducing poverty and, in particular child poverty, is high on the policy agenda in all countries, not least because poverty has a significant effect on child development (Kamerman et al., 2003). UK policy formulation is most explicit in setting quantified targets for reducing child poverty: it aims to halve the number of children living in low-income households by 2010 and eradicate child poverty by 2020. Other countries are less explicit in setting such targets (*e.g.*, Canadian policy "seeks to eliminate child poverty") or set intermediate goals such as reducing the number of social assistance recipients (Sweden) and increasing employment rates (both Finland and Sweden). Despite the differences in policy formulation, all four countries provide significant financial support to (working) parents to reduce the risk of child poverty (Chapter 5).

2.2. Demographic context

2.2.1. Populations

Of the four countries under review, Canada is by far the largest, covering almost 10 million square kilometres (the OECD covers 35 million km^2), and has the lowest population density with slightly more than three inhabitants per square kilometre. Moreover, about 85% of its 31.8 million inhabitants live within 300 kilometres of the US border. The province of Québec is the second largest province in Canada with about 7.5 million inhabitants. By European standards, Sweden is a large country (450 million km^2 and almost twice the size of the United Kingdom), but Nordic countries have relatively small populations; the United Kingdom is the most densely populated country in this review.

Table 2.2. **A considerable proportion of the Canadian population is foreign-born**

Main demographic indicators, in 2002

| | Total population | | Density | Percentage of total population | | | Foreign (-born) population[a] |
| | | | | Children | Working age | Elderly | |
	Millions	Net average annual increase over previous 10 years	Inhabitants per km^2	0-14	15-64	65+	
Canada	31.3	1.0	3	18	69	13	18.2
Province of Québec	7.5	0.5	5	17	70	14	9.4
Finland	5.2	0.4	15	18	67	15	2.0
Sweden	8.9	0.4	20	18	65	17	5.3
United Kingdom	59.1	0.3	247	19	65	16	4.5
OECD average	38.3	0.9	33	19	67	14	6.1

a) Foreign-born population in Canada; foreign population in Finland, Sweden and United Kingdom.
Source: OECD (2003b), *Trends in International Migration*, OECD, Paris; United Nations (2003), *World Population Prospects: The 2002 Revisions*, New York; Statistics Canada, CANSIM database.

In 2003, the relative proportion of population groups by age is not significantly different across Canada, Finland, Sweden and the United Kingdom. In all four countries, around two-thirds of the population is of working age (Table 2.2) and the proportion of senior citizens (ranging from 13% in Canada to 17% in Sweden) is almost as high as the proportion of children (18% to 19%). Foreigners make up around 5% of the population in Sweden and the United Kingdom, but only 2% in Finland.[7] About one-sixth of the Canadian population is foreign born and this only concerns 10% of the population in the province of Québec. Aboriginals constitute about 3% of the population in Canada.

Net population growth in the past decade was about 0.4% in Finland, Sweden and the United Kingdom and close to 1% in Canada, and between 1991 and 2001, averaged 0.5% in the province of Québec. This is largely because of relatively high immigration levels in Canada and the relatively small proportion of elderly people, which contributes to a relatively low mortality rate.[8] By 2020, however, it is expected that the share of elderly persons in British and Canadian populations will be similar (Chart 2.4).

Chart 2.4. **Finnish and Swedish populations will get old soon**

Population aged 65 and over, as a percentage of population aged 15-64

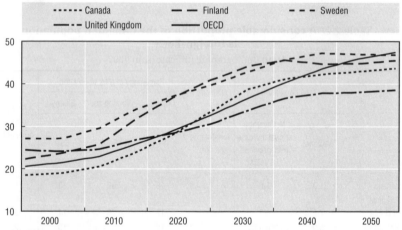

Source: United Nations (2003), *World Population Prospects: The 2002 Revisions*, New York (*www.un.org/esa/population/unpop.htm*).

The most rapid increase in the share of the elderly population is expected to materialise in Finland: by 10 percentage points starting in 2010. Already by 2035, there will be almost one senior citizen for each person of working age in Finland and Sweden. On the other hand, the British population will age at a steady and moderate pace (Chart 2.4). The demographic trends illustrate the increasing need for policies that foster a good work-life balance to ensure that future populations of working age can engage in paid work (Chapter 6).

2.2.2. Household and family structures

The prevailing notion of partnership between adults has changed. Fewer marriages are taking place than in the past (cohabitation is increasingly regarded as an alternative rather than a trial leading up to formal marriage), such that in the province of Québec and Sweden, respectively an estimated 32% and 47% of the population gets married (in the province of Québec, where the incidence of marriage is relatively low, 58% of all births are to unwed mothers). On the other hand separations and divorces are more common, so much so, that one in two marriages breaks up (Chart 2.5). On average, marriages last longest in Canada (14 years) while the average duration was 12, 10, and 8 years in Finland, Sweden and the United Kingdom, respectively, in 2000 (OECD, 2005).

Chart 2.5. **About one in two marriages breaks up**

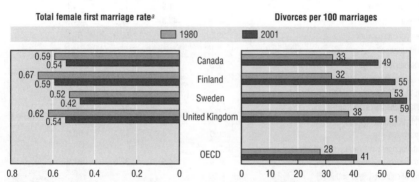

a) Total first marriage rate is the sum of age-specific first marriage rates, which is an estimate of the likelihood of getting married. Data for Canada are for 1986 and 1996.

Source: Eurostat, New Cronos database, Theme 3; Statistics Canada, Vital Statistics Compendium, 1996.

Changing family structures, ageing populations and shifting fertility patterns (see below) have led to a growing share of households without children, a decline in the average size of households and a decline in the proportion of couple families (Table 2.3). Most children still grow up in couple families, but the incidence of sole parent families has increased markedly: more than one in five children live in sole parent families in Canada (and in the province of Québec), Sweden and the United Kingdom, while this concerns one in six children in Finland.

Crucial to anti-poverty and family-friendly policy development is the fact that many children grow up in families where no parent is engaged in paid

Table 2.3. **Families are getting smaller**
Trends in households and family composition

	1980	1985	1990	1995	2000	2002
Canada[a]						
Average household size	2.9	2.8	2.7	2.6	..	2.6
Share of households in all households (percentages adding to 100%):						
Without children in all households	52.0	52.9	56.5	57.8	..	58.7
With youngest child aged 17 and over in all households	9.1	11.5	10.3	10.4	..	10.6
With youngest child aged under 17 in all households	39.0	35.6	33.3	31.8	..	30.6
Number of children (aged under 17)	7 243 050	6 832 025	6 955 635	7 304 100	..	6 488 160
Share of children living in (percentages adding to 100%):						
One-parent households	13.2	15.4	16.5	19.1	..	21.1
Two-parent households	86.8	84.6	83.5	80.9	..	78.9
Share of children in household (percentages adding to 100%):						
No parent in work	10.8	11.6	11.8	14.1	..	11.7
One parent in work	49.9	44.4	37.2	34.6	..	35.3
Both parents in work	39.3	44.1	50.9	51.3	..	53.1
Province of Québec[a]						
Average household size	2.9	2.7	2.6	2.5	..	2.4
Share of households in all households (percentages adding to 100%):						
Without children in all households	50.6	52.7	57.1	58.4	..	61.9
With youngest child aged 17 and over in all households	10.0	12.4	10.2	10.6	..	10.5
With youngest child aged under 17 in all households	39.4	34.9	32.8	31.0	..	27.5
Number of children (aged under 17)					..	
Share of children living in (percentages adding to 100%):						
One-parent households	13.4	16.7	17.6	20.1	..	22.4
Two-parent households	86.6	83.3	82.4	79.9	..	77.6
Share of children in household (percentages adding to 100%):						
No parent in work	15.5	15.6	13.8	16.0	..	12.2
One parent in work	52.7	46.3	39.8	36.7	..	35.7
Both parents in work	31.9	38.1	46.5	47.3	..	52.1

Table 2.3. **Families are getting smaller** (cont.)

Trends in households and family composition

	1980	1985	1990	1995	2000	2002
Finland						
Average household size	2.7	2.6	2.4	2.3	2.3	2.2
Share of households in all households (percentages adding to 100%):						
Without children in all households	..	53.3	58.4	61.8	65.0	66.6
With youngest child aged 17 and over in all households	..	12.0	10.4	9.1	8.5	8.0
With youngest child aged under 17 in all households	38.4	34.7	31.2	29.1	26.5	25.4
Number of children (aged under 17)	..	1 136 027	1 135 686	1 150 562	1 116 687	1 096 705
Share of children living in (percentages adding to 100%) with:						
One-parent households	..	10.1	11.2	14.5	16.4	16.7
Two-parent households	..	89.9	88.8	85.5	83.6	83.3
Share of children in household (percentages adding to 100%) with:						
No parent in work	..	4.4	4.7	12.9	9.6	..
One parent in work	..	31.1	30.0	37.5	33.4	..
Both parents in work	..	64.5	65.3	49.5	57.0	..
Sweden						
Average household size	..	..	..	..	2.6	2.5
Share of households in all households (percentages adding to 100%):						
Without children in all households	..	..	..	..	62.8	63.9
With youngest child aged 17 and over in all households	..	..	..	..	5.6	5.5
With youngest child aged under 17 in all households	..	..	..	..	31.6	30.6
Number of children (aged under 17)					1 937 015	1 934 762.0
Share of children living in (percentages adding to 100%):						
One-parent households	..	..	..	..	22.8	23.8
Two-parent households	..	..	..	..	77.2	76.2
Share of children in household (percentages adding to 100%) with:						
No parent in work	..	..	..	..	..	7.0
One parent in work	..	..	..	..	..	26.7
Both parents in work	..	..	..	..	..	66.3

Table 2.3. **Families are getting smaller** (*cont.*)

Trends in households and family composition

	1980	1985	1990	1995	2000	2002
United Kingdom						
Average household size	..	..	..	..	2.4	2.4
Share of households in all households (percentages adding to 100%):						
Without children in all households	..	..	..	..	69.8	70.1
With youngest child aged 16 and over in all households	..	..	..	..	2.4	2.7
With youngest child aged under 16 in all households	..	..	..	..	27.6	27.2
Number of children (aged under 16)	..	..	..	..	13 354 777	13 246 656
Share of children living in (percentages adding to 100%):						
One-parent households, children 15 yrs or younger	..	..	..	..	21.8	23.1
Two-parent households, children 15 yrs or younger	..	..	..	..	78.2	76.9
Share of children in household (percentages adding to 100%) with:						
No parent in work	..	..	..	..	18.3	18.5
One parent in work	..	..	..	..	32.6	33.6
Both parents in work	..	..	..	..	49.1	47.9

.. Not available.

a) In Canada, data from 1981, 1986, 1991, 1996 and 2001 census.

Source: Information supplied by national authorities.

employment (Chapter 5). Almost 19% of children in the United Kingdom live in such families compared to 12%, 11%, 10% and 7% in Canada, the province of Québec, Finland and Sweden, respectively (Table 2.3). About one-third of children live in single-earner families in Canada, the province of Québec, Finland and the United Kingdom, while the proportion of children living in a dual-earner family is highest in Sweden at 66%.

2.2.3. Family formation

Patterns of family formation are changing such that birth rate trends contributes to concerns about future labour supply and the financial sustainability of social protection systems. At an individual level, there is concern about to what extent parents are able to have as many children as they desire. Indeed, in all four countries, the number of children desired by young people is considerably above observed fertility levels. Since 1981, the average number of children desired in Canada, Finland, Sweden and the United Kingdom fluctuated around 2.5 children and averaged 2.1 children in the province of Québec, but birth rates are generally below two children per mother (Chart 2.6). In general, total fertility rates have stagnated below two children per

Chart 2.6. **Parents have fewer children than they desire**

Panel A. **Desired average number of children per women in 1981, 1990 and 2000 on the basis of survey responses**

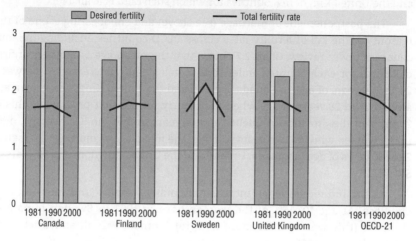

Panel B. **Completed fertility rates by year of birth of mother, 1930-1965, and total fertility rate, 1970-2002**

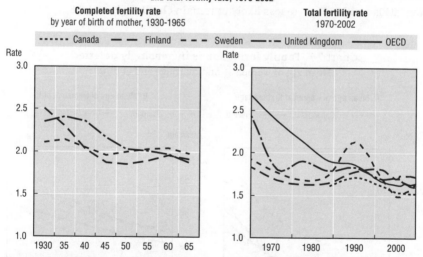

The completed fertility rate (CFR) measures the number of children that a cohort of women who have reached the end of their childbearing years had in the course of their reproductive life. The CFR is measured by cumulating age-specific fertility rates in a given cohort as they aged from 15 to 49 years.

The total fertility rate (TFR) in a specific year is the average number of children who would be born to a synthetic cohort of women whose age-specific birth rates were the same as those actually observed in the year in question.

Source: World Values Survey (1981, 1990, 2000); Eurobarometer (2001); OECD (2004), *Employment Outlook*, OECD, Paris; OECD (2005), *Society at a Glance: OECD Social Indicators*; Eurostat, New Cronos database, Theme 3; Canada: Statistics Canada.

woman since 1975 in all four countries under review. Completed fertility rates have fallen with the cohorts and, since the cohort of women born in 1950, the number of children born per woman has been below two in Finland, Sweden and the United Kingdom (countries for which such data is available).

The postponement of marriage (see above) and childbearing is one of the reasons for the fall of fertility rates across OECD countries, including the four countries under review. Chart 2.7 shows that the mean age of mothers at first childbirth for each country under review, has steadily increased to between 28 and 30 years of age. In Canada, Finland and the United Kingdom women are around 27 to 28 years of age when they marry for the first time, while this is 29 years in the province of Québec and 30 years in Sweden. On average, men marry women who are two years younger: the mean age of marriage for men is 29 to 30 years of age in Canada, Finland and the United Kingdom and 32 years in Sweden.

At the individual level, increasingly many women (and men) remain childless. At age 40, 15% of the women born in 1961 in Sweden remained childless (this was 25% for men) and, for Finnish, British and Québécois women born in 1960, this rate was 19%, 20% and 24%, respectively (data provided by national and provincial statistical offices, similar data is not available for Canada). Moreover, this proportion is increasing; women born in the 1940s and 1950s were less likely to remain childless (Chart 2.8).

Chart 2.7. **Family formation is increasingly deferred**

Mean age of women at first marriage and at birth

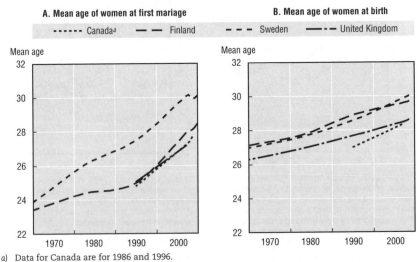

a) Data for Canada are for 1986 and 1996.

Source: Eurostat, New Cronos database, Theme 3; Statistics Canada (2004), Annual Demographic Statistics 2003, Ottawa.

Chart 2.8. **The proportion of childless women is increasing**

Proportion of childless women at age 40, born in different years, percentages

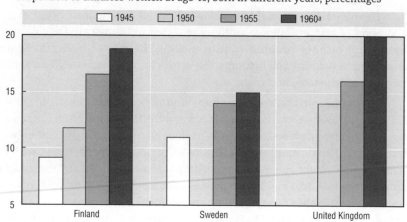

a) 1961 for Sweden.

Source: UK National Statistical Office, Statistics Finland and Statistics Sweden.

There appears to be a negative association between the number of children being born to a women and the level of maternal educational attainment: the average number of children born to a women with a high level of educational attainment in 2000 was close to 1.8 in Finland and Sweden and 1.7 in Canada, while for women with low levels of educational attainment this was greater than two children per woman in the same countries (D'Addio and Mira d'Ercole, 2005; directly comparable data for the United Kingdom is not available). Batljan (2001) finds that, while Swedish women with relatively low levels of educational attainment have always had more children on average, women born later than the 1960s and with relatively high education do not appear to have significantly less children.[9] This suggests that in Sweden at least, it seems more likely that women combine children and career opportunities than in the past (see below).

Canada, and especially the United Kingdom, have relatively high incidences of teenage motherhood with, respectively, 22 and almost 29 out of 1 000 children born to mothers in the 15 to 19 year age group. In comparison, teenage motherhood rates are much lower in the province of Québec, Finland and Sweden at 12, 11 and 7 births per 1 000 births to young mothers in the same age group, respectively. The relatively high incidence of teenage pregnancy (and often these young mothers are sole parents) has a significant negative effect on the socio-economic status of such mothers and their children (Kamerman et al., 2003), even though these effects may be associated with disadvantages built up prior to the pregnancy (low educational attainment) or limited hours work (because of sole motherhood) rather than because of teen pregnancy (Kaplan et al., 2004).

2.2.4. Is being in paid work more or less compatible with motherhood than before?

The old-fashioned male breadwinner model was defined by an explicit allocation of responsibilities: mothers provided full-time care for children at home and fathers secured family income. In this framework, female employment usually was incompatible with caring for children and fertility rates remained stable and high.

Female labour market aspirations and opportunities changed, first in Finland and Sweden, and later in Canada and the United Kingdom (Chapter 3). Not only did female labour market behaviour change, so did the link between fertility and female employment. In the 1970s and 1980s, countries with low female employment rates had higher fertility rates, but this relationship no longer holds (D'Addio and Mira d'Ercole, 2005; Sleebos, 2003): at present OECD countries with higher rates of female employment also tend to have relatively high fertility rates (Chart 2.9, Panel A). Countries with policies that facilitate female employment as through, for example, public support for childcare for 0 to 3 year olds and flexible working hours at workplaces (Castles, 2003) and individual tax systems (Apps and Rees, 2004), are also those countries with the highest fertility rates.

Public policy can lead to significant short-term effects on fertility trends. Increasing fertility rates in Sweden during the late 1980s were not only related to a booming economy but also to parental leave reform that introduced incentives to mothers to have second or subsequent children within a relatively short period of each other (Chapter 6). Public policy also temporarily affected birth rates in Québec in the late 1980s and early 1990s, when in the aftermath of the introduction of Allowance for Newborn Children in 1988 (abolished in 1997), the total fertility rate in the province of Québec increased from below 1.4 to almost 1.7 just below the Canadian average (Chart 2.9, Panel B). Although Milligan (2002) estimated that almost 15% more children were born than in the absence of the programme, the Québécois Statistical Institute estimates that the programme had a considerably smaller effect. In any case, the programme was a high cost to the Québecois Exchequer of about CAD 15 500 per child (Roy, 2002).

Chart 2.9, Panel B suggests that for *individual countries* for the period after 1985 there is no clear negative relationship between fertility and female employment (and whether or not that is on a part-time basis seems irrelevant). In the late 1980s, both birth rates and female employment increased simultaneously in all countries, while in the early 21st century, there does not appear to be a strong negative association between female employment and fertility either.[10]

Chart 2.9. **High female employment rate are not incompatible with fertility rates close to replacement level**

Panel A. **Female employment rate (age 15-64) and total fertility rates**

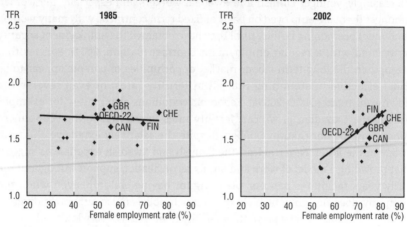

Panel B. **Trends in female employment rates by full-time/part-time for 25-54s, and total fertility rates, 1985-2002**

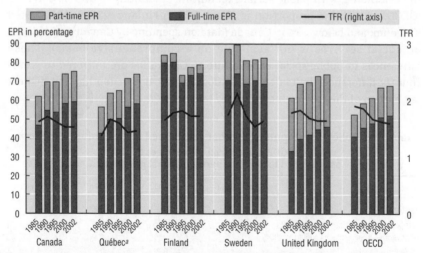

Note: As data is not available for the complete 1985-2002 period, OECD(22) does not include the Czech Republic, Hungary, Iceland, Luxembourg, Mexico, Poland, Slovak Republic and Turkey.
a) TFR in Québec for 1986, 1991 and 1996.

Source: OECD calculations based on European Labour Force Surveys; Information supplied by Institut de la Statistique du Québec (www.stat.gouv.qc.ca); OECD (2004), *Employment Outlook*; OECD (2004), *Labour Force Statistics*; and OECD (2005), *Society at a Glance: OECD Social Indicators*.

Economic and employment conditions are critical to fertility trends. In Sweden, fertility among women not in work is lower than among women in work, particularly among those who have established themselves in the labour market. Increasingly, younger Finnish and Swedish workers and especially the women amongst them are employed on basis of fixed term contracts, with many women (and men) postponing fertility until they have obtained the employment security associated with a regular employment contract (Batljan, 2001). Policies that strengthen the long-term labour market opportunities of parents appear to be most effective in stemming the fall in fertility rates, or even reverse the downward trend (OECD, 2005a). Economic conditions also matter: for example, among the Canadian provinces, fertility rates in the prospering economy of Alberta are higher than in Québec, despite the relatively extensive childcare policy in the latter. Nevertheless, the Finnish and Swedish experiences suggest that providing a model of work and family reconciliation support throughout the early years facilitates parents' planning for having children, even when the economy does not grow at high speed. Such policies also support individual fertility decisions thereby preventing fertility rates to fall to very low levels.

2.3. Social policy intervention

Sweden has one of the most comprehensive social protection systems in the OECD area, with public social expenditure amounting to over 30% in 2001 (OECD, 2004i); this proportion is about 25% in Finland, 23% in the United Kingdom, and below 20% in Canada (data on spending by Canadian provinces on social services is not available on a comprehensive basis). These differences in public social expenditure to GDP ratios are mirrored in cross-country differences in Tax-to-GDP ratios (Table 2.4): Sweden has the highest tax burden of the four countries under review.

Table 2.4. **Policy development is most centralised in the United Kingdom**
Tax to GDP ratios (2002), percentages of GDP,
as attributed to different parts of general government

	Canada	Finland	Sweden	United Kingdom
Tax to GDP ratios	33.9	45.9	50.2	35.8
Attribution of tax revenue to sub-sectors of government, percentages adding to 100%				
Supranational	–	0.2	0.8	1.3
Federal or central government	40.8	54.0	55.3	77.2
Provinces	35.5	–	–	–
Local government	8.5	21.5	32.1	4.5
Social security funds	15.2	24.4	11.9	17.0
	100.0	100.0	100.0	100.0

– Not applicable.

Source: OECD (2004), OECD Revenue Statistics, 1965-2993, OECD, Paris.

Finnish and Swedish welfare states had already "matured" by 1990 and social spending in both countries has more or less rebounded from the budget cuts during the mid-1990s: public social spending to GDP ratios in 1990 and 2001 are not very different from each other. In Canada, public social spending to the working-age population as a percentage of GDP has declined in recent years, because strong economic growth led to a reduction in spending on unemployment compensation and social assistance payments (Chapter 5). By contrast, the expansion of the British social protection system is ongoing, with tangible spending increases in the areas of health and families in recent years.

In all four countries, public spending towards those in retirement is increasing and, with the dynamics of ageing populations, this trend is expected to continue. Sweden spends most on support for the working age population and families in particular almost 4.5% of GDP in 2001 (Chart 2.10 does not account for the increase in spending on childcare with the capping of parental fees in 2003), while this is about 3% in Finland. In 2001, public spending on family benefits was just above 2% of GDP in the United Kingdom (including spending on income support for sole parent families with children), and just below 1% in Canada. However, data on public spending on family benefits in Canada do not include provincial family services, including childcare support.

Chart 2.10. **The Swedish welfare state appears to be most comprehensive**

Public social expenditure by broad social policy area, 1980, 1990 and 2001, percentage of GDP

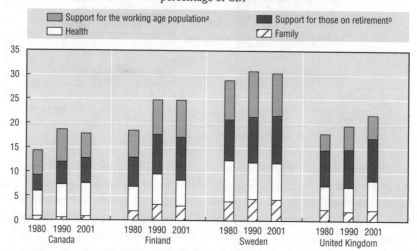

a) Incapacity, unemployment, labour market programmes, housing and other.
b) Old age and survivors benefits.

Source: OECD (2004), Social Expenditure Database (www.oecd.org/els/social/expenditure).

Alternative measures of social spending point to considerably smaller cross-country differences in social spending for two main reasons (Chart 2.10):

● Benefit income in Finland and Sweden is generally subject to income tax; and indirect taxation of consumption out of benefit income is relatively high. In Sweden, the claw back of social spending through direct and indirect taxation on transfer income amounted to about 6% of GDP in 2001, compared to 5% in Finland (Adema and Ladaique, 2005, and Eklind et al., 2003). Also accounting for the value of tax expenditures to families (non-existent in Finland and Sweden), the value of social expenditure clawed back of transfer income by the British and Canadian exchequers was between 1% and 2% of GDP in 2001.

● British and Canadian[11] authorities also use their tax systems to stimulate private arrangements of provisions for retirement. In 2001, although the system has yet to mature, private social expenditure (largely pension payments) already amounted to about 4% of GDP in these two countries, compared to 2% and 1% of GDP in Sweden and Finland, respectively.

Chart 2.11. Taxation and private spending reduce cross-country differences in social effort

Gross and net (after tax) public and private social spending, 2001, percentage of GDP

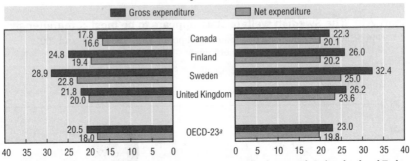

a) OECD-23 do not include, Greece, Hungary, Luxembourg, Poland, Portugal, Switzerland and Turkey.
Source: Estimates based on Adema, W. and M. Ladaique (2005), "Net Social Expenditure", 3rd edition, *Social, Employment and Migration Working Paper*, OECD, Paris.

Private pensions which constitute a large part of private social spending in Canada and the United Kingdom are often earnings-related, and favourable fiscal treatment of such arrangements disproportionately benefits the relatively well-off. In addition, private pensions are mainly paid to households without dependent children. This contributes to Finnish and Swedish tax/benefit systems having a greater impact on reducing poverty among families than for households without children (Chart 2.12: in Finland and Sweden pre-tax poverty rates are reduced by more than half for households without

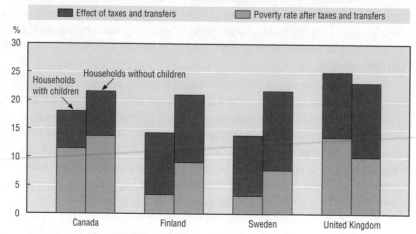

Chart 2.12. **Tax/benefit policy in Finland and Sweden re-distributes resources towards families**

Poverty rates before and after taxes and transfers, households with and without children, 2000

Source: Förster, M. and M. Mira d'Ercole (2005), "Income Distribution and Poverty in OECD Countries in the Second Half of the 1990s", *Social, Employment and Migration Working Paper*, No. 22, OECD, Paris.

children and close to 75% for families with children). The Canadian and UK tax/benefit systems appear to be more neutral in their impact on poverty reduction among households with and without children.[12] The redistributive nature of the Finnish and Swedish tax/benefit systems is further enhanced by the provision of social services (including childcare) to families with children at a low user fee (Chapter 4) and financed out of general taxation.

2.3.1. Family-friendly policy coherence

Discretion regarding policy development is linked to funding sources and, thus, it appears from Table 2.4) that among the countries under review the UK policy set-up is the most centralised: less than 5% of all tax revenue accrues to local government. In the late 1990s, devolution led to a greater role for authorities in Northern Ireland, Scotland and Wales such that the Scottish Sure Start programme for assistance to vulnerable families is different in design from Sure Start policy in England and Wales (Chapter 4). By contrast, in Finland and Sweden (municipalities) and especially Canada (provinces), lower tiers of government have a much larger tax capacity (Table 2.4) and play a larger role in social policy formulation and delivery.

In both Finland and Sweden, local (municipal) authorities are responsible for providing social and health care services. Central government identifies goals, formulates guidelines, sets financing rules and general rules on basic standards, but legislation does not provide an excessive number of detailed provisions on the nature and scope of service provision.[13] The systems thus allow for a considerable degree of local discretion in policy development, and, thus, variation in service provision across municipalities. In general, however, there is a high degree of conformity in childcare service delivery across municipalities in both Finland and Sweden as policy makers across the two countries and different levels of government generally aim to provide quality childcare services.

Nevertheless, in terms of family-friendly policy practice, the balance of tax/benefit policies that affect the parental work and care balance can differ across different levels of government and different municipalities, as it does in Finland. The national Finnish policy set-up provides financial support both for parents with very young children who use local childcare services and for those who do not. However, some (often larger) municipalities affect the balance of choice options by providing additional payments to parents who choose to not claim municipal childcare support (Chapter 4). Given the cost of providing formal childcare for very young children, this system is understandable from a narrow municipal budget perspective, but its effects on financial incentives to work make it sit uncomfortably with national policy objectives to raise female employment rates to 70% (Chapter 5).

Canada consists of 10 provinces and 3 territories and responsibility for social and family policy development is shared between federal, provincial and territorial authorities. Federal authorities in Canada are responsible for employment insurance (including parental leave arrangements, Chapter 6), while provinces are responsible for social and family services. Such provincial policies are co-financed through block grants using national frameworks as until recently the Canadian Social and Health transfer and, since fiscal year 2004/5, the Canada Social Transfer (CST). In addition there is an "equalization" grant which re-allocates resources between provinces with varying tax raising capacities, so that all provinces are able to provide a comparable level of public services as if they had similar levels of taxation (Table 2.5). There are no conditions attached to receiving equalization grants and provinces can use these resources as they see fit.[14] It is thus at the discretion of each of Canada's provinces and territories to design its own social service policy, including childcare policy.

In the late 1990s, the introduction of the federally-financed National Child Benefit freed up provincial resources for family supports, which in Québec, exceptionally for Canada, was used to co-finance expansion of the childcare system. Furthermore, within the multilateral federal/provincial Early Childhood Development Agreements (financed through the CST) and the Multilateral Framework on Early Learning and Child Care, promoting early childhood development was backed with financial support for childcare

Table 2.5. **Major federal transfers to provinces in Canada**
Value of transfers in Canadian dollars and per capita, 2003-05

		2003-04	2004-05
		Value of transfers (CAD millions)	
Canada Health and Social Transfer (CHST)		37 333	
Canada Health Transfer (CHT)			25 895
Canada Social Transfer (CST)			6 512
Health Reform Transfer (HRT)		1 000	1 500
Equilization		8 690	9 002
Territorial Formula Financing[a]		1 717	1 832
Total[b]		47 588	51 666
		Per capita value of transfers (CAD)	
Canada	Average CHST, CHT, CST, HRT	1 229	1 335
	Equilization	274	282
	Average major transfers[b, c]	1 503	1 617
Province of Québec	Average CHST, CHT, CST, HRT	1 211	1 321
	Equilization	502	497
	Average major transfers[b, c]	1 651	1 755

a) Federal transfers to the Yukon, Northwest Territories and Nunavut.
b) Equalization associated with the CHST/CST/CHT tax transfer is included under both the CHST/CST/ CHT and Equalization. The total amount has been adjusted to avoid double counting.
c) Includes Territorial Formula Financing.
Source: Department of Finance Canada (2004), *Federal Transfers to Provinces and Territories*, October, Ottawa.

programmes. The federal government has also pledged in 2004 to spent another CAD 5 billion over the subsequent five years to help develop childcare arrangements across Canada.

The province of Québec is not a signatory to these agreements as it wishes to preserve its responsibility in the family policy area. The provincial government of Québec, nevertheless, receives relevant funds as its policy is in line with the general principles embodied in Early Childhood Development Agreements and the Multilateral Framework. In fact, when it comes to policy coherence in the family-friendly policy area, particularly regarding many aspects of childcare policy, provincial policy in Québec is way ahead of other provinces and of federal policy development.

Québec's family policy has a strong focus on both supporting child development and working parents; as such, the intricacies of measures in both federal and provincial tax/benefit systems require some fine-tuning. Reform of provincial policy in Québec introduced in 2005 streamlined various measures supporting families and generally strengthened the income position of working families with children (Chapter 5).

2.4. Conclusions

Family-friendly policy development in the four countries under review has to consider the following key features within the socio-economic, demographic and political environment:

- Strong economic growth in Canada and the United Kingdom facilitated a marked rise of female employment in both countries. The economic downturn that hit Finland and Sweden in the early 1990s contributed to increasing job insecurity among younger people, which, in turn, contributed to delays in family formation and a decline in fertility.

- Notwithstanding the ability to turn economic growth into rising employment, joblessness among (sole parent) families is higher in Canada and the United Kingdom than in Finland and Sweden. This contributes to higher poverty rates in Canada and the United Kingdom, with child poverty rates in these two countries about three times as high as in Finland and Sweden.

- Although Canada, Finland, Sweden and the United Kingdom are by no means low-fertility countries by international comparison, the dynamics of rapidly ageing populations will increase the need for polices that help parents combine work and family commitments.

- Particularly in Finland, Sweden and Canada, sub-national levels of government play an important role in employment-oriented social policy development. In general, the involvement of different levels of government in policy development does not appear to lead an incoherent pursuit of policy objectives among different public authorities, although municipal policy in Finland towards parents with very young children can affect work and care decisions of such parents to the detriment of employment policy objectives.

Notes

1. Finland, Sweden and the United Kingdom are all members of the European Union, but Sweden and the United Kingdom are not part of the European Monetary Union (EMU).

2. The 1989 Canada-US Free Trade Agreement (FTA) and 1994 North American Free Trade Agreement (NAFTA – which includes Mexico) contributed to increased integration with the US economy.

3. Since the mid-1990s, the development of the information and communication technology sector contributed significantly to Finnish economic growth. However, productivity gains in this sector are likely to be smaller in future with falling ICT prices, which will add to downward pressure on the growth rate of GDP per capita (OECD, 2004a).

4. The collapse of Finland's neighbour the Soviet Union in 1991 exacerbated the effect of the global economic downturn on the Finnish economy. For the rest of the 1990s, the Finnish unemployment rate remained above 10%. Turner *et al.* (2002) estimated that the structural rate of unemployment in Finland was about 9% in 1999, compared to 7.7%, 5.8% and 7.0% for Canada, Sweden and the United Kingdom, respectively.

5. Unemployment has declined significantly in Sweden since 1997 because of employment growth and increased participation in adult education.

6. The Gini coefficient can range form 0 to 100, *i.e.*, from perfect equality to perfect inequality. The level of income inequality in Nordic countries is consistently lower than in Canada and the United Kingdom, regardless of the indicator with which income dispersion is measured (Förster and Mira d'Ercole, 2005).

7. There are about 70 000 to 80 000 Sami living in Northern Europe, of which 17 000 to 20 000 in Sweden and 6 000 to 10 000 in Finland.

8. Because of the relatively low share of the population older than 65 years of age in Canada (Table 2.2), the mortality rate is relatively low: 7.6 deaths per 1 000 persons, while this is around 10 deaths per 1 000 persons in the other three countries (the number of births per 1 000 persons is close to 10 in all four countries).

9. Comprehensive data is not available on a cross-country basis, but in general the proportion of childless women at age 40 is higher among women with higher levels of educational attainment. For example, the proportion of childless women in Finland in the 40 to 44 age group at the end of 2002 who had completed upper secondary education was 15%, compared to almost 27% for those who had completed the second stage of tertiary education (information provided by Statistics Finland).

10. Cross-country studies by Engelhardt *et al.* (2001) and Kögel (2002) also suggest that the relationship between fertility rates and female employment is still negative in any single country, but that the extent of incompatibility had diminished in Scandinavian countries.

11. The net social expenditure indicators for Canada as presented in Chart 2.1 do not account for the effect of provincial tax systems on the value of social support.

12. The data for 2000 which underlie Chart 2.12 suggest that the UK tax/benefit system has a slightly stronger effect on reducing poverty among households without children compared to families. However, this finding does not account for post-2000 reform that strengthened the income position of families with children.

13. Recent reform in Sweden capped the parental childcare fee, which is established by municipalities, thereby reducing variation of childcare fees across the country (Chapter 4).

14. Under the "equalization" rules only the Canadian provinces of Alberta and Ontario do not receive grants. Territorial governments do not receive "equalization" funding; Territorial Formula Financing in Canada provides financial assistance towards public service delivery by territorial Governments; the Yukon, Northwest Territories and Nunavut (Department of Finance Canada, 2004).

ISBN 92-64-00928-0
Babies and Bosses: Reconciling Work and Family Life
Canada, Finland, Sweden and the United Kingdom
© OECD 2005

Chapter 3

Mothers and Fathers in Work

This chapter discusses parental employment patterns in Canada and the province of Québec, Finland, Sweden and the United Kingdom. The presence of children in household hardly affects labour market behaviour of fathers but has a significant impact on maternal employment patterns. In general, working mothers are in full-time employment in Canada, the province of Québec, Finland and Sweden, even though many Swedish mothers make use of their entitlement to reduce working hours until children go to school. By contrast, working mothers in the United Kingdom often work part-time. Apart from the comprehensive discussion of employment trends and how employment outcomes vary with the age and number of children, the chapter also considers gender wage gaps and gender differences in the contribution to household earnings.

Canada and the province of Québec, Finland, Sweden and the United Kingdom have labour markets that are performing well. Employment rates are high for both sexes and female employment in all four countries is at least 10 percentage points above the OECD average. The development of the service sector has contributed hugely to female employment growth, but whereas such employment is often in the private sector in Canada and the United Kingdom, public services have a much greater role in Finland and Sweden. In all four countries under review, female employment remains concentrated in certain occupations and sectors. Gender differences in employment and pay are smallest in Finland and Sweden, but they seem difficult to erase. While such differences are bigger in Canada and the United Kingdom, they are smaller at the top end of the earnings distribution and a higher proportion of women in these two countries seem to get through to managerial positions.

To a considerable extent, these and other differences in labour market outcomes of fathers and mothers are related to the presence of children in families: compared to fathers, mothers are much more likely to reduce working hours after childbirth (Sweden and the United Kingdom) or temporarily drop out of the labour force (all four countries). Working hours for men generally remain largely unaffected by the presence of children in Canada, Finland and Sweden, while fathers in the United Kingdom appear to increase hours at the workplace.

This chapter first presents some key labour market indicators and differences between men and women in terms of the economic sectors in which they are employed, the jobs they occupy, the number of hours they work and the employment status they have. The chapter then goes on to show how the presence of children and household status may affect maternal employment behaviour and considers trends in work and family formation. Before summarising, the chapter discusses gender wage gaps and differences in the contributions fathers and mothers make to family income in couple households.

3.1. Key labour market outcomes

Overall, labour market performances in all four countries under review compare favourably to those in many other OECD countries (Table 3.1). Female labour force participation rates in particular are high from an international perspective: they range from 69% in the United Kingdom to 77 % in Sweden,

Table 3.1. **Canada, Finland, Sweden and the United Kingdom: high employment among men and women**
Key labour market indicators, 2003

	Canada					Finland				Sweden				United Kingdom				OECD			
	1980	1990	2000	2003	Province of Québec	1980	1990	2000	2003	1980	1990	2000	2003	1980[a]	1990	2000	2003	1980	1990	2000	2003
Labour force participation (percentage of working age population 15-64)																					
Men and women	71.5	76.6	76.3	78.1	77.0	74.3	76.6	74.3	74.1	81.7	84.6	78.9	78.9	74.8	77.8	76.6	76.6	68.1	70.0	70.1	69.8
Men	85.7	84.9	82.1	83.2	82.3	79.2	79.6	76.4	76.1	87.9	86.7	81.2	80.8	87.9	88.3	84.3	83.9	83.9	82.1	81.0	80.2
Women	57.2	68.3	70.5	73.0	71.6	69.4	73.5	72.1	72.1	75.3	82.5	76.4	76.9	61.7	67.3	68.9	69.2	52.9	58.1	59.3	59.6
Employment rate (percentage of working age population 15-64)																					
Men and women	66.0	70.3	71.1	72.1	69.9	70.7	74.1	67.0	67.4	79.9	83.1	74.2	74.3	65.9	72.5	72.4	72.9	64.2	65.6	65.7	64.9
Men	79.6	77.8	76.3	76.5	74.3	75.5	76.7	69.4	69.0	86.2	85.2	76.1	75.6	77.4	82.1	79.1	79.3	79.5	77.5	76.3	74.7
Women	52.5	62.7	65.8	67.7	65.4	66.1	71.5	64.5	65.7	73.4	81.0	72.2	72.8	54.5	62.8	65.5	66.4	49.3	53.9	55.3	55.3
Women, aged 25-54	55.7	69.7	74.0	75.7	74.7	79.8	85.1	77.6	78.8	81.6	89.7	81.7	81.7	60.3	68.6	73.1	74.1	53.6	61.6	64.0	64.1
Women, aged 30-34	56.1	69.5	74.7	75.3	75.1	80.8	82.4	71.3	73.9	..	89.1	80.1	79.2	52.3	64.4	71.3	70.3	52.4	60.2	61.5	61.1
Share of part-time (under 30 hours)[b] employment in percentage of total employment, aged 15 and over																					
Men and women	14.4	17.1	18.1	18.8	18.4	..	7.6	10.4	11.3	16.8	14.5	14.0	14.1	19.6	20.1	23.0	23.3	9.6	11.1	12.2	14.8
Men	6.9	9.2	10.3	11.0	11.0	..	4.8	7.1	8.0	4.9	5.3	7.3	7.9	4.2	5.3	8.6	9.6	5.2	5.0	5.9	7.2
Women	26.0	26.9	27.3	27.9	27.0	..	10.6	13.9	15.0	29.8	24.5	21.4	20.6	41.2	39.5	40.8	40.1	15.7	19.5	20.7	24.8
Unemployment rate (percentage of labour force 15-64)																					
Men and women	7.6	8.2	6.9	7.7	9.2	4.7	3.2	9.9	9.1	2.3	1.8	5.9	5.8	11.9	6.8	5.6	4.9	5.8	6.3	6.2	7.1
Men	7.1	8.3	7.0	8.1	9.7	4.7	3.6	9.2	9.3	2.0	1.8	6.3	6.4	12.0	7.1	6.1	5.5	5.2	5.7	5.8	6.9
Women	8.3	8.1	6.7	7.3	8.6	4.8	2.7	10.6	8.9	2.6	1.8	5.4	5.3	11.6	6.6	4.8	4.1	6.7	7.1	6.8	7.3
Long-term unemployment (percentage of total unemployment)[c]																					
Men and women	5.3	7.2	11.2	10.1	6.7	27.0	9.2	29.0	24.7	5.5	12.1	26.4	17.8	46.3	34.4	28.0	23.0	12.7	31.2	31.6	31.0
Men	5.6	7.9	12.2	11.4	8.5	25.5	9.7	32.2	27.7	6.8	12.3	29.3	19.6	52.7	41.8	33.7	26.5	12.5	30.0	30.2	30.2
Women	5.0	6.2	10.0	8.4	4.3	28.3	8.4	26.2	21.4	4.4	11.8	22.8	15.3	35.7	23.7	19.0	17.1	12.9	32.5	33.1	31.9

.. : Data not available.
a) United Kingdom: 1984 instead of 1980.
b) Part-time employment refers to persons who usually work less than 30 hours per week in their main job.
c) Long-term unemployment: 12 months and over; 1991 instead of 1990 in Finland.
Source: OECD (2004), Employment Outlook, OECD, Paris; Statistics Canada for data on the province of Québec.

compared to a proportion close to 60% in OECD member countries in 2003. As a result, gender employment gaps are relatively small: from about 3% in Finland and Sweden to 9% in Canada (and the province of Québec) to 13% in the United Kingdom. In line with patterns of education and early retirement, employment rates for prime-age women (ages 25-54) are about 10 percentage points above those for the working-age population as a whole. However, employment rates of women in their early thirties are (except for Canada) significantly below that of prime-age women. In part this reflects the rise in the age at which women have their first child (Chapter 2), but it also suggests that a significant number of women (re-)enter the labour force when their children grow up.

As in most OECD countries, there appears to be a trend of declining male participation rates in all four countries under review (Table 3.1). Female employment trends, however, vary from country to country. Before formal childcare system development was initiated in the late 1960s (Chapter 4), employment rates of prime – age female workers were already high at 55% (Sweden) and 65% (Finland).[1] This appears comparable to the female employment situation in Canada and the United Kingdom of the early 1980s. Yet, the experience of these two groups of countries continues to be different, as in the early 1990s the economic crises in Finland and Sweden involved a serious employment shake out: in Finland the employment/population ratio fell from 74% in 1990 to 60% in 1994 and in Sweden from 83% in 1990 to 71% in 1997 (male and female employment trends were the same). By contrast, in Canada and the United Kingdom, female employment rates held up (male employment rates fell by 4 percentage points in the early 1990s) and resumed their upward trend before the mid-1990s. In all, private service sector growth facilitated a considerable increase in female employment since 1980 in the United Kingdom and especially Canada. On the other hand, in Finland and Sweden, employment levels have not yet recovered to 1990 levels: at more or less constant participation rates in these two Scandinavian countries, this translates into significantly higher unemployment rates than in the past (Table 3.1).

Private service sector expansion facilitated growth of part-time employment in proportion with full-time employment in both Canada and the United Kingdom.[2] Part-time employment is particularly widespread among women in the United Kingdom where two out of five women work part-time, while this is almost one in four in Canada. The incidence of part-time employment among women in Sweden has fallen since 1990, which partly reflects the decline in employment opportunities since that year, given the drop in labour force participation rates. In Finland where labour force participation rates are now back at 1990 levels, part-time employment has increased, but remains at a very low level (15% of all female employment).

The Canadian labour market appears to have the highest degree of labour market turnover as indicated by the low incidence of long-term unemployment in all four countries (the OECD average is 32%). Nonetheless, Canadian and especially Québécois unemployed women often move in (and out) of jobs and/or the labour force.

3.1.1. *Worker qualifications: educational attainment and employment*

The likelihood of being in employment increases with educational attainment level, particularly for women. Education outcomes have changed most significantly for women, but nowhere was the change as profound as in Canada over the last 20 years or so. In the beginning of the 1980s, the proportion of the population with tertiary education varied from 16% (United Kingdom) to 22% (Finland), while in 2002 this ranged from 27% (United Kingdom) to a very high 43% in Canada (almost twice the OECD average). In all countries except the United Kingdom, female levels of educational attainment are above those of men and are high: in Canada, 45% of women possess a university degree, compared to 35% in Finland and Sweden and 26% in the United Kingdom (Table 3.2).

Compared to massive gains in educational attainment in Canada, gains in female employment rates for women with at least secondary education have been limited to 5 to 6 percentage points. By contrast, the increase in the likelihood of being employed at higher levels of educational attainment was most pronounced in the United Kingdom (Table 3.2). Compared to 1980, employment rates declined across all levels of educational attainment in Finland and Sweden and not surprisingly the decline was steepest among women with less than secondary education. Nevertheless, employment rates for Finnish and Swedish women compare well to their counterparts in Canada and the United Kingdom, particularly among those with less than secondary education.

Women may generally have higher levels of educational attainment compared to men, but they are less likely to be in employment. For those with at least upper secondary qualifications, the gender employment gap has been very small for some time in Finland and Sweden (at below 5 percentage points) and is narrowing rapidly in Canada and the United Kingdom. For those with lower levels of educational attainment, the gender employment gap is smallest in Finland (6 percentage points) and Sweden (12 percentage points) and much higher in Canada and the United Kingdom (22 percentage points).

There are, however, crucial gender differences in the subject in which a degree is obtained. In all four countries under review, women still make up the overwhelming majority of students who complete their studies in the areas of health and welfare, arts and humanities, education and, to a lesser extent, in other social sciences and business law and services (Table 3.3). Male graduates

Table 3.2. **Advances in educational attainment appear most pronounced in Canada**

Distribution of population and employment rates by level of educational attainment and gender, 25 to 64 years old, 1981, 2002

	Both sexes			Men			Women		
	Less than upper secondary education	Upper secondary education	Tertiary education	Less than upper secondary education	Upper secondary education	Tertiary education	Less than upper secondary education	Upper secondary education	Tertiary education
A. Distribution of population by level of educational attainment									
2002									
Canada	17.4	39.9	42.6	18.1	42.0	39.9	16.8	37.9	45.3
Finland	25.2	42.0	32.6	26.6	43.6	29.6	23.8	40.4	35.6
Sweden	18.4	49.0	32.6	20.2	49.4	30.3	16.6	48.6	34.9
United Kingdom	35.6	37.4	26.9	30.4	42.2	27.2	41.4	32.0	26.4
OECD	35.1	41.8	23.0	33.1	43.4	23.4	37.1	40.2	22.6
1981[a]									
Canada	34.7	45.0	20.3	35.2	42.2	22.6	34.2	47.8	18.0
Finland	48.6	29.7	21.6	47.3	32.1	20.5	50.0	27.3	22.7
Sweden	44.4	36.5	19.1	43.7	37.2	19.1	45.1	35.7	19.2
United Kingdom	42.2	41.9	15.9	35.2	47.6	17.3	49.2	36.2	14.6
OECD	..	..	..	..	..	..	..	..	..
B. Employment rates									
2002									
Canada	55.3	75.9	82.0	66.0	82.1	86.1	43.9	69.1	78.3
Finland	57.7	74.4	85.1	60.7	76.9	86.8	54.2	71.6	83.8
Sweden	68.2	81.8	86.5	73.8	83.5	87.2	61.0	80.1	85.8
United Kingdom	52.9	79.4	87.8	59.1	84.4	89.7	47.5	73.3	85.6
OECD	56.8	73.3	82.0	73.5	81.9	88.7	41.5	64.5	74.8
1981[a]									
Canada	64.9	76.9	85.5	83.8	92.4	95.2	45.1	63.0	73.2
Finland	84.1	85.6	94.4	89.0	89.3	97.9	79.4	81.1	91.0
Sweden	84.0	90.7	93.1	90.5	95.3	94.7	77.5	85.7	91.4
United Kingdom	64.4	77.8	84.4	77.9	89.8	94.0	54.8	62.0	72.9
OECD	..	..	..	..	..	..	..	..	..

a) 1982 for Finland and 1984 for the United Kingdom.

Source: OECD (2004), *Employment Outlook*, OECD, Paris; OECD (2004), *Education at a Glance*, OECD, Paris.

Table 3.3. **Women mostly obtain arts, humanities, health, welfare, education and law degrees**

Percentage of tertiary qualifications awarded to females,
by type of tertiary education and by field of study, 2002

	Health and welfare		Life sciences, physical sciences and agriculture		Mathematics and computer science		Humanities, arts and education		Social sciences, business, law and services		Engineering, manufacturing and construction	
	Tertiary-type B education	Tertiary-type A and research	Tertiary-type B education	Tertiary-type A and research	Tertiary-type B education	Tertiary-type A and research	Tertiary-type B education	Tertiary-type A and research	Tertiary-type B education	Tertiary-type A and research	Tertiary-type B education	Tertiary-type A and research
Canada (2000)	84	74	50	53	29	28	70	68	62	58	17	23
Finland (2001)	87	86	54	54	48	39	75	79	58	68	18	21
Sweden	95	81	54	57	42	40	55	77	69	59	31	28
United Kingdom	85	74	44	54	27	28	61	67	54	55	14	20
OECD	84	70	41	49	31	30	67	70	59	53	18	23

Source: OECD (2004), *Education at a Glance*, Annex 3 for notes, OECD, Paris (*www.oecd.org/edu/eag2004*).

dominate in mathematical sciences and engineering, but Finnish and Swedish women are more likely to have such degrees than women in Canada and the United Kingdom. Evidence of student performance by gender shows that young women in general have better results than young men (OECD, 2004b). However, gender differences remain: 15-year old female students score significantly better on combined reading literacy in all OECD countries, while males on average had the edge in terms of mathematical literacy in most OECD countries, including Canada, Sweden and the United Kingdom, but not in Finland. Given this, there seems ample reason for policy to be more persistent in trying to change attitudes among younger women when they choose their field of study.

3.1.2. *Where and under which conditions do men and women work?*

Service sector employment plays an important role in all four countries under review, but particularly in Canada, the province of Québec, Sweden and the United Kingdom where three out of four workers are employed in the service sector. Shares of workers in industry (26%) and agriculture (5%) are largest in Finland, but nevertheless below the OECD average. More than in most other OECD countries, female employment is heavily concentrated in service activities and accounts for about 85% for female employment in Canada, the province of Québec and Finland and almost 90% in Sweden and the United Kingdom. The difference is that Finnish and Swedish women are public sector employees more often their counterparts in Canada and the United Kingdom: 40% of female employees in Finland and 50% of female employees in Sweden work in the public sector (Table 3.4). In all four countries, there are many nurses and teachers in public sector employment: whereas predominantly female childcare workers are employed by local governments in Finland and Sweden, they are in private sector employment in Canada, the province of Québec and the United Kingdom (Chapter 4).

The Canadian labour market has the lowest degree of occupational concentration across the OECD area: 75% of women work in 32 occupations and 75% of men work in 50 occupations (OECD, 2002a). On average across the OECD, women are concentrated in 19 out of 114 occupations, while 75% of male workers can be found in 30 of these occupations (Table 3.2). In Finland, Sweden and the United Kingdom, occupational concentration is around OECD average and strongest for women: in the United Kingdom, 17 occupations account for 69% of female employees, while in Finland 77% of female workers can be found in 22 occupations.

Women clearly face difficulties in climbing the hierarchy: the number of women in management positions in Finland and Sweden is not much higher than the OECD average. Canadian women, who hold 38% of all management jobs, seem to do somewhat better.[3]

Non-standard forms of employment

Work practices have changed and employment relationships have become more flexible over the last few decades with ongoing technological progress, product market deregulation and the expansion of the service sector. The nature of labour markets in Finland and Sweden changed forever in the aftermath of the crisis in the early 1990s, leading to an increased proportion of employees working under "non-standard" (casual, atypical, non-regular) employment conditions, who may have less than complete access to family-friendly workplace support (Chapter 6).[4]

Since the early 1990s, temporary employment contracts have become prevalent in Sweden and are highest in Finland at 16% among the countries under review (Table 3.4; among OECD labour markets, only Turkey, Mexico, Korea and Spain have higher incidences of temporary employment, OECD, 2002a). The crisis of the early 1990s, stringent employment protection legislation and costs considerations contributed to a greater use of temporary employment contracts for younger workers by local governments (who are responsible for health, education and social services and also employ many women, see above). In Finland, 37% of all female employees between ages 25 and 29 and 23% of those between ages 30 and 34 have a temporary contract (Forssén et al., 2003). Many municipalities in Finland hire their

3. MOTHERS AND FATHERS IN WORK

Table 3.4. **Women are most likely to work in certain occupations at low levels of the hierarchy under precarious employment conditions**

Employment structure

	Canada				Finland			Sweden			United Kingdom			OECD	
	1990	2000	2003	2003 Province of Québec	1990	2000	2003	1990	2000	2003	1990	2000	2003	2000	2003
Share of agriculture in percentage of civilian employment															
Men and women	3.4	2.5	2.2	1.6	8.9	6.1	5.1	3.3	2.4	2.1	2.2	1.5	1.3	8.0	7.2
Men	4.3	3.2	2.9	2.2	11.0	8.1	6.8	4.7	3.5	3.2	3.1	2.2	1.8	8.9	8.3
Women	2.3	1.6	1.4	0.9	6.6	3.9	3.3	1.8	1.1	0.9	1.1	0.8	0.6	7.6	7.0
Share of industry in percentage of civilian employment															
Men and women	25.4	23.4	23.2	24.0	30.4	27.6	26.3	29.1	24.6	22.7	30.0	25.2	23.3	28.5	27.4
Men	35.5	33.5	33.4	33.7	42.5	40.1	39.2	43.1	36.7	34.7	41.4	36.5	34.6	38.0	37.3
Women	12.7	11.6	11.4	12.7	17.4	13.9	12.5	14.0	11.4	9.9	16.2	12.0	10.2	16.7	15.4
Share of services in percentage of civilian employment															
Men and women	71.2	74.1	74.7	74.4	60.7	66.3	68.5	67.4	72.9	75.1	67.1	73.0	75.3	63.3	65.2
Men	60.2	63.2	63.7	64.1	46.4	51.8	54.0	52.0	59.7	62.0	54.6	61.0	63.4	52.6	54.1
Women	85.0	86.8	87.2	86.4	75.9	82.2	84.1	84.2	87.3	89.2	82.1	87.0	89.0	75.7	77.5
Occupational concentration – number of occupations that employ at least 75% of wage and salary employees															
Men	..	53.0	..	..	..	29.0	..	..	31.0	..	..	29.0	..	30.0	..
Women	..	32.0	..	..	..	21.0	..	..	20.0	..	..	17.0	..	19.0	..
Occupational concentration – average male / female share in the occupations that employ at least 75% of male / female wage and salary employees															
Men	..	71.0	..	..	..	75.0	..	..	71.0	..	..	70.0	..	73.0	..
Women	..	68.0	..	..	..	77.0	..	..	75.0	..	..	69.0	..	70.0	..
Share of women in managerial occupations and in jobs with a supervisory role	..	37.8	..	..	..	29.8	..	..	31.6	..	..	33.4	..	29.1	..
Prevalence of managerial occupations among workers															
Men and women	..	7.7	..	..	..	6.1	..	..	4.0	..	..	14.5	..	5.2	..
Men	..	9.3	..	..	..	8.6	..	..	5.6	..	..	18.4	..	6.9	..
Women	..	6.1	..	..	..	3.6	..	..	2.5	..	..	10.2	..	3.3	..
Share of temporary employment in total employment[a]															
Men and women	..	12.5	12.5	13.6	..	16.5	16.3	..	14.6	..	4.7	6.0	5.1	..	..
Men	..	11.8	12.0	12.6	..	13.0	12.6	..	..	..	3.6	5.0	4.3	..	..
Women	..	13.3	13.0	14.7	..	19.9	20.0	..	..	..	6.1	7.1	6.1	..	..
Share of self-employment in civilian employment															
Men and women	9.5	10.7	9.7	..	15.6	13.7	12.9	9.2	10.3	9.6	15.1	12.3	12.7	18.3	17.8
Share of public employment in total employment[b]															
Men and women	21.0	18.7	19.0	21.0	23.5	24.8	25.6	40.6	35.4	34.7	..	23.1	23.4	..	..
Men	17.3	14.0	14.0	15.7	19.1	15.8	15.6[c]	23.9	19.1	18.5	..	15.9	15.7	..	..
Women	25.5	24.2	24.8	27.0	38.3	40.1	39.6[c]	57.1	51.5	50.5	..	31.4	32.4	..	..

..   Data not available.

a) Canada, Finland and Sweden: seasonal, term/contract, casual and other temporary; United Kingdom: non permanent employment.

b) CANSIM for Canada; UK: Labour Force Survey (LFS) Historical Quarterly Supplement, Table 22 "All in employment by industry sector"; Finland: Analytical Database for both genders, Ministry of Social Affairs and Health by gender; Sweden: Statistics Sweden.

c) Data for 2002.

Source: Data supplied by national statistical offices based on Labour Force Surveys; Self-employment: OECD (2004), Labour Force Statistics, OECD, Paris; Occupational data: OECD (2002), Employment Outlook, OECD, Paris.

younger education and childcare workers on contracts that span the period between the long summer holidays (Chapter 6).[5]

The incidence of temporary employment in Canada, the province of Québec and the United Kingdom is much lower (Table 3.4). Apart from the United States, these countries have the least strict employment protection legislation among OECD countries. The cost of dismissing regular workers is relatively small and, hence, British and Canadian employers do not need to hire on a temporary rather than a regular basis in the same way as their Finnish and Swedish counterparts (OECD, 2004).

Regular hours worked

Since 1979, average weekly working hours per worker have fallen in most OECD countries, including Finland, the United Kingdom and, to a lesser extent, Canada. Sweden bucks this trend: average working hours were already low in 1979 but, while working hours seem to have fallen somewhat in recent years, they remain above the 1979 level (OECD, 2004g). Swedish women in particular have increased their average weekly working hours during the second part of the 1990s from 32.9 to 34.1 hours per week. This feature contributes to explaining the increase in long-term sick leave in Sweden (ESO, 2002)[6] and a relatively high incidence of parents reporting work and family life pressure (Chapter 6).

The average working week for women is shorter than for men for two reasons: men are more likely than women to work long hours, while women are most likely than men to work part-time. Chart 3.1 illustrates that this pattern is most relevant to the situation in the United Kingdom, where average female working hours are just above 31 hours per week (see also Table 3.1 on the incidence of female part-time employment), while male hours average about 42.5 hours per week. The long working hours culture among British men partly explains why in the United Kingdom 24% of males work more that 50 hours per week, compared to 12.5% in Finland, 7.7% in Canada and a mere 2.3% in Sweden (Chapter 6). In fact, in these last three countries, male working hours are below the OECD average (Chart 3.1).

British and Finnish women are more likely to work long hours: 6.8% and 4.3% of female employees work more than 50 hours per week in Finland and the United Kingdom, respectively, compared to 1.9% in Canada and only 0.6% in Sweden (see Chapter 6). As women in Finland work on average close to 36 hours per week, the ratio of female-to-male average weekly working hours in that country is very high at 92%. Gender working hours gaps are also small in Canada (15 percentage points) and Sweden (11 percentage points), but considerable in the United Kingdom at 26 percentage points.

Chart 3.1. **The gender working hours gap is largest in the United Kingdom**
Average weekly usual hours of work, age 15+, by gender, 2002

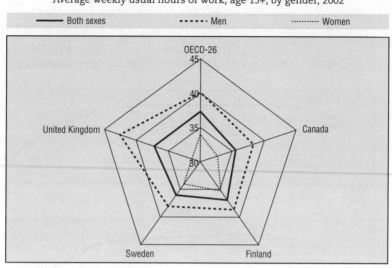

Source: OECD Database on Usual Weekly Hours of Work, Paris. Data on the province of Québec that is fully compatible with data in the OECD Database on Usual Weekly Hours of Work is not available. However, national data suggest that the distribution of working hours is not very different from that in the rest of Canada (Chapter 6).

Estimates of full-time equivalent employment rates can be generated, accounting for the incidence of long hours and of part-time employment by comparing actual hours with a 40-hour working week. These equivalised employment rates, are below orthodox employment rates, especially in the United Kingdom, where female part-time employment is widespread by 15 percentage points. Overall, cross-country differences in female employment rates increase (Table 3.1) when measured in full-time equivalents and range from 62.0% in Sweden and 59.4% in Finland to 54.8% in Canada and 51.7% in the United Kingdom.

Changes in working patterns during the life course

Although maternal employment rates can vary markedly from one year to another (see below) and fluctuations cannot always be gleaned from five-year cohort data, age-related employment rates can be used to illustrate general shifts in employment behaviour of workers over the life cycle. As in other OECD countries, male employment patterns vary little across the four countries under review, particularly for prime-age workers (Chart 3.2). Male employment rates go up until men become fathers of young children and start to drop, particularly from age 55 onwards, even though effective retirement ages seem to be even lower in Finland and the United Kingdom. In general, the presence of children

Chart 3.2. **Since 1980, male and female employment behaviour in Canada and the United Kingdom has become more similar**[a]

Cross-cohort comparisons of employment rates by age, percentages

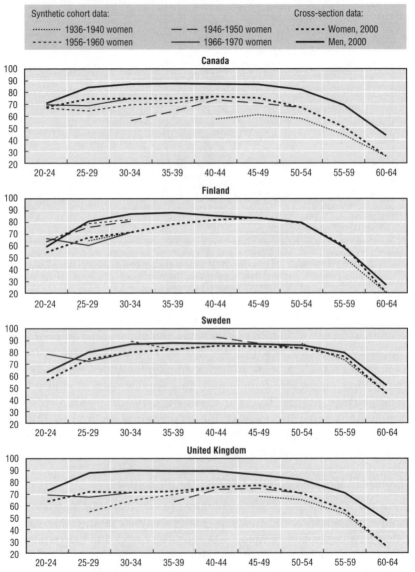

a) The chart combines cross-sectional data by age and gender for the year 2001 with "synthetic cohort" data for women belonging to selected age cohorts.

Source: OECD (2002a), *Employment Outlook*, OECD, Paris.

does not seem to have a big impact on paternal working hours in Canada, Finland or Sweden, but British fathers work on average a few hours more per week than men without children (Anxo *et al.*, 2002; Stevens *et al.*, 2004).

There is much more variation in employment behaviour of women across both across age-cohorts and across countries. Data for British and Canadian women in employment show the flattening of the M-curve that results from younger women increasingly remaining in the labour force around the time of (marriage and) childbirth. For younger Canadian women, their lifetime employment pattern appears as flat as that for men, but is at an employment level which is 10 percentage points lower. Female profiles in the United Kingdom are not dissimilar, except that employment among women appears to peak around age 45. In both countries, increasing female employment rates among younger cohorts have led to a greater similarity in male and female employment patterns over their life course.

The information that is available for Finnish and Swedish cohorts clearly shows the impact of the economic crisis on the cohort of women born in 1966-70. Nevertheless, the cohorts of women born in 1946-50 and 1956-60 had higher employment rates than both the older and younger cohorts and much more closely reflected male employment behaviour. The limited number of observations makes it difficult to determine whether the drop in female employment rates among the youngest cohort reflects a permanent change.[7] Institutional changes, however, have weakened the labour force attachment of younger Finnish women who are increasingly in temporary employment and are likely to drop out of the labour force for several years until their youngest child turns 3 or goes to school (Chapter 6). These features contribute to a profile of increasing female employment rates, which peak around age 45.

3.2. Mothers in employment

This section illustrates how maternal employment patterns may differ with the age of the youngest child, the number of children, partnership status and patterns in family formation (see Chapter 2).

3.2.1. Maternal employment and the age of the youngest child

By 2003, almost two out of three mothers with dependent children in the United Kingdom were in paid work. In the other three countries, however, maternal employment rates were either more than 70% (Canada) or 80% (Finland and Sweden) and were higher than employment rates for women generally. Since the 1980s, gains in maternal employment rates have been most significant in Canada and the United Kingdom, although rates in both Sweden and Finland were already very high in 1980. These increases were strongest in Canada and particularly in the province of Québec, where maternal

Table 3.5. **Mothers with very young children are least likely to be in employment**
Maternal employment rates by age of the youngest child

| | | Women | | Mothers with youngest child aged: | | | | | | | | | | | |
| | | | | | 0-16 years old[a] | | | Under 3 years old | | | 3 to not yet 6 years old[a] | | 6 to 16 years old[a] | |
		All :	Part-time share[b]	(On maternity/ parental leave)[c]	All, of which:	Part-time share[b]	(On maternity/ parental leave)[b]	All, of which:	Part-time share[b]	(On maternity/ parental leave)[b]	All, of which:	Part-time share[b]	All, of which:	Part-time share[a]
Canada[d]	1981	53.5	27.7	..	49.4	34.1	..	39.6	33.3	..	46.7	36.9	55.4	33.6
	1986	57.1	30.1	..	56.5	36.2	..	49.0	34.1	..	54.8	38.8	61.4	36.2
	1991	62.6	27.0	1.2	64.1	29.4	3.3	54.0	31.2	11.3	61.5	33.7	70.6	27.5
	1996	62.1	30.7	1.0	65.4	31.4	2.7	56.2	32.5	10.0	62.5	34.5	71.1	30.0
	2001	66.3	27.9	1.9	70.5	27.4	5.4	58.7	30.4	22.0	68.1	30.2	76.3	25.7
Province of Québec	1981	46.4	23.0	..	41.7	29.8	..	37.4	28.1	..	39.9	32.8	44.6	29.6
	1986	50.1	26.6	..	50.8	32.1	..	49.0	29.7	..	50.3	32.4	51.9	33.2
	1991	57.1	25.0	..	60.4	26.0	..	53.7	26.0	..	58.2	27.4	64.3	25.7
	1996	57.0	28.4	..	62.4	26.8	..	55.4	27.7	..	59.3	27.4	66.8	26.2
	2001	63.4	25.5	..	70.3	22.1	..	61.1	23.1	..	68.1	23.4	74.8	21.5
Finland	1995	58.9	11.7	..	65.8	..	..	40.8	..	..	68.4	..	78.4	..
	2000	64.5	13.9	..	73.1	..	..	47.0	..	..	77.2	..	83.2	..
	2002	66.1	14.8	1.5	76.0	..	4.2	52.1	..	18.3	80.7	..	84.2	..
Sweden[b]	1980	73.4	46.2	..	78.8	58.3	..	72.6	60.7	..	74.2	64.8	73.3	62.9
	1985	77.4	43.7	..	85.5	54.4	..	79.5	58.9	..	83.3	63.4	81.3	61.3
	1990	81.0	40.4	..	88.7	50.5	..	82.0	51.2	..	88.7	60.2	85.0	55.6
	1995	70.8	40.3	..	77.9	46.3	..	67.5	47.2	..	78.5	53.7	72.5	50.6
	2000	72.2	34.9	..	80.7	39.0	..	71.3	41.0	..	80.7	46.0	75.9	43.8
	2001	73.4	34.2	..	81.9	37.2	..	72.3	40.3	..	82.9	43.5	77.5	42.1
	2002	73.3	34.2	..	82.5	36.9	..	72.9	38.1	..	82.5	44.0	77.4	41.3
	2003	72.8	34.1	2.6	81.5	36.5	7.0	71.9	37.0	26.8	81.3	45.2	76.1	41.1
United Kingdom	1995	65.6	39.3	..	58.5	58.0	..	44.4	57.7	..	55.1	65.1	69.5	55.7
	2000	69.0	39.4	..	64.0	55.9	..	52.3	59.3	..	60.4	62.7	72.4	52.2
	2001	69.3	38.8	..	64.1	55.6	..	51.6	60.8	..	60.0	63.3	72.8	51.0
	2003	69.5	38.5	..	64.2	55.5	..	49.9	61.3	..	60.4	63.0	73.3	50.9
	2003	69.7	38.6	2.0	64.2	54.8	5.2	49.2	61.6	18.7	59.7	60.2	74.1	50.6

.. : Data not available.
a) Instead of 16 years old: 15 years old in the United Kingdom; instead of 6 years old: 7 years old in Sweden.
b) Data regarding part-time work for Sweden reflects persons working less than 35 hours per week, but less than 30 hours for the other countries and the province of Québec.
c) We assume all mothers on maternity/parental leave are full-time workers.
d) Leave data based for 1996 based on 1995 child-related EI claimants.
Source: Information provided by national authorities.

employment rates shot up from 42% in 1981 to 70.3% in 2001 (Table 3.5). In the United Kingdom, maternal employment growth has been substantial and is currently close to 70%, up from about 50% in 1980 (Gregg et al., 2003). More recently, employment among Finnish mothers increased markedly in the aftermath of the 1990 crisis from 66% in 1995 to 76% in 2002.

The age of the youngest child has a significant impact on maternal employment rates in all countries under review. In Canada, the province of Québec, Sweden and the United Kingdom, employment rates of mothers with very young children (i.e., less than 3 years old) are about 10 percentage points below that of mothers with children in the 3-6 age group. This employment differential appears largest at almost 30 percentage points in Finland, as many mothers withdraw from the labour force for the first two to three years after the child's birth. This behaviour is related to the strong financial incentives for one parent in Finnish (couple) families to not use childcare and instead provide full-time parental care (Chapter 5). Moreover, while in Canada, Sweden and the United Kingdom all parents on employment-protected child-related leave are counted as employed, parents in Finland on child-related leave are not always regarded as such (Box 3.1). Even when such differences are accounted for, however, employment rates for mothers with very young children are a poor indicator of the extent to which mothers are actually engaged in paid work. Although available information concerns estimates, they suggest that mothers with very young children are more likely to be in work in Canada, the province of Québec and the United Kingdom than in Finland and Sweden (Box 3.1).

In all four countries, the age of the child does not appear to be a very critical factor in determining working hours of mothers in employment. About 55% of mothers in employment in the United Kingdom work on a part-time basis, and this share is only somewhat higher among mothers with very young children (ages 0-2). In the United Kingdom, mothers in part-time employment often keep this employment status for a long time. In Canada, the incidence of part-time employment among mothers has fallen only slightly over the years, and most Canadian mothers (73%) work full-time from an early age of the child onwards. Trends in Sweden involve greater change: at similar employment rates (around 80% in both 1980 and 2003) the incidence of mothers with children working less than 35 hours per week has fallen from 58% in 1980 to 37% in 2003. Nevertheless, this proportion is relatively high compared to the incidence of part-time employment among all women in Sweden (21%): mothers rather than women appear to work reduced hours in Sweden. Also, the incidence of reduced working hours appears to be highest among mothers whose child is 3 to 6 years of age, which suggests that a significant proportion of mothers in Sweden do so in line with their entitlement until their child is 8 years of age (Chapter 6).

Box 3.1. **Being on child-related leave, employed and/or in work**

Labour force surveys of the four countries under review all regard people as employed persons if they have a job but are on leave for "family reasons" (Canada), "care of children" (Sweden) or with explicit reference to "maternity and parental leave" (Finland and the United Kingdom). Hence, differences in the length of child-related leave arrangements affect the interpretation of employment rates (especially for young women) across countries. The situation is further complicated because those who are using certain long leave benefits that last until a child is about 3 years of age as in Finland (but also Austria, Germany, France and Spain) are by convention *not* counted as employed in labour force surveys (ILO, 2004).

The table below shows the estimated effects. The female employment rate for mothers with a child not yet 3 years of age is lowest in the United Kingdom and Finland at respectively 49% and 52%, in contrast to 59% in Canada and highest in Sweden at 72%. If mothers on home care leave with job protection (more than 20% of all mothers with a child aged 0-2) are taken into account, then the maternal employment rate in Finland would be higher than in Sweden (data for 2002 provided by Finnish authorities along with definitions as in Haataja, 2001; see also Forssén *et al.*, 2003). Accounting for mothers on leave in the employment rate allows for considering the extent to which mothers with very young children are actually at work: this share is about 45% of mothers with very young children in Sweden, 40% in Canada, one-third in Finland and the United Kingdom.

Swedish mothers with very young children are most likely to be in employment and in paid work

	Canada	Finland	Sweden	United Kingdom
	2001	2002	2003	2003[a]
Mothers with a child 0-3	866 305	142 000	267 300	1 898 754
of which (in percentages):				
in work[b]	39.1	33.8	45.1	30.5
on maternity/parental leave	22.0	18.3	26.8	18.7
in employment[c]	58.7	52.1	72.0	49.2
on home care leave[d]	..	21.8	..	..

.. Not applicable.
a) Maternity/parental leave estimates for the United Kingdom are from 2003/04.
b) "In work" estimates indicate mothers who have returned to work after birth and are no longer on leave. These figures also include mothers who might be absent from work due to sickness leave.
c) The category in employment includes all women in work. In addition, this category includes women on maternity and parental leaves in Canada and the UK; women with valid employment contracts during their full-day parental leave in Sweden; and women with valid employment contracts before birth and on maternity and/or parental leave in Finland. The Finnish definition of the employment rate excludes those mothers from the labour force which are on job-protected *home care leave.*
d) On home care leave indicates those mothers who receive home care allowance and are in an employment-protected status. There is no comparable system in the other countries in this review.

Source: Finland, Labour Force Survey; Canadian and Swedish maternity/parental leave rate, OECD Secretariat calculations; other data, national authorities.

3.2.2. Total working hours of mothers in employment decline as family size increases

The effect of family size on maternal employment rates and length of working time is illustrated in Table 3.6. In all four countries under review, the probability of mothers not being in employment increases with family size, although the effect appears weak in Finland (where there is no clear relationship between part-time work and family size either). In Sweden, there does not seem to be a dramatic drop in maternal employment rates irrespective of the number of children, while in Canada (and the province of Québec) maternal employment rates only drop markedly for mothers with four children. In Canada, part-time employment increases steadily with family size and Swedish mothers reduce working hours most with their second child. In the United Kingdom, maternal employment rates drop significantly for mothers with three children and, while almost half of the mothers with one child work part-time, this share increases to at least 60% for two children.

Table 3.6. **Mothers of large families are least likely to be in paid work on a full-time basis**
Maternal and female employment rates (EPR) and share of part-time (PT) employment[a]

	Canada		Province of Québec		Finland		Sweden		United Kingdom	
	2001				2002		2003		2003	
	EPR	Share PT	EPR	Share PT	EPR	Share PT	EPR	Share PT	EPR	Share PT
1 child	70.1	22.8	71.3	18.9	71.2	7.5	80.6	30.3	68.5	47.2
2 children	73.2	27.6	73.2	21.9	70.9	6.0	84.7	38.9	66.4	60.5
3 children	68.4	32.7	65.4	28.2	60.3	9.1	75.6[b]	44.8[b]	51.8	63.5
4+ children	58.0	36.1	53.3	31.6	59.3	6.3			32.1	67.4
All mothers	70.5	27.4	70.3	22.1	69.0	7.0	81.5	36.5	64.2	54.8
All women	66.3	27.9	63.4	25.5	61.6	9.5	72.8	34.1	69.7	38.6

a) Data regarding part-time work for Sweden reflects persons working less than 35 hours per week, but less than 30 hours for the other countries and in the province of Québec.
b) Three or more children.
Source: Information supplied by national statistical offices.

3.2.3. Maternal employment and household status

Dual earners in couple families are the norm: in Canada (and the province of Québec), Finland and the United Kingdom, both adults are in employment in two-thirds of the couple families, while in Sweden both spouses work in five out of six couples (Table 3.7). Students and older workers may engage in part-time employment, but this is less often the case for Finnish mothers with dependent children: in almost 60% of all couple families (and 91% of all dual earner families) both adults work full-time (even though

Table 3.7. **One-and-a-half-earner families are most common in Sweden and the United Kingdom**

Employment status of couple families with dependent children[a]

	No one in employment	One in employment[b]				Both in employment[b]				
		All	FT	PT	Unknown	All	2 FT	1 FT, 1 PT	2 PT	Unknown
Canada										
1981	5.4	48.1	45.5	1.9	0.7	43.5	26.9	16.2	0.5	3.0
1991	6.3	33.0	30.5	1.8	0.7	58.2	39.1	18.6	0.6	2.5
1996	7.7	29.7	26.5	2.4	0.7	60.3	39.1	20.4	0.9	2.3
2001	6.1	27.1	24.5	1.9	0.6	64.6	44.6	19.2	0.7	2.2
Province of Québec										
1981	8.7	52.3	49.2	2.2	0.8	36.6	24.1	12.0	0.4	2.5
1991	7.9	35.5	32.7	2.0	0.8	54.0	38.1	15.3	0.6	2.6
1996	9.2	31.6	28.3	2.5	0.8	57.0	39.6	16.5	0.9	2.2
2001	6.4	27.0	24.4	1.9	0.7	64.3	48.2	15.5	0.7	2.4
Finland[c]										
1990	1.3	24.9	24.3	0.6	–	73.8	67.8	5.6	0.4	–
1995	7.6	35.3	34.1	1.2	–	57.2	52.4	4.6	0.2	–
2000	5.4	32.0	31.2	0.9	–	62.6	57.6	5.0	0.0	–
2002	4.8	31.2	29.7	1.5	–	64.1	58.9	5.0	0.2	–
Sweden										
2002	2.9	13.0	8.7	4.3	–	84.1	39.4	39.1	5.6	–
United Kingdom										
2000	6.5	26.8	23.2	3.0	0.7	66.7	27.6	36.6	0.7	1.8
2003	5.6	27.2	23.4	3.0	0.7	67.2	28.3	36.3	0.8	1.7

a) Children aged 16 years old or younger, 15 years or younger in the United Kingdom.
b) PT = part-time, working less than 30 hours per week, except for Sweden where it is 35 hours per week; FT = full-time, working 30 or more hours (35 or more for Sweden) per week.
c) Finnish data on employment by household status are taken from the income survey and over the last ten years, the number of employed persons according to this survey was about 6 to 8% below that as suggested by the labour force survey. This is because the income survey does not regard a person as employed if that person was in employment for less than six months during the survey year.

Source: Information supplied by national statistical offices.

the data underestimate dual earner couples, see notes to Table 3.7). In Canada, both adults in two-thirds of dual earner families work full-time (this is 75% in the province of Québec), while this is only 42% in the United Kingdom. Indeed, the majority of dual earner couples in the United Kingdom are so-called "one-and-a-half earner families", i.e., one parent works full-time and the other works on a part-time basis. In about 40% of the dual earner couples, Swedish mothers with young children reduce their hours of work to below 35 hours per week and, in 6% of couple families, both partners work less than 35 hours per week.

Historical data is not available for Sweden and the United Kingdom (see Table 3.A.1 at the end of this chapter), but maternal employment trends suggest that dual earners in couple families have long been the norm in Sweden and are a relatively recent feature in the United Kingdom. Indeed, the United Kingdom is the one country in this review where main earner families (including single earner couples and one-and-a-half earner families) are the most predominant type of couple family. Trends reveal that the proportion of single earner families has almost halved since 1981 in Canada, with an almost proportional increase in dual full-time earner families: in the province of Québec these trends were even more pronounced. Finnish data suggest that both adults working full-time in couples has been the norm for some time and that its prevalence is growing again after the labour market shake out during the early 1990s.

At 2.9%, Sweden has a very low level of joblessness among couple families with dependent children. In the other countries, the joblessness rate is almost twice as high, raising serious poverty concerns (Chapter 2). Improved economic conditions have contributed to a decline in the incidence of joblessness in couple families with dependent children in Finland, Canada, the province of Québec and the United Kingdom since the mid-1990s.

Employment in sole parent families

There are very significant differences in the employment (and poverty) situation of sole parent families in the four countries under review (Table 3.8). Employment rates among sole parents are highest in Sweden at more than 80% (with many sole parents work less than 35 hours per week). In Finland and Canada sole parent employment rates are somewhat lower at around 70% and 68%, respectively, but in contrast to Sweden, about 75% of sole parents in Canada and the province of Québec work full-time while this is almost 95% in Finland. In the United Kingdom, sole parent employment rates are at 54.3% in 2004 (up from 45% in 1997) of which about half concerns part-time employment. The Québec experience has been significant in that the employment rate of sole parents increased from 47% in 1981 to 67.8% in twenty years. This trend can be related to improved economic circumstances (Chapter 2), childcare policies (Chapter 4) and a tightening of benefit generosity (Chapter 5).

3.3. Gender differences in pay

Women generally earn less than men because of their economic concentration in employment sectors/occupations with relatively low pay, the nature of their employment contracts, the relatively small number of hours of paid work they engage in and because mothers rather than fathers reduce

Table 3.8. **A rapid increase of employment among sole parents in the province of Québec**

Employment status among sole parents[a]

	In employment		Not in employment
	All	PT share[b]	
Canada			
1981	58.7	17.3	41.3
1991	59.3	17.1	40.7
1996	57.5	22.3	42.5
2001	67.6	19.2	32.4
Province of Québec			
1981	47.0	15.3	53.0
1991	58.0	15.1	42.0
1996	55.5	17.9	44.5
2001	67.8	15.6	32.2
Finland			
1990	87.3	2.9	12.7
1995	63.7	6.9	36.3
2000	66.7	4.8	33.3
2002	70.0	5.4	30.0
Sweden			
2002	81.9	40.7	18.1
United Kingdom			
2000	51.2	50.7	48.8
2003	53.1	48.7	46.9

a) Children aged 16 years old or younger, 15 year old or younger in the United Kingdom.
b) Part-time share in total employment: PT = part-time, working less than 30 hours per week (except for Sweden where it is less than 35); full-time, working 30 or more hours per week (except for Sweden where it is 35 or more).

Source: Information supplied by national and provincial statistical offices.

their labour force participation in the presence of children. Older women have relatively low levels of educational attainment, but the education gap for younger women has, if anything reversed. Yet, as shown in Table 3.3, there still is a gender gap in the field of studies that are pursued, which contributes to the gravitation of women towards female-dominated sectors such as education, health or childcare services. Cross-country comparable data on gender wage gaps suggests that gender wage gaps are largest in the United Kingdom, smallest in Finland and Sweden with Canada holding a middle position (OECD, 2002a). In Finland and Sweden gender wage gaps are smallest at *lower earnings* levels: The gender wage gap at the bottom quintile is only 8% compared to 14% across the OECD. However, when moving up the income distribution, gender wage gaps widen and at *high earnings* levels are about 19%

Table 3.9. **Small gender wage gaps in Sweden and Finland, but not at higher earnings levels**

Female and male earnings ratios[a]

	Hourly earnings, full-time wage and salary employees[b]				Hourly earnings, all wage and salary employees[b]			
	Ratio of mean	Ratio of median	The gap at the bottom quintile[c]	The gap at the top quintile[c]	Ratio of mean	Ratio of median	The gap at the bottom quintile[c]	The gap at the top quintile[c]
Canada	82	81	81	86	81	78	81	81
Finland[d]	82	87	92	77	82	87	92	77
Sweden	86	90	92	84	83	88	91	81
United Kingdom[d]	80	85	85	80	75	79	79	76
OECD[e]	84	86	86	85	84	85	86	84

a) Percentage ratio of female to male wage.
b) Persons aged 20 to 64 years old.
c) Ratio between the upper earnings limits of, respectively, the female and male earnings distributions' quintiles.
d) 1998 for Finland and the United Kingdom.
e) Unweighted average for 19 OECD countries: Australia, Austria, Belgium, Canada, Denmark, Finland, France, Germany, Greece, Ireland, Italy, the Netherlands, New Zealand, Portugal, Spain, Sweden, Switzerland, the United Kingdom and the United States.

Source: OECD (2002), *Employment Outlook*, OECD, Paris.

in Canada and Sweden and 23-24% in Finland and the United Kingdom, and well above the OECD average of 16%.[8]

Evidence from national studies in the four countries under review finds that individual worker characteristics and workplace differences between women and men explain a large proportion of the gender wage gap, especially in the United Kingdom.[9] About half of the Finnish gender wage gap and 61% of the Canadian gender wage gap can be explained by occupational and sectoral segregation of women (Drolet, 2002; and Kuusisto, 2004), while in Canada gender pay differences are also related to part-time employment status.[10] In Sweden, the gender wage gap is halved when accounting for sectoral differences, such that the wage differential is reduced to 1% in the municipal sector, 8% in the central government sector and 10% in the private sector (Berg, 2004). Meyerson and Petersen (1997) find that the unexplained gender wage gap is only 1.4% in Sweden when all differences in employment and worker characteristics are taken into account. Wally and Olsen found for the United Kingdom that 72% of the wage gap can be explained by employment experience (26%), interruptions due to family care (15%), part-time employment (12%), education (6%) and occupational segregation (26%).

In both Canada and the United Kingdom, gender wage gaps have narrowed over time, but only in Canada has this led to a reduction in the unexplained pay differences (Mumford and Smith, 2004; and Shannon and Kidd, 2001).[11] By contrast, gender wage gaps have not narrowed in Finland and Sweden since the 1970s and the 1980s, respectively (Albrecht *et al.*, 2001; and

STM, 2003). Evidence for the United States and Denmark, which respectively experienced a decrease and stagnation in the gender wage gap, finds that positive wage effects of increased human capital are conferred to American women (as in Canada and the United Kingdom) but not to Danish women, providing strong evidence of the existence of a glass ceiling in Denmark (Datta Gupta et al., 2001). Similarly, gender wage gaps in Finland and Sweden (Table 3.8) are largest at higher earnings levels. Albrecht et al. (2001) suggest that the glass ceiling is partly due to the extensive parental leave system, which may reduce the leave taker's career commitment and/or depreciate his/ her human capital (Albrecht et al., 1999; Phipps et al., 2001; and Datta Gupta and Smith, 2000).[12] At the same time, as mothers rather than fathers tend to take leave to care for young children, employers come to expect less from female workers, which can reduce investment in their training and reduce their long-term career prospects (Lommerud and Vagstad, 2000).

The family gap, which estimates the female wage penalty due to the decision to have children (as opposed to remaining childless), is low in Sweden and Finland (Jansson et al., 2003; and Vartiainen, 2001). In the United Kingdom, wage differences between mothers and non-mothers are estimated at between 10% and 22% and are related to the relatively high incidence of mothers in part-time employment (Viitanen, 2004; Joshi and Paci, 1998). Having children reduces cumulative earnings of mothers compared to men and childless women in all four countries. Sigle-Rushton and Waldfogel (2004) find that the estimated cumulative earnings of childless women (by age 45) with educational attainment levels up to and including upper secondary education are 70% (Sweden) and 77% (Finland) of men's earnings; this proportion is 62% (Sweden) and 63% (Finland) for mothe rs with two children. Similarly, in Canada and the United Kingdom, childless women earn 67% (Canada) and 73% (United Kingdom) of men's cumulative earnings, while this proportion was only 51% (Canada) and 41% (United Kingdom) for mothers with two children.

3.3.1. The differences in earnings between mothers and fathers in a couple family

In all countries the norm is that husbands work full-time and, because of that, they are most likely to be the highest earner in families. On average, earning differentials between married partners are smallest in Sweden, where women contribute 63% of their husband's earnings to household income, in contrast to 58% in Canada and the province of Québec, 53% in Finland and 45% in the United Kingdom. Much of the difference in Sweden is related to the limited number of women who are not in employment or earn less than 10% of what their husbands earn (Chart 3.3).

Chart 3.3. **Women generally earn less than their husbands**

Distribution of dual earner couples where the husband worked full-time by the ratio female-to-male of annual income from work, latest year

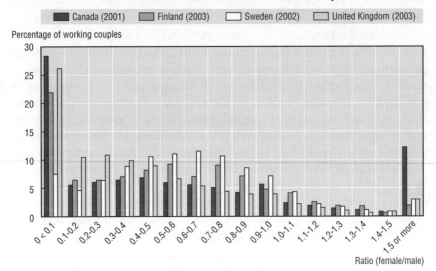

Ratio (female/male)

Source: Data supplied by national authorities based on Statistics Canada (Census 2001), Statistics Finland and UK Labour Force Survey.

The distribution of earnings within couple families varies considerably among countries. Not surprisingly, however, given their low part-time employment participation, one-quarter of Finnish mothers with dependent children (and one-fifth of Canadian mothers) contribute more to family income than their husbands in full-time work. Moreover, one in eight married Canadian women earns more than 1.5 times what the husband in full-time work earns. In Sweden, the high proportion of women working less than 35 hours per week contributes to maternal earnings concentrating in the upper half of what their husbands earn, while maternal part-time employment in the United Kingdom is much more likely to involved in low-wage employment and/or limited hours of work (Chapter 6).

3.4. Conclusions

Labour markets in all four countries under review perform rather well in comparison to other OECD member countries. Female labour force participation rates in particular are high from an international perspective: they range from 70% in the United Kingdom to 77 % in Sweden, compared to 60% for the OECD area in 2003. As a result, gender employment gaps are relatively small: from about 3% in Finland and Sweden to 9% in Canada (and the province of Québec) to 13% in the United Kingdom. Employment outcomes for sole parents are also generally better than in most OECD countries, except for the United Kingdom, where the employment rate is just above 50% and mainly concerns part-time employment. The increase in employment among sole parents in Québec has been impressive: the employment rate increased from 47% in 1981 to 68% in 2001.

These high female employment rates mask, however, considerable differences in work and family outcomes of parents in the four countries under review. High employment rates of mothers in Sweden (and to a lesser extent Finland) reflect long leave periods during which they are counted as employed. Nonetheless, mothers are highly likely to be in work in Canada (the province of Québec) and the United Kingdom as well as in Sweden due to the availability of part-time employment in these countries. Mothers in the United Kingdom are the most likely to work part-time and many Swedish mothers work less than 35 hours per week. Finnish women are most likely to withdraw from the labour market after childbirth to return when their youngest child is generally 3 years of age. The expectation that mothers provide personal care for very young children on a full-time basis contributes to the high incidence of temporary employment among young Finnish women (Chapter 6).

The trend in educational attainment has been towards the establishment of a "positive" female gender education gap. The fields of study pursued by women, however, still reflect a tendency to obtain certificates in female-dominated areas, including health, humanities and education rather than, say, mathematics and engineering. This contributes to a high level of gender segregation in employment occupations/sectors in Finland, Sweden and the United Kingdom, but less so, in Canada. For Canada and the United Kingdom, this means that many women are in low-paid private sector jobs that contribute to relatively large wage gaps at bottom quintiles. In Finland and Sweden, wage gaps are generally smaller, but not at the higher income quintiles. Relatively limited labour force withdrawal, a low incidence of part-time employment, limited gender segregation by sector and a low gender wage gap at the top quintile all point to Canadian women having a fairly equal chance compared to men of getting through to the top.

Dual earners in couple families are the norm in all four countries. At 84%, Sweden has the highest percentage of couples in which both parents work, while this is about two-thirds of all couple families in Finland, Canada and the province of Québec and the United Kingdom. But whereas in Finland (92%) and the province of Québec (75%) these are families in which both parents work full-time, the most common type of working couple in both Sweden and the United Kingdom are those where second earners reduce working hours. At almost 6%, Sweden has the highest incidence of couples wherein both partners reduce their working hours. Sweden also has the best record in generating high employment rates among sole parents (82% in 2002): employment rates in Canada and Finland are about 10 percentage points lower (but with more sole parents working full-time) and, in the United Kingdom, slightly more than half of sole parents are in paid work (half of them part-time). The change in employment outcomes among sole parents in the province of Québec has been most significant: the increase from 47% in 1981 to 68% in 2001 will no doubt contribute to a reduced poverty risk among sole parents, their children and their children's children.

Notes

1. Because of Finland's involvement in wars from 1939 to 1945, Finnish women engaged in the labour market on a large scale. Compared to Sweden, which was not engaged in military conflict at the time, there was thus a relatively strong tradition of female employment which continued during the post-war period: female employment rates in Sweden only overtook Finnish rates during the late 1970s.

2. Full-time and part-time employment in this review is based on a common definition of 30 usual weekly hours of work in the main job, unless otherwise noted.

3. A comparison of women in management positions across countries is fraught with difficulties as the categorisation of similar jobs may be different from one country to another. This feature is likely to contribute to the relatively high prevalence of managerial occupations among workers in the United Kingdom (almost 15% of workers are in "managerial" jobs) compared to the other three countries.

4. Non-standard workers include: temporary employees (i.e., workers with an employment contract of fixed duration), seasonal workers, workers who engage in self-employment or work on a contract basis ("own account workers"), on-call workers and workers employed by a temping agency. Because of cross-country differences in definitions and measurement, there is no comprehensive set of information on the prevalence of non-standard employment.

5. During the period between two temporary contracts of about 9 to 10 months, Finnish workers are generally entitled to unemployment benefits. This feature exerts upward pressure on female unemployment rates in Finland (Table 3.1).

6. During the 2000-03 period, the number of workers who reported sick per annum increased from 140 000 to 175 000, while the number of sick people not in employment increased to almost 400 000 or 3.5% of the labour force (OECD, 2004l).

7. The one observation available for the 1976-80 cohort suggests a sharp drop in employment rates among 20-24 year olds, especially in Sweden. This change is likely to be influenced by changes in educational patterns, and does not necessarily affect the employment profile for the rest of the life course.

8. At higher earnings gender wage gaps are smallest in Portugal at about 2% (OECD, 2004).

9. For example, gross wage differences in Finland are about 30% for salaried manufacturing workers and 25% for central government workers and private service sector companies; in Sweden, the difference for white-collar workers (24%) is higher than for central government staff (16%) and blue collar workers (11%) (Statistics Sweden, 2004; Vartiainen, 2003).

10. Drolet (2002) found that the proportion of part-time work in a workplace even when controlling for industry and occupation, has a more significant negative wage impact for women than for men and contributes to about 11% of the gender wage gap.

11. The evidence in Canada (as in the United States) suggest that the decline in the gender wage gap since the late 1970s reflects the improvement of female workers wage-determining characteristics (e.g., education, experience, union membership) and the fall in the unexplained portion (Shannon and Kidd, 2001). By contrast, Harkness (1996) found that the unexplained part of the gender wage gap in the United Kingdom increased between 1974 and 1992.

12. In Canada, career interruptions due to maternity leave and childcare have lower wage penalties than demand-related interruptions such as unemployment and lay-offs (Phipps et al., 2001), while the same applies to career interruptions other than taking parental leave in Sweden (Albrecht et al., 1999).

Table 3.A.1. **Employment in households with children**
Canada

A. Census families[a] with youngest child 16 years old or less

		With two parents							With one parent			
	No one in employment	One in employment			Both in employment				Not in employment	In employment		All
		FT[b]	PT[b]	Who did not work[c]	2 FT[b]	1 FT, 1 PT[b]	2 PT[b]	Who did not work[c]		FT	PT	
1981	4.7	39.5	1.6	0.6	23.3	14.0	0.4	2.6	5.4	7.7	17.3	100
1986	5.1	32.2	2.1	0.7	25.7	15.8	0.6	2.5	6.5	8.9	18.3	100
1991	5.2	25.5	1.5	0.6	32.6	15.5	0.5	2.1	6.7	9.8	19.3	100
1996	6.2	21.5	2.0	0.6	31.6	16.5	0.7	1.9	8.1	11.0	20.3	100
2001	4.8	19.3	1.5	0.5	35.2	15.2	0.6	1.7	6.8	14.3	21.3	100

B. Census families[a] with youngest child not yet 3 years old

1981	5.0	50.2	1.8	0.7	20.5	11.3	0.3	2.8	4.4	3.1	17.3	100
1986	5.8	40.3	2.3	0.9	24.2	13.8	0.5	2.8	5.6	3.8	18.3	100
1991	6.5	33.6	1.7	0.7	28.9	14.3	0.4	2.5	7.1	4.1	19.3	100
1996	7.9	28.0	2.3	0.8	29.6	15.5	0.7	2.2	8.3	4.6	20.3	100
2001	6.2	28.0	1.9	0.8	31.3	14.7	0.6	2.3	7.8	6.6	21.3	100

C. Census families[a] with youngest child 3 to not yet 6 years old

1981	4.6	42.0	1.5	0.6	20.9	14.2	0.3	2.9	6.0	6.9	17.3	100
1986	5.0	33.8	2.1	0.8	23.4	16.2	0.6	2.7	7.4	8.1	18.3	100
1991	5.2	27.0	1.6	0.6	29.1	17.1	0.5	2.2	7.8	8.9	19.3	100
1996	6.2	22.6	1.9	0.6	28.8	17.3	0.7	2.0	9.8	10.0	20.3	100
2001	4.9	20.4	1.5	0.5	32.9	16.2	0.6	1.9	7.9	13.2	21.3	100

a) Census families where adults are between 15 and 64.
b) PT = Part-time = employment of less than 30 hours a week; FT = Full-time = employment of 30 hours or more per week.
c) Those who were employed but did not work includes persons who were absent from their job or business, with or without pay, for a variety of reasons (illness, maternity leave, vacation, a labour dispute at their place of work, bad weather, personal or family responsibilities or any other reasons).

Source: Statistics Canada, Census: 1981, 1986, 1991, 1996, 2001.

Table 3.A.1. **Employment in households with children** (cont.)
Province of Québec

A. Census families[a] with youngest child 16 years old or less

| | With two parents | | | | | | | | With one parent | | | All |
| | No one in employment | One in employment | | | Both in employment | | | | Not in employment | In employment | | |
		FT[b]	PT[b]	Who did not work[c]	2 FT[b]	1 FT, 1 PT[b]	2 PT[b]	Who did not work[c]		FT	PT	
1981	7.5	42.6	1.9	0.7	20.9	10.4	0.4	2.1	7.1	6.3	17.3	100
1986	7.1	34.1	2.2	0.8	23.8	12.5	0.6	2.2	8.7	8.0	18.3	100
1991	6.5	27.0	1.7	0.6	31.4	12.6	0.5	2.1	7.4	10.2	19.3	100
1996	7.4	22.6	2.0	0.6	31.7	13.2	0.7	1.7	9.0	11.2	20.3	100
2001	4.9	18.9	1.5	0.5	37.4	12.0	0.5	1.8	7.2	15.2	21.3	100

B. Census families[a] with youngest child not yet 3 years old

1981	7.3	49.6	2.0	0.8	21.0	9.4	0.3	2.2	4.9	2.3	17.3	100
1986	7.7	38.0	2.5	1.1	25.5	12.1	0.6	2.5	6.8	3.3	18.3	100
1991	8.1	32.8	1.9	0.8	30.8	11.9	0.5	2.7	7.0	3.5	19.3	100
1996	9.8	27.0	2.4	0.9	31.7	13.2	0.8	2.2	8.5	3.6	20.3	100
2001	7.2	25.0	1.9	0.9	36.7	11.9	0.6	2.7	7.5	5.4	21.3	100

C. Census families[a] with youngest child 3 to not yet 6 years old

1981	7.4	44.9	1.7	0.8	19.3	10.9	0.4	2.4	7.2	5.1	17.3	100
1986	7.0	35.1	2.0	0.9	23.6	12.6	0.6	2.3	8.8	7.0	18.3	100
1991	6.7	28.1	1.7	0.8	30.1	13.2	0.5	2.2	8.4	8.4	19.3	100
1996	7.7	23.9	1.9	0.7	30.8	13.0	0.7	1.9	10.5	9.0	20.3	100
2001	5.3	19.1	1.6	0.5	36.8	12.3	0.5	1.8	8.4	13.6	21.3	100

a) Census families where adults are between 15 and 64.
b) PT = Part-time = employment of less than 30 hours a week; FT = Full-time = employment of 30 hours or more per week.
c) Those who were employed but did not work includes persons who were absent from their job or business, with or without pay, for a variety of reasons (illness, maternity leave, vacation, a labour dispute at their place of work, bad weather, personal or family responsibilities or any other reasons).

Source: Statistics Canada, Census: 1981, 1986, 1991, 1996, 2001.

Table 3.A.1. **Employment in households with children** (*cont.*)

Finland

A. Households[a] with youngest child 16 years old or less

	With two parents						With one parent			All
	No one in employment	One in employment		Both in employment			Not in employment	In employment		
		FT[b]	PT[b]	2 FT[b]	1 FT, 1 PT[b]	2 PT[b]		FT	PT	
1990	1.1	21.1	0.5	59.0	4.9	0.3	1.6	11.3	17.3	100
1995	6.4	28.8	1.0	44.4	3.9	0.2	5.6	9.8	18.3	100
2000	4.5	25.9	0.7	47.9	4.1	0.0	5.6	11.2	19.3	100
2001	4.0	25.2	0.7	50.1	3.6	0.2	4.9	11.3	20.3	100
2002	4.1	25.3	1.3	50.2	4.2	0.2	4.4	10.3	21.3	100

B. Households[a] with youngest child not yet 3 years old

1990	2.4	46.5	0.6	41.8	2.9	0.6	2.9	2.4	17.3	100
1995	10.8	52.4	1.8	25.9	2.4	0.0	5.4	1.2	18.3	100
2000	9.5	53.7	0.7	28.6	2.7	0.0	4.1	0.7	19.3	100
2001	7.3	54.3	0.7	29.8	2.0	0.0	4.0	2.0	20.3	100
2002	8.3	56.9	0.7	26.4	2.8	0.0	3.5	1.4	21.3	100

C. Households[a] with youngest child 3 to not yet 6 years old

1990	0.8	15.0	0.8	65.0	8.3	0.0	0.8	9.2	17.3	100
1995	5.7	25.7	1.0	50.5	5.7	0.0	5.7	5.7	18.3	100
2000	2.9	20.0	1.0	54.3	6.7	0.0	7.6	7.6	19.3	100
2001	3.1	19.6	0.0	54.6	6.2	1.0	7.2	8.2	20.3	100
2002	4.0	19.2	1.0	56.6	6.1	0.0	6.1	7.1	21.3	100

a) Age criteria applied in couple households: at least one of the spouses aged 15-64.

b) PT = Part-time = employment of less than 30 hours a week; FT = Full-time = employment of 30 hours or more per week.

Source: Statistics Finland: Income Distribution Statistics.

Table 3.A.1. **Employment in households with children** (*cont.*)

Sweden

A. Households[a] with youngest child 16 years old or less

	With two parents						With one parent			All
	No one in employment	One in employment		Both in employment			No one in employment	In employment		
		FT[b]	PT[b]	2 FT[b]	1 FT, 1 PT[b]	2 PT[b]		FT	PT	
2001	2.2	6.8	2.5	30.7	31.0	3.2	4.1	19.6	17.3	100
2002	2.2	6.6	3.3	30.0	29.8	4.2	4.3	19.6	18.3	100

B. Households[a] with youngest child not yet 3 years old

2001	3.4	7.2	3.3	29.9	41.2	6.1	2.1	6.7	17.3	100
2002	2.6	6.5	4.9	28.2	40.4	6.8	3.1	7.6	18.3	100

C. Households[a] with youngest child 3 to not yet 7 years old

2001	3.0	8.4	2.8	26.6	37.2	3.9	3.0	15.1	17.3	100
2002	2.3	8.3	3.6	25.4	38.4	4.2	4.0	13.9	18.3	100

a) Age criteria applied in couple households: at least one of the spouses aged 15-64.
b) PT = Part-time = employment of less than 35 hours a week; FT = Full-time = employment of 35 hours or more per week.

Source: Statistics Sweden.

Table 3.A.1. **Employment in households with children** (cont.)

United Kingdom

A. Households[a] with youngest child 15 years old or less

	With two parents								With one parent		All
	No one in employment	One in employment			Both in employment				No one in employment	In employment		
		FT[b]	PT[b]	Who did not work[c]	2 FT[b]	1 FT, 1 PT[b]	2 PT[b]	Who did not work[c]		FT	PT	
2000	5.1	18.3	2.4	0.5	21.9	29.0	0.5	1.4	10.7	10.1	17.3	100
2001	5.0	18.2	2.2	0.6	21.8	29.2	0.5	1.5	10.6	10.3	18.3	100
2002	4.9	18.2	2.2	0.7	21.1	28.7	0.6	1.7	10.6	11.2	19.3	100
2003	4.4	18.3	2.3	0.6	22.1	28.4	0.6	1.4	10.9	11.0	20.3	100

B. Households[a] with youngest child not yet 3 years old

	No one in employment	FT[b]	PT[b]	Who did not work[c]	2 FT[b]	1 FT, 1 PT[b]	2 PT[b]	Who did not work[c]	No one in employment	FT	PT	All
2000	5.9	27.9	2.4	0.5	18.5	28.2	–	1.8	10.8	4.1	17.3	100
2001	5.6	27.7	2.3	0.8	17.8	29.2	–	1.6	11.0	4.0	18.3	100
2002	6.3	28.9	2.6	1.0	17.2	27.0	0.6	1.1	10.7	4.6	19.3	100
2003	5.4	29.6	2.3	0.9	17.0	26.9	0.7	1.0	11.9	4.2	20.3	100

C. Households[a] with youngest child 3 to not yet 6 years old

	No one in employment	FT[b]	PT[b]	Who did not work[c]	2 FT[b]	1 FT, 1 PT[b]	2 PT[b]	Who did not work[c]	No one in employment	FT	PT	All
2000	5.1	20.2	2.1	0.6	17.6	32.3	–	1.2	12.3	8.6	17.3	100
2001	4.2	20.9	2.0	0.7	17.1	31.1	–	2.0	12.3	9.6	18.3	100
2002	5.1	19.7	1.9	0.8	16.5	31.3	–	2.0	12.5	10.2	19.3	100
2003	4.4	21.1	2.5	0.8	18.0	29.5	–	1.9	12.3	9.3	20.3	100

a) Age criteria applied in couple households: at least one of the spouses aged 15-64.
b) PT = Part-time = employment of less than 30 hours a week; FT = Full-time = employment of 30 hours or more per week.
c) Those who were employed but did not work includes persons who were absent from their job or business, with or without pay, for a variety of reasons (illness, maternity leave, vacation, a labour dispute at their place of work, bad weather, personal or family responsibilities or any other reasons).

Source: ONS Labour Force Survey.

ISBN 92-64-00928-0
Babies and Bosses: Reconciling Work and Family Life
Canada, Finland, Sweden and the United Kingdom
© OECD 2005

Chapter 4

Childcare Support

Both in the province of Québec and the United Kingdom public investment in childcare has increased rapidly since the late 1990s to 0.8% GDP in the province of Québec, and 0.4% of GDP in the United Kingdom. The long-established municipal day-care systems in Nordic countries (including OSH-care) are more costly: 1.1% of GDP in Finland and 2% of GDP in Sweden. Compared with the other countries the Swedish system is expensive because of its intensive use by very young children: almost 85% of 2-year olds use formal childcare in Sweden while this is about half that in Finland, the United Kingdom, the province of Québec, and considerably lower in the rest of Canada. The countries under review are thus at different stages of childcare system development and therefore often face different policy challenges. This chapter discusses these and other outcomes, in view of differences in public policy approaches towards the development of childcare capacity, reducing the costs of access for families and promoting high-quality childcare services.

There are different reasons for investing in formal childcare. Public policy generally wishes to increase female labour supply, enhance child development and education, tackle poverty, and, in some countries, help parents to have as many children as they desire. Different emphases on these policy objectives (as related to different histories of policy development) help explain the considerable cross-country variation in the nature of formal childcare systems and the intensity with which they are used. For example, a very high proportion of 2-year olds in Sweden use formal childcare (85%), while this is about half that in Finland, the province of Québec and the United Kingdom.

This chapter discusses differences in the nature of childcare systems and their effect on the reconciliation of work and family life. To highlight cross-country differences the chapter first illustrates the relationship between female employment trends and childcare development leading into a discussion of childcare policy objectives. It then gives an overview of existing systems and their use, and goes on to relate cross-country differences in public policy approaches towards the provision of childcare services that are simultaneously affordable, accessible and of high quality.

4.1. Female employment and public childcare investment: chicken and egg

It appears that changing female labour market behaviour preceded and indeed, was a key driver for initiating the development of broadly accessible childcare systems. Subsequently, the development of formal childcare allows female employment to expand further, both in terms of the number of female workers and the hours they engage in paid employment. The Swedish experience – the only country for which long time series on childcare use is available – illustrates the case.[1] In the late 1960s/early 1970s, female employment rates were around 60-65% and only increased above this level when facilitated by childcare expansion that started in the late 1960s (Chart 4.1). In 1965, about 3% of all very young children in Sweden used a public childcare place, and this proportion grew rapidly, especially in the late 1970s and early 1980s, to 50% in 1985 (Chart 4.1). The proportion of very young children using childcare has been in excess of 60% since 1996, and with recent reform extending access to childcare to almost four out of five children not yet 6 years of age. In turn, the expansion of childcare capacity facilitated female

Chart 4.1. **Female employment growth in Sweden
preceded childcare development**

Share of children aged 0-6 and prime age (25-54) female employment rate in Sweden,
percentages

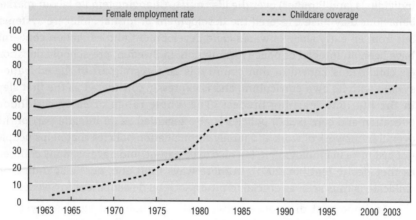

Source: Female employment rates from OECD (2004), *Labour Force Statistics*, OECD, Paris; childcare data
provided by the Swedish authorities.

employment to increase to very high levels: employment rates for prime-age females increased to 90% at peak in 1990, and despite the recession in the early 1990s prime-age female employment rates are still high at around 80%.

The extent to which parents have access to affordable high quality childcare is one of the factors that explain cross-country differences in female labour market outcomes (Chapter 3). As the more comprehensive and longer established Swedish and Finnish (for kids 3 years and older) childcare systems facilitate working full-time, the female employment differential across countries is significant: in full-time equivalents, female employment rates are 62.0% in Sweden, 59.4% in Finland, 54.8% in Canada, and 51.7% in the United Kingdom. Moreover, employment rates among mothers with young children in Sweden (although many are on leave) are at least 20 percentage points higher than in the other countries. Nevertheless, these differences in female employment rates are much smaller than one might expect on basis of differentials in public spending on childcare which amounts to 2%, 1.1%, 0.8%, 0.4%, and 0.2% of GDP in Sweden, Finland, the province of Québec, the United Kingdom and Canada as a whole respectively. Public spending on childcare does not only depend on female labour supply objectives and the pursuit of economic growth, but should also be regarded in the much wider mix of policy objectives that underlie childcare policy development.[2]

4.2. Childcare policy objectives

In Nordic countries such as Finland and Sweden, childcare policy is part of the universal welfare policy models that provide comprehensive support to individuals (and families) over the life course. Changing female labour market behaviour may have triggered the development of formal childcare systems, but from an early stage onwards child development and education concerns have been an integral of policy formulation. In Sweden, pre-school education (as childcare is known in that country) is an integral part of the education system with its own curriculum, and is expressly considered as the first step in the life-long learning process. The whole range of early childhood education and care (ECEC) policies is also regarded as an integral part of the overall framework of work and family reconciliation policies that helps people not just to be in employment, but also to be parent, and have as many children as they desire (Batljan, 2001). In more ways than one, public spending on childcare is thus seen as crucial to future societal development in Sweden.

An important difference between the Finnish and Swedish systems concerns the age of the child at which public policy starts to encourage the parental return to the workplace: this is around 12-18 months in Sweden, and involves two stages in Finland: first, at age 9.5 months (when parental leave expires), and, second, at age 3 when the less generous, but still considerable Home Care Allowance payments are no longer available (Chapters 5 and 6).

Fertility issues are expressly not regarded to be of concern to public family and childcare policy in the United Kingdom. However, greater political significance is attached to tackling child poverty as the primary policy objective. Other policy objectives as, for example, promoting female employment and gender equity are regarded as instrumental in achieving this, but they are not the principal objectives of policy. Very substantial childcare subsidies have been put in place since 1997 to reduce barriers to paid work, while at the same time income-tested child benefits have been expanded to address poverty more directly. These efforts have been complemented by the *Sure Start* and subsequently the Children's Centre programmes initiating the development of expanded and integrated family support services (including childcare). Initially, such services were restricted to relatively deprived areas but it is planned to have 3 500 Children's Centres across England by 2010 (see below). The free part-time (2.5 hours per day) early education offer for 3 and 4 year olds is aimed at *all* children to strengthen child development, but also to reduce the overall costs of childcare to parents. This free education offer will be extended to 15 hours per week for 38 weeks per annum, and by 2010, UK policy aims for full-day care services to be available to all parents with children aged 3-11 who wish to make use of it (HM Treasury, 2004).

To support vulnerable children and families and facilitate employment among parents in low-income families, federal policy in Canada financially supports provincial governments who are responsible for design and delivery of family services, including childcare.In many Canadian provinces public childcare support is limited and childcare coverage is patchy (OECD, 2004m).[3] In addition to existing initiatives (Box 4.1) a new federal initiative has been announced to improve access to affordable, quality childcare services among a broader group of Canadians.[4] Compared to other provinces, public family policy in Québec is more interventionist and family policy reform in 1997/ 98 led to a rapid expansion of affordable quality childcare services (with more subsidised childcare places being projected). This expansion is driven by a strong focus on both supporting *all* working parents and enhancing child development of *all* children (MESSF, 2003 and 2004). There is an aspirational reflex in Québec policy to be as universal in family support as Nordic countries.

4.3. Childcare services: governance, type of service and use

There are marked differences in the governance, provision and use of childcare services across countries. In Sweden and Finland there is by now a tradition of public childcare provisions while in Canada, the province of Québec, and the UK provision is mixed, but predominantly private (both commercial and not-for-profit providers). By nature, private provision allows for a greater diversity in services, as reflected in the UK set-up. Swedish parents and children are the most intensive users of formal childcare among the four countries.

4.3.1. *Childcare governance*

The Finnish and Swedish models of childcare operations are not dissimilar. In both countries local (municipal) authorities are responsible for providing social and health care services, including childcare. Childcare is provided under the aegis of the Ministry of Social Affairs in Finland. In Sweden, all childcare services are considered preschool facilities since the 1996 reform that brought all such services under the supervision of the Ministry of Education. In these frameworks, Central Government identifies goals, formulates guidelines and sets financing rules. In both countries, municipalities have to provide pre-school services and out-of-school-hours care as required by parental work commitments (this extends to parental education commitments in Sweden). In Sweden, this obligation concerns all children of one year and older, but unlike Finland, parents do not have recourse to the judicial system to exercise this right. In Finland, the childcare guarantee concerns *all* children who are not yet old enough to go to primary school (age 7 in both countries).[5] Throughout the year, Swedish municipalities

Box 4.1. **Childcare policy in Canada**

The federal government in Canada does not have direct responsibility for childcare services, except for specific target groups (first nations on reserve, families of military staff and new immigrants). Chapter 2 illustrated how federal Government contributes to the general financing of provincial delivery of social and family services. However, in recent years the federal Government has become more directly involved in childcare funding, and recent initiatives reflect the development of a more active federal policy approach in childcare support for a broader group of Canadian parents.

In the late 1990s, two initiatives increased public support for families: the National Child Tax Benefit (NCTB) improved the income position of families, but also freed up provincial resources for family supports (see the Québec experience below), while the policy framework as established under the National Children's Agenda (NCA) focuses on the enhancement of health, safety and overall development of all young children.

The National Child Tax Benefit, launched in 1998 is a joint federal/provincial/territorial initiative to assist lower income families regardless of whether they are in work or in receipt of benefits. The introduction of the NCTB allowed provinces to reduce the child supplements within social assistance payments, and the provincial funds thus "freed up", could be reinvested elsewhere. It is estimated by federal authorities that about 30% of provincial/territorial reinvestments in 2002/03 were directed to childcare services, subsidies and support.

The Early Childhood Development Agreement launched in 2000 aims to improve and expand support for young children (birth to age 6) and their families. In 2003/04 federal funding of CAD 0.5 billion was allocated to the provinces and territories through the Canada Social Transfer (CST) towards support for four key areas: 1) health in pregnancy and infancy, 2) parenting and family supports, 3) community supports and 4) "Strengthening early childhood development, learning and cares". The initiative is jointly implemented by Social Development Canada and Health Canada, at the federal level. Provinces have discretion in the setting programme priorities, but seven provinces have spent additional funding for extending childcare support (e.g., increasing fee subsidies, new spaces, educator training).

In March 2003, the federal/provincial/territorial Multilateral Framework on Early Learning and Child Care was initiated to make further investment in promoting early childhood development and the support of parental workforce participation or employment training. Over five years about CAD 1.05 billion will be transferred to provinces and territories to invest in regulated childcare programmes.

The provincial government of Québec has not signed these agreements as it wishes to preserve its responsibility in this policy area. However, as its policy is in

Box 4.1. **Childcare policy in Canada** (cont.)

line with the general principles embodied in these two initiatives, it receives federal funding through the Canada Social Transfer. In 2003/04 CAD 118 4 million was transferred to the province of Québec in the framework of Early Childhood Development and about CAD 6 million in the context of the Multilateral Framework on Early Learning and Childcare (over five years until 2008/09 the province of Québec is scheduled to receive almost CAD 250 million).

Apart from these earmarked funds towards support for young children, it is at the discretion of each of Canada's 13 provinces and territories to design its own social and family policy, including childcare policy. OECD (2004m) provides an overview of the different nature of childcare systems across Canada, in terms of, for example, public spending (which is relatively low at 0.2% of GDP), quality, parental fees, and other pertinent information. The province of Québec is outstanding in the Canadian environment, as since 1997, it has increased investment in childcare in contrast to other provinces.

Provincial childcare spending per child aged 0-12 across Canada, 1995 and 2001,[a] in 2001 Canadian dollars

Province/territory	1995	2001
Newfoundland and Labrador	33	101
Prince Edward Island[b]	74	187
Nova Scotia	73	91
New Brunswick	28	105
Québec	**190**	**980**
Ontario	318	232
Manitoba	258	338
Saskatchewan	74	97
Alberta	146	110
British Columbia[c]	169	274
Northwest Territories[d]	87	..
Nunavut	..	..
Yukon Territory[d]	574	..
CANADA	**220**	**386**

.. Not available.

a) Estimates based on total provincial and territorial allocations and total number of children age 0-12 years.

b) The 2001 figure for Prince Edward Island includes kindergarten, which is under child care legislation. As a result, the 2001 figure is not comparable to the figures in the previous years.

c) Figures for British Columbia for fee subsidies are estimated because British Columbia allows subsidies to be used in both regulated and unregulated care. These figures have been adjusted accordingly.

d) Figures for the Northwest Territories and the Yukon are based on estimated numbers of children age 0 – 12 and therefore are not directly comparable to the figures given for the other jurisdictions.

Source: Friendly, M., J. Beach and M. Turiano (2003), Early Childhood Education and Care in Canada 2001, Childcare Resource and Research Unit, University of Toronto, Toronto.

> ## Box 4.1. **Childcare policy in Canada** (cont.)
>
> As a result, coverage of formal childcare is patchy across Canada, except for Québec (OECD, 2004m): 40% of Canadian childcare capacity is in this province, while Québec's very young children account for only 22% of the Canadian total. Taking a leadership role in the development of childcare capacity and improving access among Canadians, federal authorities have announced to spend additional funding of CAD 5 billion over the next five years. How exactly this funding will be allocated is subject of study, but ideally funding should follow parental choice, and use could be made of a mix of financing tools, as in the United Kingdom (see below) and other OECD countries that are in the process of building up their childcare capacity (OECD, 2002 and 2004). For example, there could be direct subsidies to providers towards capital investment, providers in deprived and/or scarcely populated areas or those who provide services to children with special needs. In addition, earmarked childcare (and out-of-school-hours care) support could also be directly awarded to parents. The certainty that public childcare support is available to parents helps attract private providers into the market and funding parents does not favour one provider over another, improves efficiency in delivery through competition and gives parents more choice in type of care and provider. However, such demand-side funding should be strictly tied to providers adhering to pre-set quality standards (*e.g.*, rules on the number of certified staff among personnel, staff-to-child ratios, but also on parental involvement in childcare provision, etc). Demand-side support for childcare can be made income-tested to achieve an equitable allocation of public resources, and, linked to working hours, to pursue employment policy objectives.

have to provide a childcare place "without unreasonable delay", i.e. within three to four months upon application. In practice entry into to the Swedish pre-school system often takes place in August or January. In Finland, parents have to register their child four months before intended use, but only two weeks if the reason for application is employment or study related. The situation varies across municipalities, for example, in Helsinki, parents generally register their child two months before intended use.

Legislation on local service provision may set general rules on basic standards, but otherwise does not provide an excessive number of detailed provisions on the nature and scope of service provision (Box 4.2). Hence, the systems allow for variation in service provision across municipalities. For example, municipalities can, and often do, provide childcare themselves (or in association with adjacent municipalities), but they may also buy such services from other local authorities or private service providers. Nevertheless there is

Box 4.2. **The governance of quality**

Quality is a key factor in the use of formal childcare. Assessment of quality is, however, difficult as it refers to many dimensions: standards of hygiene and safety, the number of children per staff member, training of staff members and, in some countries, compliance with educational policies as laid down in a pedagogical curriculum. Across the four jurisdictions there are considerable differences in the way quality is fostered (see for a detailed discussion of different quality aspects in formal childcare policy, OECD, 1999, 2000, 2000a, 2001 and 2004m).

In Finland, the Ministry of Social Affairs and Health leads and steers childcare policy, while preschools for children of 6 years of age and out-of-school-hours services are the responsibility of the Ministry of Education. The National Board of Education and the National Research and Development Centre for Welfare and Health (Stakes) developed a *Core Curriculum for preschool education* which was adopted in 1996 to enhance the transition into primary school. The core curriculum also serves to recommend standards in day-care for which municipalities are also responsible. Each municipality can implement local standards (in addition to what is laid down in the curriculum), under supervision of the Provincial State Offices. Since 1999, evaluation of education is a statutory requirement and the National Board of Education regularly evaluates all schools. Standards in childcare institutions are evaluated along municipal practice, with a detailed assessment only taking place upon receipt of complaints.

In Sweden, the Ministry of Education and Science is responsible for childcare services to strengthen the pedagogical links of ECEC, school and school-age childcare, and integrate childcare provision into a lifelong learning framework. Since 1998, there is a national curriculum for pre-schools (which in Sweden encompasses all formal childcare), which establishes a set of pedagogical orientations. However, implementation of standards is at the discretion of the 290 municipalities. The Swedish National Agency for School Improvement (NASI) has consultations with municipalities on quality issues, and the agency also plays a key role in providing information on childcare and supports teacher training. Furthermore, the National Agency for School Improvement has been instructed to produce quality indicators at national and local level and to produce general guidelines for quality in preschool to support municipalities in their endeavours to improve quality. Each municipality and school has to prepare annual quality reports, which should (but not always do) contain an assessment (and advice where necessary) of the extent to which the educational objectives have been achieved. In 2002, about 97% of municipalities and schools had prepared quality reports for 2001. Preschools and out-of-school-hours services do not have to prepare such quality reports (as is proposed in new pre-school legislation), but their activities are included in most municipal reports. Childcare facilities do make individual plans that set targets for each individual child. For example, plans identify areas where progress should be made (mathematics, languages, etc.).

Box 4.2. **The governance of quality** (cont.)

In the province of Québec, registered childcare services receive subsidies if they comply with quality standards (e.g., staff-to-child ratios). The Ministry of Employment, Social Solidarity and Families (MESSF) promotes an "educative programme" which sets out the principles and objectives of childcare operations and that have to be agreed by each "centre de la petite enfance", and licensed private garderies. Qualification and training of the childcare workers form an integral part of the mandatory prescribed childcare standards, which, for example, requires that two out of three childcare workers in "centre de la petite enfance" and one out of three childcare workers in "garderies" have to be fully qualified as such. In April 2002, the proportion of qualified childcare workers was 68% in "centres de la petite enfance", and 43% in garderies (MESSF, 2003). The Ministry assesses the quality of childcare services not only through a narrow focus on health and safety standards, but by also considering the organisation of childcare activities and other parameters that influence childcare worker performance, e.g., staff-to-child ratios and group size, the level of training and remuneration of childcare workers (Tremblay, 2003).

The current regulatory landscape is complex in England and involves a number of different agencies: i) the DfES sets the standards and detailed regulations for childcare registration and jointly with the Qualifications and Curriculum Authority is responsible for producing guidance on the foundation stage of the National Curriculum; ii) the Office for Standards in Education (Ofsted) which registers childcare providers, and iii) a separate registration scheme for independent schools, many of which offer early years services.

Until recently, there were no national standards, but in England some important steps have been made towards quality improvement since 2001. In that year, 14 National Standards for under Eights Day Care and Childminding were introduced for inspecting childcare provision with separate standards for nurseries, childminders and out-of-school-hours services. These standards require childcare providers to ensure that premises and people who work with children are suitable, set minimum ratios between staff and children, and take steps to secure the safety of children, to keep records and to ensure that children have activities that are suitable to their ages. Since April 2003, Ofsted assesses childcare providers against these national Standards for the purpose of initial registration, with re-assessment at least once every two years. Ofsted also inspects nursery education providers against early education outcomes as set out in the foundation stage of the national curriculum for children aged 3 and over (these inspections take place every four years, or more frequently when necessary). This curriculum encompasses "six early learning goals" for different areas of learning that can be adapted to the needs of each child in the form of "Stepping Stones", which help practitioners to identify progress being made. In Scotland registration and inspection is the responsibility of the Care Commission that works to standards developed and published by the Scottish Executive. There are differences with rules that prevail in England and Wales. For example, childminders working with children up to age 16 (including out-of-school services) have to register in Scotland, while in England only childminders working with children up to 8 years old have to register.

Box 4.2. **The governance of quality** (cont.)

In England, Local authorities have the statutory obligation to monitor and improve the quality of education and care services in their area. Local quality assurance schemes are intended to facilitate the improvement of quality and professional training of early years workers. Ofsted expected that by 2004 at least 40% of providers had been accredited by a quality assurance scheme, but this target was not met because accreditation procedures took longer than expected, or because there were no quality assurance schemes to which providers (including childminders) could sign up to (NAO, 2004). Extending the application of quality assurance is a matter of priority, and to that end, the government intends to: i) upgrade the quality of the early years workforce through reform of the qualification and career structure; ii) spend GBP 125 million through the "Transformation Fund" so that quality improvements do not impinge on affordability of childcare; iii) reform the regulatory and inspection framework; and, iv) improve access for childminders to services that improve their standards. Local authorities and Children's Centres (Box 4.5) are expected to play a key role in raising quality of local childcare (HM Treasury, 2004).

a high degree of conformity across municipalities as policy makers in Finland and Sweden generally aim to provide access to affordable quality ECEC-services. Hence, municipal rules with respect to settings, quality standards, the pedagogical curriculum and maximum fee regulations do vary (e.g., some municipalities in Finland and Sweden do not charge a parental fee at all), but not that much.

In the province of Québec, the Ministry of Employment, Social Solidarity and Families (MESSF) is responsible for childcare policy operations, including the granting of licenses and the allocation of funding to mostly non-public childcare providers. In contrast to the other jurisdictions, local authorities play a limited role in the provision of childcare services, except for out-of-school-hours care services and leisure time activities during school holidays (see below).[6]

In England, each local authority is now expected to develop, plan and co-ordinate childcare and early years services including nurseries, children's centres, day-care services, playschools and out-of-school-hours care, as described below. Working with their partners through Children's trusts (partnerships[7] including local community representatives, Jobcentre Plus, schools, health agencies, NGOs and commercial private childcare providers) local authorities are responsible for local childcare facilities to serve local needs.

4.3.2. Types of childcare service

The provision of childcare services in Finland differs across municipalities, but broadly speaking there are three types of childcare: centre-based day-care facilities, group family day-care centres, and home-based family day care (Table 4.1). Most of centres provide full-time care, i.e. services that start at 7am until the late afternoon (5 or 6pm). Finnish municipalities also organize supervised play activities and open day-care centres, providing social networks for parents (and their children) who otherwise provide personal care at home on a full-time basis. In 2000, Finland launched its "preschool programme" for 6-year olds and municipalities have to offer this pre-school education for free and comply with the new core preschool curriculum. In general this type of pre-school education is provided for five hours per day starting at 9am. There are a few private day-care centres in Finland, covering 2% of children under age 3 and 4% of 3 to 6 year olds. Often such private centres provide specific services (e.g., an emphasis on music classes or foreign languages), and they are generally more expensive than municipal day care.

About 84% of childcare places in the province of Québec are in "Centres pour la petite enfance" that are operated by non-profit organisations through centre-based care (38%), or family-based childcare places (46%).[8] These so-called "chartered" childcare institutions adhere to provincial quality regulations and provide subsidised childcare for a flat-rate fee of CAD 7 per day (up to a maximum of 10 hours). Commercial day-care providers cover about 16% of the market.[9] Children can also attend nurseries (garderies), halte-garderies, private home-based support and jardins d'enfants (Table 4.1). Garderies can provide services with great flexibility: when the need arises they may on occasion provide a 24-hour care service; the "jardins d'enfants" serve 2 to 5 year olds for up to four hours per day. Free access to full-time "Maternelles" has been available to all 5 year olds since 1997, while 4 year olds in deprived areas may have access to free part-time care.

In Sweden, municipalities operate the pre-school facilities which are largely centre-based day-care facilities.[10] The obligation for municipalities to provide day care in line work requirements means that in general childcare centres are open from about 6.30am or 7am to 6.30pm. Since 2003, municipalities also have to provide free access to preschool centres to all four to 5 year old children and pre-school classes for 6 year olds. To complete the scope of service provision, there are open pre-school services for parents who otherwise provide full-time parental care, but who wish their children to interact with their peers for a few hours per day (in 2002, about 43% of these open preschools were open for more than 16 hours a week).

Table 4.1. **Diverse child care services**

Main characteristics of care facilities for children

	Age group	Type of providers	Overview of the service
		FINLAND	
Children aged 0-6			
Day-care centres	4 months-6 years	Mainly run by municipalities	
Family day care		Operated by municipalities or private	
Three-family day care			Two or three families alternate to take care of children in a home-based environment. Generally on a full-time basis
Group family day care			Two or three childminders provide care in a facility generally provided by local authority. Generally full-time care
Playground activities		Operated by municipalities or private	
Open day-care centre		Operated by municipalities or private	Care provided until 10 continuous hours
Preschool classes	6 years	Public	
Children aged 7-12			
		Mainly based in schools	Free "morning and afternoon" sessions provided in comprehensive schools for pupils in grade 1 and 2 (7 and 8 years old). Three hours per day arranged between 7am and 5pm
		PROVINCE OF QUÉBEC	
Children aged 0-5			
Regulated services			
Centres de la Petite Enfance	0-5 years	Can be centre or family-based. Non-profit organisation. A majority of parents are represented on the Administrative board	Care is provided most often on a full-time basis. Maximum capacity of 350 places for each centre
Garderies	0-5 years	Can be chartered or not. Generally for-profit organisation. Consultative role of a committee of parents	Maximum capacity of 80 places for each centre
Non-regulated services			
Garde familiale	0-5 years	Service provided in private home	
Halte-garderies	0-5 years	Centre-based	Care provided occasionally and with flexible hours. Care can be provided for 24 continous hours when necessary
Jardins d'enfants	2-5 years	Centre-based	Regular attendance for four hours per day
School aged children (6-12)			
Out-of-school care in schools and childcare centres		Mainly provided in schools under the responsibility of the Ministry of Education	Daily care is provided mostly for at least 2 h 30 per day, avalaible from 6.30/7 a.m., at lunch time and at the end of the school day
Leisure activities		Provided by municipalities during school holidays	Activities surrounded by students

Table 4.1. **Diverse child care services** (cont.)

Main characteristics of care facilities for children

	Age group	Type of providers	Overview of the service
		SWEDEN	
Children aged 0-5			
Preschool centres		Centre-based facilities mainly run by municipalities	Full-day care provided from 7 a.m. to 6.30 p.m.
Family-based		Family-based care provided by childminders	
Open preschool		Services providing collective activities for children who otherwise do not use pre-school facilities	Services provided for a couple of hours per day
School aged children (6-12)			
Out-of-school care		Provided mainly in schools but also in childcare centres ("leisure time activities" centres)	
		UNITED KINGDOM	
Children aged 0-5			
Full day-care centre	0-5 years	Includes services provided outside the home. Most frequent are day nurseries (for-profit or not), Children's centers and family centers. Nursery schools can also provide care for children between 3 and 5	Childcare provided for at least four hours per day
Sessional care	0-5 years	Includes playgroups or Crèches that offer short term childcare while parents are unable to look after children.	Childcare is organised by session of less than four continuous hours per day. Children can attend two session per day but not more than five sessions per week
Nursery schools	3-4 years	Provided by public, private sector and voluntary sector (in Scotland). Free of charge for parents when provided by the public sector and often at only a residual charge in the private sector	Educate preschool aged children. Generally open school hours (9 a.m. to 3.30 p.m.) during term time, sometimes morning only. Children usually attend for half a day
Childminders	Usually up to 8 years	Private service of a self-employed person who provides day care for more than two hours per day; usually based in the childminder's own home, with flexible hours	Childcare is provided according to parents needs
School aged children (5-12)			
Out-of-school care	5-12 years	Includes summer camps, Holiday play schemes, breakfast clubs, after-schools clubs. A range of activities are offered including sports, drama, arts and crafts and music	

Source: Information supplied by national authorities.

UK childcare policy has traditionally relied on private sector provision of day-care facilities, and as a result there is great variety in the type of childcare services that is available (see Table 4.1 and Table 4.A.1 at the end of this chapter). The multitude of services includes day care centres as, for example, day nurseries, children centres and family centres, and family day care services through childminders all registered with the Office for Standards in Education (Ofsted). "Sessional" day care, for example, in playgroups is typically available for children from 2 years old, for about 4 or 5 hours per day. In addition, there is the (to be extended, see below) free early education offer for all 3 and 4 year olds of 55 free 2½ hour sessions per term for six terms before reaching statutory school age – the first term following their fifth birthday. In the United Kingdom, the prevalence of providers varies with the type of service. Full day-care services are largely commercial private (75%), while play groups are often organised by NGOs and churches. Out-of-school-hours care is likely to be organised by either NGOs or local authorities, while the free early education offer is predominantly organised by local authorities.

Table 4.2 shows that recommendations set by local and/or central authorities towards staff-to-child ratios and group size vary. In all countries, most staff per child is required for younger children that need more intensive and personalised care. Group size and the qualification of childcare workers are generally seen to indicators of quality in childcare delivery. A lower number of children per childcare worker, for example, generally has a positive effect on child development (OECD, 2001a).[11] Staff-qualifications are also positively associated with the observed quality profile of childcare facilities. For example, a recent study for the United Kingdom found a significant positive relationship between the percentage of highly qualified staff in centres and young children's intellectual and social/behavioural development (Sylva et al., 2004).

In Sweden, about 95% of pre-school workers (and 70% of family day-care workers) have recognised qualifications, and just over half of staff in pre-school (51% in 2002) and out-of-school-hours care facilities (56%) hold higher education degrees (NAER, 2004). In Finland, at least every third employee in a childcare facility has a recognised college degree, or a diploma from a vocational institute, while other staff has to have at least a diploma at school level (family day care workers have to have gone through extended training programmes for 1 660 hours). In Canada, more than four out of five childcare centre workers has at least one year of post secondary training in early childhood education, while two out of five family day-care workers had some type of family care specific training (OECD, 2004m). About 20% of childcare staff in the United Kingdom have graduate level education; at least 50% of childcare staff have not gone through specialist training (Bertram and Pascal, 2000).

Table 4.2. **Most intensive service provision for the youngest children**

Staff-to-child ratios in childcare facilities

	Finland	Province of Québec	Sweden	United Kingdom	
				England and Wales	Scotland
Children aged 0 to 3	1:4 in municipal day care 1:4 in family day-care home, + 1 child who has started preschool or comprehensive school and is in part-time care	1:5 for children under 18 months 1:8 for children between 18 months and 4 years 1:10 for children between 48 and 71 months 1 : 4 for children cared by nannies (family day care) 3:12 in group day family care	1:5.4 for children from age 1 to 5.	1:3 for full-time day care children under 2 for full day care 1:4 for children age 2-3	1:3 for full-time day care for children under 2 1:5 for children age 2-3
Children aged 3 to 6	1 : 13 for less than five-hour sessions	1:10 for children between 4 and 5 years	Average group size is 17 children in 2003, but the size varies mainly between 15 and 20 depending on the age	1:8 for children 3-5 either in full-day or sessional care	1:10 for children 3-5 either in full-day or sessional care
Staff-to-child ratio in preschool facilities	1 :7 for full-day care	1:20 for children older than 5		1:10 in nursery schools and 1:13 in classes	1:15 for children over 8

Source: Information supplied by national authorities. For all countries except Sweden, information refers to recommended ratios by either central or local government. Swedish data concern the actual average ratio, as reported by the National Agency for Education.

4.3.3. Participation in childcare

The use of childcare services by very young children is highest in Sweden (Table 4.3 Panel A). In 2002, about 370 000 children or 80% of all 1-5 years olds in Sweden made use of a formal childcare service. Already 45% of children not yet 2 years of age use childcare, and childcare attendance grows rapidly when children get older: about 85% of the 2-year olds use formal childcare. In the other countries, the use of childcare among children not yet 3 years of age is much more limited. In Finland, the province of Québec and Scotland about 45% of 2-year olds use a formal childcare service, while in these three countries, the use of childcare by children before their first birthday is highest in Scotland at 12%. In both England and Scotland just over a quarter of all children under age 3 use formal childcare. By contrast childcare use among older children generally exceeds 90% in the year directly prior to entering school (Table 4.3).

Table 4.3, Panel B shows that in Sweden almost 90% of children age 1-5 are in centre-based care while only 10% use a family-based setting (use of

Table 4.3. **Use of childcare**

Panel A. Participation of children in formal childcare is highest in Sweden

Participation rate in education and care facilities, % of the child population concerned

	Age 0- < 3	Age 3 to age of compulsory school[a]	Children under school age
Finland	25%	68%	50%
	1% for < 1 year old children	61% for 3- < 4 years old children	
	28% for 1- < 2 years old children	68% for 4- < 5 years old children	
	44% for 2- < 3 years old children	72% for 5- < 6 years old children	
		94% for 6- < 7 years old children are enrolled in free preschool[b]	
Province of Québec	34%	49%[c]	40%[c]
	16% for 1.5 to < 2 years old children	50% for 3 to < 4 years old children	
	45% for 2 to < 3 years old children	48% for 4 to < 5 years old children	
		87% for 5 to < 6 years old children in preschool	
Sweden	65%	89% of 3- < 4 years old children	81%
	45% for children under 2	91% of 4 and 5 years old children	
	85% of children at age 2- < 3		
England	26%[d]	82%	
		97% for 3-4 years old children[c]	
		93% for 3- < 4 years old children	
		100% for 4- < 5 years old children	
Scotland	27%	80%	
	12% for < 1 year old children	94% for 3- < 4 years old children	
	23% for 1- < 2 years old children	100% for 4- < 5 years old children	
	47% for 2- < 3 years old children	40% for 5- < 6 years old children	

Table 4.3. **Use of childcare** (cont.)
Panel B. Children of all age-groups use centre-based care
Proportion of children in each type of care

	Age 0- < 3	Age 3 to age of compulsory school[a]
Finland		
Family-based care	48%	30%
Centre-based care	43%	62%
Other	9%	7%
Province of Québec		
Family-based care	50%	34%
Centre-based care	50%	66%
Sweden		
Family-based care	10%	10%
Centre-based care	90%	92%
England		
Family-based care	9%	10%
Centre-based care	26%	40%
Preschool	6%	48%
Other (nannies, au pair)	10%	14%
Scotland		
Family-based care	18%	6%
Centre-based care	82%	16%
Preschool facilities		78%

a) Mandatory school age is 7 in Finland and Sweden, and 5 in England and Scotland.
b) Preschool is provided at age 6 in Finland and Sweden, 5 in the province of Québec (4 for vulnerable children), 3 in the United Kingdom.
c) Office for National Statistics, Provision for children under 5 years of age in England, January 2004 (provisional). Available data for England is not directly comparable with information for the other countries, as data include non-regular care (e.g. baby-sitting services not included elsewhere), and because data have not been adjusted for multiple use of formal childcare services by one and the same child.
d) Estimates for year 2001 from Woodland, S., M. Miller and S. Tipping (2002), "Repeat Study of Parents' Demand for Childcare", Department for Education and Skills Research Report, No. RR348, London.
Source: Information supplied by national authorities.

family day care is particularly low among those not yet 2 years of age). Formal care in a family-based environment is also uncommon in England and Scotland. By contrast, formal family-day care is common in both Finland and the province of Québec, where half of the children not yet 3 years of age who participate in formal childcare use a home-based facility.

4.3.4. Childcare use and parental employment

The daily opening hours of subsidised childcare services in Finland, the province of Québec and Sweden (see above) facilitate full-time employment of both parents in couple families if they have access to such support, and in all three jurisdictions there is a significant concentration of working hours around 38 to 40 hours per week, for many men and women (Chapters 3 and 6). Many parents with younger children only use childcare services for up to 6 hours a day as that is often considered long enough for young children. In couple families where both parents work full-time, parents adjust their work-schedules so that one parent brings children to the childcare centre with the other parent responsible for the pick-up later in the day. Another solution is that one parent reduces working hours, and this helps explain why so many Swedish mothers with children age 3 to 6 work less than 35 hours per week. On average children of working parents attend childcare for 32 hours per week, while this is 23 and 21 hours per week for children of unemployed parents and parents in parental leave, respectively.

Mothers in England are most likely to reduce working hours, which contributes to the high use of childcare on a part-time basis: in 2001 the average number of hours of childcare use was slightly above 21 hours per week in England (Woodland et al., 2002). Both in terms of participation and the number of hours of use: attendance of childcare services in the United Kingdom varies strongly with parental employment status: 62% of children in households where both parents are in paid work use childcare (including free nursery classes for 3 to 4 year olds); this proportion is only 41% for households where the mother is not in paid employment, and 23% for jobless couple families (Barnes and Willitts, 2004). Dual earner couples and sole parents in full-time employment make the most intensive use of childcare: on average 25 and 31 hours per week, respectively (ibid.).

The increased prevalence of atypical working hours (Chapter 6) has an effect on childcare demand. In Finland, where the childcare guarantee stipulates provision of childcare in line with workplace requirements at all hours, parents who work along irregular schedules accounted for 8% to 9% of all children in day care (MSAH, 2000). Larger municipalities (e.g., Helsinki) can with some difficulty cater for childcare needs in evenings, at night, and over the weekend, but many smaller municipalities cannot address these challenges to their service capacity. In Sweden too, the demand for childcare in the late afternoon/evening increased during the 1990s, and by the year 2000 around 3 000 children were involved in night care. About half of the municipalities provide childcare services for parents working at atypical hours.

In the province of Québec, where about 20% of children not yet 5 years of age attended childcare services on a non-regular or occasional basis in 2001 (ISQ, 2001), a recent survey among childcare users found that 13% of parents would like to have more flexible opening times of centre-based facilities (ISQ, 2004). However, many atypical workers are called up at short notice, so that it is difficult to find a provider, and parents working under such conditions often rely on their ability to synchronise working hours with their partner and/or use informal childcare.[12] Parents working atypical hours use formal childcare thus less intensively than parents with regular work schedules (Rochette and Deslauriers, 2003). Also, 70% of parents with children up to one year using irregular formal childcare have a preference for more flexible family day care provision, compared with 55% of parents with regular use of childcare (ISQ 2004).

In England, about a quarter of parents of preschool children had experienced problems in finding childcare solutions outside normal working hours, and sole parents are most likely to encounter such a problem (NAO, 2004). Solutions are often found in the informal sector: Barnes and Willitts (2004) reported that when mothers in families are in work the use of informal childcare (58% of the cases) was much higher than the use of formal childcare arrangements (22%). Indeed, informal care is still the most common form of care provision in the United Kingdom. Woodland *et al.* (2002) report that around 65% of children under school age in England (also) use an informal provider, grandparents for 55% of the children, 23.5% by other family members and 15% by friends and neighbours. Sole parents in full-time employment make frequent use of informal carers (41%) compared to only 29% of dual full-time earner couples.[13]

Because the free early education offer only covers 2.5 hours per day, parents often have to supplement such care with informal and/or private formal care; almost three-quarters of families using childcare rely on more than one provider. Many parents have complicated work-life schedules, as they arrange to transport children from one source of care to another, with care and schooling hours often being different among siblings. For example in a family with two children of different ages (attending different childcare facilities, with different opening hours) there can be a great many separate movements from one place to another to ensure that children are looked after on a constant basis. Parents frequently have to rely on a complex patchwork of arrangements, mixing different childcare sources, and this irregularity in care provision is hardly beneficial to the child (Barnes and Willitts, 2004). Not surprisingly, there are parents who decide that the organisational challenge involved are such that it is not worth the hassle to try and find (full-time) employment, until their children are at least in the same primary school. This underscores the importance of childcare being close to schools and other early education services that children use (see below).

4.4. Policy issues in childcare investment

Public policy intervention is a key determinant of childcare use as it affects price, quality and accessibility of formal childcare care arrangements. Public spending on childcare services is highest in Sweden at 2% of GDP, while spending in other countries is at most half of that, and about a quarter in the United Kingdom (Table 4.4). The key factor in explaining cross-country differences in public childcare spending is the use and cost of childcare services for very young children (0-3): 1 and 2 year old Swedish kids use formal childcare at least twice as much as their counterparts in the other countries. Public spending per child enrolled in day-care is higher in Finland than in Sweden (as related to the relatively small number of children per staff member in Finland (see Table 4.2), the province of Québec and, particularly, the United Kingdom (Table 4.4).

Table 4.4. **High public investment in childcare services in Sweden**

	Finland (2002)	Province of Québec (2001)	Sweden (2002)	United Kingdom (2003)
Spending as % of GDP	1.1%	0.8%	2.0%	0.4%
Childcare only[a]	0.9%	0.6%	1.4%	0.1%
Pre-primary education only[b]	0.1%	0.12%	0.2%	0.2%
Out-of-school-hours care	0.03%	0.01%	0.4%	–
Percentage of total spending on families	38%	37%	44%	16%
Annual spending in millions USD (PPP)	1 535	1 453	4 559	6 576
Childcare only	1 303	–	3 464	2 182
Pre-primary education only	192	–	383	4 283
Annual spending per child enrolled in USD (PPP)	7 665	–	6 496	2 629
Childcare only	11 251	8 791	10 074	1 529
Pre-primary education only	2 823	–	4 096	3 986
Out-of-school-hours care[c]	5 427	5 981	3 057	–
Spending per child enrolled as % of GDP per capita	29%	–	24%	9%
Childcare only	42%	32%	37%	5%
Pre-primary education only	11%	–	15%	14%
Out-of-school-hours care[c]	20%	21%	11%	–

– Not available.
a) Childcare concern 0 to 5 year olds in Finland (i.e., does not include 6 year old children in preschool classes); in Sweden, spending on childcare gathers all public funds devoted to preschool (excluding those devoted preschool classes the year before primary school); in the province of Québec, childcare spending includes funds directed to chartered childcare services, mainly for children ages 1 to 4; in the United Kingdom, it includes all programs funding childcare support, but not grants directed to nursery schools to provide education services to 3 and 4 year old children.
b) Spending on pre-primary education corresponds to preschool classes for the 6 year old children in Finland and Sweden (year 2003, for children age 6 in Sweden); it refers to children in maternelles in the province of Québec (mostly 5 year old children) and to 3 and mostly 4 year old children in nursery schools in the United Kingdom.
c) For Sweden, estimation of the cost per child enrolled in leisure time activities.
Source: OECD estimates based on information supplied by national authorities.

There are also important trend differences in public childcare spending. In Finland, public spending on childcare services has grown in the second part of the 1990s despite a decline in overall demand (see below and MSAH, 2003). In Sweden, childcare spending has largely recovered from the decline in spending in the aftermath of the economic crisis of the early 1990s, while in the province of Québec and the UK public childcare spending has expanded rapidly in recent years. Spending trends in both Québec and the United Kingdom reflect a rapid increase in public childcare spending: from about 0.2% of GDP in 1995 to 0.8% in 2003 in the province of Québec; and from 0.2% of GDP in 1998/98 to 0.4% of GDP in 2003/04 in the United Kingdom, and in both jurisdictions public spending is expected to rise (MESSF, 2004; and HM Treasury, 2004).[14] Childcare systems are thus in different stages of development, and this contributes to there being a different emphases in national policy debates. In Sweden, capacity issues remain in that some municipalities cannot always provide a childcare place at the first birthday, but the debate largely focuses on improving the quality of already high quality services. Recent childcare expansion in the province of Québec and the United Kingdom allows for reflecting on what has been accomplished in recent years and how to go forward in view of emerging pressure points, as equity in access (Québec) and the desirability for further development of affordable, sustainable and flexible childcare services in the United Kingdom. In the latter country, the development of out-of-school-hours care has also emerged as a key new policy issue (Box 4.3).

4.4.1. Parental contribution to childcare fees

Another reason for relatively high public childcare spending in Sweden is that public support for parents towards their childcare costs is most extensive in that country. In all four countries, free access to preschool education is provided when children are of an age immediately prior to entry in primary school However, there are marked differences in the extent to which public funds serves to alleviate parental childcare costs for younger children. On average, parental fees in Sweden amount to about 11% of childcare costs and this is about 16% in Finland and 19% in the province of Québec; by contrast, estimates on the average parental share in childcare costs in the United Kingdom range from 45 to 75% (NAO, 2004; and Daycare Trust, 2004, respectively).

Parental fees for child care services are set by municipal authorities in both Finland and Sweden. However, legislation regulates the maximum fee municipalities are allowed to charge to parents (and receipt of central government grants is tied to adherence to the maximum fee legislation). In Finland, day care fees vary across municipalities with family income and composition: the maximum fee is about EUR 200 a month for the first child, EUR 180 for the second and EUR 40 for each subsequent child. With the introduction of the Maximum parental fee elgislation in 2002 (see below), the parental fee in Sweden cannot exceed 3% of gross household income (or EUR 140 at maximum) for the first child, 2% of gross household income for the

Box 4.3. **Care for children out of school-hours**

Out-of-school-hours care services (OSH) provided at school-facilities or elsewhere are key in helping parents combine their family and (full-time) work commitments when children get older. These services are relatively cheap, for example, costs per child amount to one-third of the cost in day-care in Sweden. Nevertheless, these services are underdeveloped in Canada (except Québec), Finland and the United Kingdom. The absence of such services contributes to the existence of so-called "latch-key kids"; many US-based evidence reports behavioural problems for kids who are in "self care" after school hours (e.g., Blau and Currie, 2004).

In Sweden, OSH-care services are generally provided in leisure time centres whose number has increased significantly over the last ten years. OSH-services are available to children from age 6 onwards until age 12. In general, OSH-services are provided from 2 p.m. onwards when school finishes, until around 5 p.m. depending on parental working hours. 80% of all 6, 7 and 8 year olds, use an OSH service, but from age 9 onwards the desire to uses an OSH services diminishes rapidly (as a about 40% of all 6 to 12 year olds make use of OSH care). For OSH-care the maximum fee for the fisrt child is 2% of gross family income (with a maximum of EUR 93 per month), and half that for second and third children, other children are not charged fees. The management of leisure time centres is integrated with primary school management to a large extend and both institutions are supervised by the National Agency of Education. Such integration facilitates the use of school facilities for out-of-school-hours services, but has contributed to the emerging concern of "schoolification" of leisure activities: some parents wonder if their children have enough time to play.

In the province of Québec, family policy reform in 1997 instigated a rapid growth of OSH-care provision at subsidised fees, but at CAD 7 for three hours of care, OSH-care is relatively expensive to parents (in comparison to 10 hours in a day-care place for the same fee). In 2003, there were 1 579 registered out-of-school care services in Québec (some of them covering several of the 2000 primary schools in the province) which catered for 174 548 regular users (and 57 667 non-regular users), or about 38% of children the aged 5 to 12. In 2001, this was considered somewhat below demand for OSH-care which was around 50% of all children in that age group. Most of these services that involve leisure time activities but also facilitate preparing homework, are provided within the school system; OSH services are carried out under supervision of the Ministry of Education. Municipalities are obliged to provide OSH places when there are at least 15 children in the area who require the service. Care is delivered for at least 2 h 30 per day, and about 80% of these services are available from 6.30 or 7 a.m., while school days generally start at 8 or 8.30 a.m. OSH services are also available for 90 minutes at lunchtime (when attendance is at maximum), and at the end of the school day from about 16 p.m. to 18 or 18.30 p.m. The majority of children use OSH-places regularly, i.e. for than three days per week and/or over 2 h 30 per day). During the summer school holiday, which lasts nine weeks, municipalities often organise leisure activities (or financially support the organising NGO), for which

Box 4.3. **Care for children out of school-hours** (*cont.*)

parents can claim tax relief. Such services are often not provided until the end of summer as the students who supervise leisure activities start their academic year before the primary school year commences.

Because of municipal spending cuts in the 1990s, municipal OSH-care capacity in 2002 was low in Finland: 3.7% of 7 to 12 year olds. Churches and other NGOs have stepped into the breach to some extent, but 70% of parents of children in the first two grades of primary school would like to use OSH-care. In response, reform in August 2004, obliges municipalities to provide at least 570 hours (three hours per day) of OSH-care in the school environment for each child at some point between 7 a.m. and 5 p.m.; School hours are generally from 8 a.m. or 9 a.m. to 1 p.m. or 3 p.m., while standard working hours starting from 8 a.m. until 4 p.m. Municipalities may provide he service themselves or contract it out; central government co-finances the scheme for 57%; municipalities fork out the rest, but can charge parents a maximum fee of EUR 60 per month.

In England, the most significant increase in childcare places has concerned OSH-care: a 134% increase in the number of OSH and holiday scheme places (*i.e.* over 300 000 places) is estimated to have occurred over the 1999-2003 period (NAO, 2004). Nevertheless, OSH-care capacity in 2001 was estimated to cover about 7% of children in the age group 3 to 5, and 19% of the 6 to 12 year old children. Because of the low coverage, the development of OSH-care services has been identifies as a new childcare policy priority (DfES, 2004). From 2003 onwards, public funds worth GBP 63 million are available to create 95 000 new out-of-school childcare places (and additional capital and revenue funding for disadvantaged areas). However, much more needs to be done to improve OSH-service capacity in the United Kingdom, and to address the parental need for affordable care that wraps around the school day and the school year. The government wishes more parents to have access to "extended schools" including services as for example, breakfast clubs, and music or sports activities, and by 2010 parents of all children aged 5-11 should have access to affordable care facilities from 8 a.m. to 6 p.m. on weekdays all year round (HM Treasury, 2004).

second child (or EUR 93 at maximum), and 1% of gross household income for the third child (or EUR 46), with no charges for fourth or subsequent children (the three-hour pre-school session for all children aged 4-5 is free of charge).

In the province of Québec, since 1997 subsidised childcare places are provided at a flat rate fee: CAD 5 per child per day, whis was increased to CAD 7 in January 2004. Parents with access to subsidised place pay a fee that as a percentage of net income is comparable with rates being charged in Finland (Table 4.5), except for sole parents with two children. For parents in the province of Québec without access to a subsidised childcare place, there is a federal tax credit and a refundable provincial tax credit for eligible childcare expenses. The measure latter is important as it allows childcare cost up to CAD 7 000 to be claimed to be reimbursed for 26 to 75% depending on family

Table 4.5. **Parents pay considerable childcare fees in the United Kingdom**

Parental fee in per cent of net earnings, by income group and family type[a]

	Average gross earnings[b, c]	Finland	Province of Québec	Sweden	United Kingdom
Lone parent, one child	0.67	4.7%	4.9%	2.7%	18.2%
Lone parent, two children	0.67	5.8%	9.5%	2.7%	24.3%
Lone parent, one child	1	7.9%	4.8%	3.4%	23.4%
Lone parent, two children	1	11.2%	9.3%	3.4%	30.8%
Couple, one child	1.33	6.9%	3.9%	3.9%	7.1%
Couple, two children	1.33	10.7%	7.7%	3.9%	9.9%
Couple, one child	1.67	5.7%	3.4%	4.0%	11.8%
Couple, two children	1.67	10.8%	6.8%	4.0%	16.5%

a) General assumption: first child at age 1 and second child, if any, at age 4.
b) "Average earnings" refer to the annual earnings of the "average production worker" in the manufacturing sector (see OECD, 2005, *Taxing Wages 2004 2005*, OECD, Paris). In 2004, these were USD 34 358 (CAD 41 574) in Canada; USD 29 966 (EUR 29 779) in Finland; USD 26 313 (SEK 254 544) in Sweden; and, USD 33 210 (GBP 21 359) in the United Kingdom.
c) It is assumed that hours of work changes while the hourly wage rate is constant. This is particularly important for the United Kingdom, where the cost of childcare is defined according to the use.

Source: OECD Secretariat calculations.

income. Nevertheless, for most families this support is not worth as much as a subsidised childcare place, although in certain circumstances, it may be financially advantageous to use a non-subsidised childcare place (Chapter 5).

In the United Kingdom, there are no nation-wide rules on fee setting, but low and middle income households can claim support towards the parental costs of childcare through the Working Tax Credit. A tax credit award involves several elements. In general, the childcare element in the working tax credit can be claimed when parents are employed for at least 16 hours per week[15] and use formal or registered childcare. Childcare fees can be compensated for 70% of eligible childcare cost up to certain limits: GBP 135 a week for the care of one child or GBP 200 for two or more children (these amounts were changed to GBP 175 and GBP 300, respectively in April 2005, Chapter 5). An income related award, tax credits are tapered by 37 pence for every pound of income over the relevant threshold (GBP 5 060). Despite this support, parental contributions are considerably higher in the United Kingdom than in the other three countries (Table 4.4). Moreover, Table 4.4 may well underestimate the cost of childcare to parents. Daycare Trust (2004) reports a typical cost for a full-time nursery place at GBP 128 (instead of the GBP 100 used for the calculations in Table 4.4), with considerable variation across the country. In January 2003, average childcare fees were GBP 168 per week (50 hours) in inner London (the highest fee recorded in inner London was GBP 338 for a 50-hour week) and GBP 107 in the West Midlands.

4.4.2. Finland: financing full-time parental care or formal childcare for very young children

Finland is quite unique among OECD countries in that it faces a potential decline in childcare demand. At a more or less constant fertility rate, the number of births is declining (Chapter 2), and the number of children not yet 7 years of age will reduce by a further 11 000 children over the 2001-2005 period (MSAH, 2003). The decline in the annual number of births is expected to lead to a decline in childcare demand of about 5 000 places, largely because of the high incidence of full-time parental care provision for very young children (and the introduction of pre-school classes for 6-year olds, see above).

The single most distinctive feature of the Finnish set-up is the Home Care Allowance (HCA) which financially supports parents of very young children who care for their own child up to age 3 (see also Chapter 5 and the Background Annex to the review). Parents are eligible for such support, if, and only if, they do not use municipal childcare facilities. At the same time, the Finnish system contains a childcare guarantee: municipalities have to provide all children not yet of school age access to a subsidised childcare place when asked. To further enhance choice, it is possible for parents to claim a private childcare allowance (of a maximum of EUR 252 per month) towards the cost of using a private childcare centre (this covers a small group of about 4% of children under school age. Thus, the Finnish system appears to provide parents with fairly comprehensive choice options: use municipal of private formal day care services, or care for children themselves on a full-time basis (to what extent the financial incentive structure that parents with very young children face favours work or providing personal care is discussed in Chapter 5).

Municipalities, however, have very strong financial incentives to get parents with children not yet 3 years of age to care for children themselves (or get them to use private providers). From a narrow budgetary perspective this makes some sense: parental care is cheaper to public budgets in the short-term. In 2002, the annual spending on childcare per child under school age was about EUR 7 467 i.e. more than twice the amount spent per child with the home care allowance (EUR 3 206). With central government covering 30% of spending on both the Home Care Allowance and a childcare place, and the former costing less than half of the latter, municipalities have a very strong financial incentive to discourage parents with young children from using childcare. Most of the larger municipalities (including Helsinki) further discourage the use of public childcare by very young children, by paying their parents an additional "home care payment" (EUR 2 600 per annum in Helsinki). This makes sense from a budgetary perspective, as the cost of a childcare place in Helsinki is relatively high (around EUR 11 000 per annum, of which parents can be asked to pay up to EUR 2 400 at maximum). Even when paying an additional EUR 2 600 per annum savings are around EUR 1 000 per child.[16] Hence, abstracting from (future) tax revenue foregone because of non-employment, it pays for municipalities to provide substantial additional home care supplements. Home care allowances were paid to about 64% of families with a one-year old child, while this was 47% for 2 year-olds. Table 4.2 illustrated the effect of the Home Care allowance on the use of childcare: in 2003, only 1% of the children in Finland attend formal childcare before their first birthday, while this was 44% of 2 year olds. By financially encouraging parents to mind their own children until age 3, in practice the Finnish Home Care Allowance policy regards this as the age at which it is most beneficial for the children's development to attend formal childcare facilities (see Box 4.4).

As noted above many smaller municipalities in Finland cannot address the demand for childcare at all hours and while budgetary considerations also contribute to the childcare guarantee being challenged in the Finnish policy debate. Suggestions have been made to restrict the scope of the childcare guarantee by limiting access for certain groups (e.g., only a part-time guarantee only for children in jobless families or parents on parental leave), but the scope of this issue is limited and access restrictions would not generate substantial spending reductions.

During the 1990s, municipalities generally adjusted childcare capacity by cutting back on family day care for younger children, rather than destroying municipal capital investment in centre-based facilities. This is because municipalities (as in Sweden) experience difficulties in recruitment and despite a preference among Finnish parents for home-based care and the fact that such care is relatively cheap for very young children, EUR 8 425 per annum, compared with EUR 9 157 for kindergarten. Another advantage of family-day care is that little capital investment has to be made to create new places, and an expansion of capacity can thus help serve childcare needs that may arise from a possible gradual reduction in the generosity of the Home Care Allowance.

4.4.3. Increasing access in Sweden

Participation in good quality formal childcare in Sweden is widely regarded beneficial to children as from age 1. In this perspective, access to childcare is a public good that should be universally available. However, for childcare participation to enhance child development, participation does not have to be on a full-time basis. Reform in July 2001 extended access to subsidies for childcare for a minimum of three hours per day to children (age 1 to 5) of unemployed parents while since January 2002 this also extends to children whose parents are on parental leave. Because of this the number of children in childcare increased by 6% from 2000 to 2002, while the average

Box 4.4. **Parental employment and child development**

Parental employment reduces the risk of children growing up in poverty (Chapter 5) and, hence, reduces the likelihood of deprivation hampering child development. At the same time, child development is promoted by quality care, if not by a parent, then by professional carers. As from what age onwards parental (usually "maternal") employment has no negative effect on children's cognitive development is a matter of debate (while it is generally accepted that from a child development perspective, regular work-schedules are better than non-regular (and/or very long) working hours, see Kamerman et al., 2003). For example, Ruhm (2004) finds for the United States that maternal employment when children are not yet 2-3 years old may negatively affect child development. For older children access to pre-school/kindergarten is generally regarded as beneficial to child development, which underlies, for example, the provision of free preschool on a part-time basis in the province of Québec and the United Kingdom (Ermish and Francesconi, 2001; and Lefebvre and Merrigan, 2002). Sylva et al. (2004) conclude on the basis of a recent longitudinal survey conduced in the United Kingdom that: i) pre-school experience, compared to none, had a significant positive effect on child development; ii) an earlier start (before age 3) is better for intellectual development at age 6 and improved independence, concentration and sociability at that age; iii) part-time attendance was no better or worse than full-time attendance. Vulnerable or disadvantaged children benefit most from good quality pre-school experiences (e.g., Oreopoulos, 2003), especially if the children in the group are of different social backgrounds. Gregg and Washbrook (2003) estimated for Avon in England that full-time maternal employment in the first 18 months of the child's life may have a small negative effect on children's cognitive development, but only if care arrangements exclusively concern unpaid care by a friend, relative or neighbour on a long-term basis. A key explanation for this is thought to be that although mothers who return early to full-time work may have fewer interactions with children, this is compensated by the strong positive effect of increased paternal interactions with children: in households where mothers return early to work, fathers are substantially more engaged in parenting. Support offered to low income families and single parents to combine work and family commitments has a positive effect on child development (Currie, 2004), and Morris and Michalopoulos (2000) found that the Canadian Self Sufficiency Project (Chapter 5) which helped sole parents to leave social assistance registers for full-time jobs and had beneficial effects on cognitive outcomes and schooling achievement of their children.

There is no longitudinal panel data evidence on child development underpinning the policy choices embedded in Finnish and Swedish formal childcare systems. The guiding principle is that as long as formal childcare services are of good quality its use is beneficial to the child, and in Finland the right of each child (regardless of age) to access childcare, suggests childcare is

Box 4.4. **Parental employment and child development** (cont.)

considered beneficial at all ages. In Sweden, the extension of access to subsidised care for those on parental leave, also suggests that entry into formal care can benefit children prior to the first birthday. In practical terms, however, the two systems have a rather different perspective on the age of the child as from which maternal employment is encouraged. The system of paid parental leave and homecare allowances in Finland financially encourages (one of the) parents to provide full-time parental care until the child turns 3, while in Sweden paid parental leave expires upon 18 months, of which two months reserved for the father (Chapter 6).

hours of attendance per child declined by one hour to about 30 hours per week (NAER, 2004).[17]

In Sweden, the introduction of maximum fee legislation in 2002 (or Maxtaxa) together with other reform increased access to childcare services (see below), considerably reduced the parental share in the costs of childcare: from about 20 to 25% prior to reform to 11% at present, reduced fee variation across municipalities, and may have contributed to increased labour supply among sole parents (Chapter 5). In line with its objectives, the introduction of the maximum fee increased equity among childcare users in Sweden by reducing the degree of regional variation in parental fees. In 1999, annual parental childcare fees for a family with two children at average earnings could vary by up to EUR 5 390 in 1999, in 2002 the variation was reduced to EUR 1 078 per annum at maximum.

Budgetary pressures in the 1990s led to an increase in the number of preschool children per employee of 4.4 in 1990 to 5.7 children in 1998, but have since fallen to 5.4 in 2003. In leisure centres (out-of-school-hours care) the number of children per staff member increased from eight in the early 1990s to 18 children in 2003 (NAER, 2004). More resources (SEK 1 billion in 2005 and SEK 2 billion in 2006 and 2007) will be made available to municipalities to reduce the size of children's groups through employment of an additional 6 000 preschool staff (an increase of almost 10%). It is estimated that the number of children will be reduced from 5.4 to 5 per teacher on average.

Given the considerable public outlays on childcare in Sweden a key challenge is to enhance efficiency in provision so as to ensure long-term financial sustainability of the comprehensive high quality system. Given the large public subsidies towards parental fees, it is difficult to improve efficiency in use of the system through price signals. For example, introducing a fee structure that accounts for part-time or full-time use of care services (as exists in 49% of municipalities in Sweden) makes little difference to the overall parental contribution. Hence, such fee differentiation has little impact on marginal childcare use decisions.

There has been a significant decline in the use of family day care since the mid-1980s (Chart 4.2). In particular in urban areas the use of family day care has declined with a professionalisation of the early years workforce, difficulties in recruitment of home-based care workers (as in Finland) and a preference among many parents for centre-based care (in contrast to Finland). Family-day care might be more difficult to organise for municipal staff than centre-based care, but otherwise home-based care is cheaper (SEK 70 700 per child) than centre-based care (SEK 91 000 per child). Maintaining, where possible, the role of family day-care could relieve budgetary pressure on the overall childcare system (without fundamentally changing its nature) and simultaneously increase choice options for parents.

Chart 4.2. **Swedish children increasingly use centre-based care**
Number of Swedish children using childcare facilities, 1975-2003

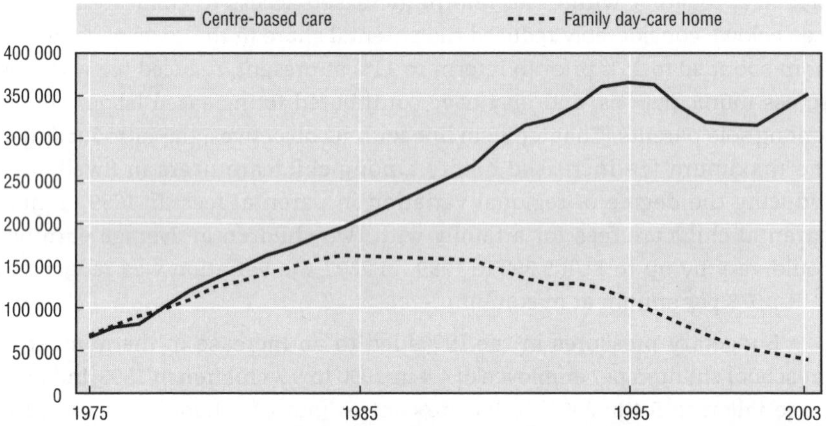

Source: Data provided by the Swedish authorities.

4.4.4. Increasing equity in the province of Québec

In the province of Québec, childcare capacity development started in the mid-1980s, but really took off during the second part of the 1990s, when Québec's family policy obtained a strong focus on both supporting working parents and child development.[18] Almost all 5-year olds attend the "Maternelle" (or kindergarten), and since 1997, public spending on childcare increased to 0.8% of GDP and in terms of childcare places for children in the age group 0-5, capacity more than doubled from 78 864 in 1997 to 179 755 in March 2004; and the proportion of young children who use formal childcare increased from 19% to 45%. As a result, about 40% of all subsidised official childcare places available in Canada (and 22% of children age 0-5) are in the province of Québec (Box 4.1).

The rapid expansion of affordable quality childcare services was accomplished by subsidising childcare places for which parents only had to pay a flat rate of CAD 5 per day for up to 10 hours of use (CAD 7 since January 2004), and for parents with access to these places, public funds cover 81.4% of the childcare costs on average. The capacity of such subsidised childcare is intended to grow by another 20 000 places in 2005-06 to in total about 200 000 subsidised places in the regulated (registered) childcare sector for a total of about 370 000 children. With this additional investment, overall formal childcare capacity in the province of Québec will be close to childcare demand (ISQ, 2001; and MESSF, 2005).

The situation in the province of Québec raises different equity issues. First, the flat-rate fee structure reduces childcare costs most for richer households, although progressivity in the tax system significantly reduces the magnitude of this effect (see Table 4.5). Second, subsidised places are allocated on a "first-come, first-serve" basis. As parents in relatively rich households seem to be either more assertive and/or have better access to information, their children are much more likely to use a subsidised place than children in poorer income groups. Lefebvre (2004), finds that take-up rates are highest among children in higher income families: 28% in families earning at least CAD 80 000 (about twice average earnings) have access to a subsidised place while this only concerns 4% of couple families where income is below CAD 30 000 per annum.[19] Third, for parents without access to a subsidised place, there is a federal income tax deduction and a refundable provincial tax credit, which subject to an income test reimburses childcare costs up to CAD 7 000 at maximum. At present, spending on the refundable tax credits is about 10% of what is spent on flat-rate subsidised childcare places (MESSF, 2003). In general, financial support towards childcare costs through the federal and provincial tax systems is not worth as much as a subsidised childcare place. However, depending on family composition and the fees charged in the private sector, families with incomes of around CAD 70 to 85% of average earnings may well be financially better off if they do not use a CAD 7 dollar per day place (Chapter 5).

Another source of inequity is that the subsidised places that have been created since 1997 are largely in the not-for-profit sector, and the share of commercial private sector provision has decreased from 50% in 1997, to about 16% in 2004. That providers who do not adhere to the regulated standards of care, do not obtain the same subsidy as those who do, is perfectly understandable. However, commercial providers who do adhere to the set quality standards also receive less funding than non-commercial providers. Lefebvre (2004) reports that over the year 2002-03, a non-profit childcare centre (Centre pour la Petite Enfance) received CAD 60 per day for each child not yet 18 months old and CAD 44 for a child aged 18-60 months. A commercial private centre received about CAD 32 to CAD 49 per day per child, while corresponding amounts for family day care providers ranged from CAD 30 to CAD 35.

The differentiation in public support unnecessarily adds to financial pressure on commercial providers which may affect the quality of care. The Longitudinal Study of Child Development conducted on-site quality evaluations of childcare facilities which provide care for children aged 30 to 48 months. Data from the 1998 evaluation visits show that not-for-profit centres are of better quality than for-profit centres. Nevertheless, overall quality is not high: one-third of the not-for-profit centres were found to be of good quality compared with only 7% of the for profit centres. Moreover, about one-third of the for-profit centres are of poor quality, compared with only 7% of the not-for-profit centres. Disadvantaged children are more likely to be cared for in poor quality services than are children from more affluent families. It is estimated that private centres who comply with the quality standards pertinent to subsidised places (at CAD 7 for parents) would have to charge CAD 35-40 to parents, while limited public subsidies also contribute to childcare workers in the commercial sector receiving less pay while the nature of employment is more precarious (Tougas, 2002).

4.4.5. Childcare expansion in the United Kingdom: encouraging providers and targeting low-income families

The National Childcare Strategy launched in 1997 aims to deliver quality, affordable and accessible childcare in every neighbourhood, and its introduction kick-started the increase in the supply of childcare in England, while similar initiatives were launched in Scotland, Wales and Northern Ireland (DfES, 2002, 2004a).[20] Public spending on childcare in the United Kingdom rapidly increased from 0.2% of GDP in 1998/99 to 0.4% of GDP 2003/04, and the UK government now influences the childcare market through a complex framework. This framework intends to encourage and support local authorities to develop new capacity and stimulate demand through direct subsidies towards care provision, and enhance their role as childcare information providers and co-ordinators. At the same time, childcare demand is stimulated by reducing parental childcare costs through the childcare element in the working tax credit (see below).

In the past, public resources were often used as seed funding to encourage community-based initiatives, but also towards business start-up, especially in disadvantaged areas.[21] UK policy continues to be attracted to the idea of "partnership" with local NGOs, parents and business in delivering family services and childcare (DfES, 2004), but funding mechanisms have moved towards a more conventional model of financing. A large part of the public sector subsidy comes through local authorities, who on basis of grants (and a specific subsidy towards the "free educational offer") finance Sure Start Local Programmes, Children's centres, and Neighbourhood Nurseries which are are key elements of local partnerships (Box 4.5).

The need for an expansion in formal childcare provision in the United Kingdom is based on a belief that lack of affordable childcare is a constraint on taking paid work. As discussed above, UK policy provides financial childcare support targeted at working low and middle-income households. This support was recently extended and the number of recipients of the childcare element of the working tax credit has drastically increased from 180 000 in October 2002 to over 317 000 families in April 2004, and payments increased from GBP 380 million in 2002/03 to GBP 700 million in 2003/04 (Inland Revenue, 2004). The average amount of help received was GBP 50 a week. Two-thirds of eligible parents pay less than GBP 80 per week for child care, and less than 6% of recipeints had childcare costs of more than GBP 150 a week.[22] For low-income families, the childcare element in the Working Tax Credit (WTC) covers up to 70% of the childcare costs (to be extended to 80% in 2006, see Chapter 5). This nevertheless implies significant out-of-pocket expense for low-income families, which contributes to many such families continuing to use cheap informal care arrangements.

Otherwise the evidence that costs are a major deterrent to the use of formal childcare is not overwhelming. NAO (2004a) finds that among parents of 0 to 4 year olds, very few (between 1 and 3%) say they do not use formal childcare because it is too expensive, but 14% of parents said the setting they used was the only one available locally.[23] Woodland et al. (2002) report that in England 29% of parents and 22% of sole parents had not always been able to get childcare when they wanted it. Moreover, low-income families with access to cheap informal childcare have limited incentives to use formal childcare: even if they could claim 70% of the formal childcare costs the residual costs are still much higher than their expense on current childcare arrangements. However, with increasing numbers of mothers in work, that source of care is likely to dry up.

Location, reputation, quality and the suitability of hours are important factors in determining the limited use of formal childcare among families In the past formal childcare in the United Kingdom was either very expensive while cheaper private childcare services did not have a good reputation. Reform since 1997 has reduced the cost of childcare to parents, while quality is also improving (although much remains to be done in terms of quality assurance systems, see Box 4.2): 58% of the parents surveyed in 2001 thought the quality of nursery education was excellent or very good, compared with less than 50% of parents in 1997 (NAO, 2004). Nevertheless, past features of the

Box 4.5. **Sure Start and Children's Centres**

A centrepiece of UK anti-poverty policy is the Sure Start policy which through its Children's Centres programme offers integrated day care and early learning, health, family and parenting support, initially in the most disadvantaged areas but policy aims to establish 3500 Children's Centres across England by 2010. The Policy objectives underlying Sure Start are threefold: i) increase the availability and sustainability of affordable childcare places for children, especially those who are disadvantaged, ii) provide integrated services for health, education and emotional development of young children; and iii) provide services to parents to support them as parents and to help them becoming job-ready. To co-ordinate all early childhood related policies and programmes in England a Sure Start Unit has been created in central government which is accountable to both the Department for Education and Skills and the Department for Work and Pensions.

Sure Start local programmes were set up in 1998 with the initial intention for 250 local (community level) programmes, but this soon increased to 524 programmes in the most disadvantaged communities across England delivering services to families to about 400 000 children and their families (i.e. about 16% of all children under 4 in England and one-third of all children living in poverty). Spending on these 524 *Sure Start* local programmes amounted to GBP 304 million in 2003. Local Sure Start programmes and Children's Centres, as for example the Seacroft Children's Centre in Leeds, include the provision of childcare places (with a focus on cognitive development), but also, for example, ante-natal support, advice to parents-to-be and general parenting and family support. In deprived areas, family workers often have to deal with debt-related issues, depression, stress and abuse issues. Moreover, there is a generation of children who were not stimulated at school and whose parents do not provide a role model of work and/or strong work ethos. It is important to build up confidence among children and parents to stimulate people to pursue success, to make their own decisions, and to break the pattern of intergenerational welfare dependency.

Sure Start Local Programmes, and other relevant services as, for example, neighbourhood nurseries are being reformed, and by the end of 2005 all remaining Sure Start local programmes will have become a Children's Centre delivering holistic family support services for children and families from pregnancy through to starting school. By March 2006, Children's Centres are expected to reach at least 650 000 pre-school children in the 20% of wards, identified as the most disadvantaged; by 2008 there are projected to be 2 500 such centres, to be increased to 3 500 by 2010.

> ### Box 4.5. **Sure Start and Children's Centres** (cont.)
>
> In the 2002-03 school year, the Department for Education and Skills (DfES) sponsored twenty five local education authorities (LEAs) to develop extended schools pathfinder projects (Cummings *et al.*, 2004). Initiatives differed in focus, but generally involved delivery of community and family services, often in areas of deprivation. In addition to their "core business of teaching", extended schools offer services to pupils and their families, before and after school hours, at weekends and during school holidays. The government is committed to guaranteeing all parents of children age 3-11 to have access to care services from 8 a.m. to 6 p.m. on weekdays by 2010. Extended schools and Children's centres are central planks in the Government strategy to enhance child development, strengthen families and communities, and help parents in England to reconcile their work and care commitments.
>
> In Scotland, the arrangements for Sure Start are different. Local Sure Start services are not limited to particular geographical areas (as the local Sure Start programmes were in England), but focus instead on the vulnerability of the family. For example, the "Stepping Stones" initiative in Edinburgh, focuses on helping people to overcome issues with respect to relationships, education, and personal problems (rather than focusing on job-readiness, for which they refer to other projects such as "Working Link"). Sure Start services include social care, health and early education programmes, and are generally integrated with the mainstream family support and childcare services provided by local authorities, sometimes through voluntary organisations. The annual budget for Sure Start Scotland is scheduled to increase from around GBP 23 million a year in 2003/04 to around GBP 50 million a year in 2005/06.
>
> In addition, some GBP 20 million a year of Social Justice funding is available to help disadvantaged parents with training and childcare under the auspices of forty-eight Social Inclusion Partnerships (SIPs). These were set up by the Scottish Executive in 1999 to deliver a multi-agency approach to the problems of deprivation. There are 34 area-based partnerships focusing on a set geographical area and 14 concentrating on a specific theme, for example, young people and young carers. SIP funding has been granted to after-school clubs, play schemes, nurseries and crèches, but also to projects that provide training to prospective childcare workers.

childcare system (a very high price/quality ratio) are still reflected in attitudes that lead many parents to prefer to mind their own children, especially when very young. This attitude still persists (NAO, 2004; and Woodland *et al.*, 2002), but is likely to change with increasing affordability and quality of formal childcare. However, such an attitudinal change will take some time to take effect.

That the current formal childcare system is not used more intensively is also related to gaps in the knowledge of both providers and users. Local authorities help parents find their way through the patchwork of mainly private service providers, through the "Children's Information Services" (which at the expense of GBP 31.2 million deal with about 750 000 enquiries per annum) that provide advice on how to find childcare in their area. There are also "Childcare Partnership Managers" who may help the Childrens Information Services co-ordination with *Jobcentre Plus* (the integrated benefit and employment service) to help those in training or seeking work to find suitable care arrangements.[24] Some *Jobcentre Plus* provide "childcare tasters" that give unemployed parents the opportunity to test local childcare services.

Local and central authorities in joint-policy development should also provide better information to providers so that they can establish more realistic business plans: at present too many providers go out of business when start-up funding runs out. In 1997, there were about 520 000 children using childcare on a full-time basis, while the NCS has since then contributed to an estimated net increase of another 520 000 childcare full-time equivalent places (NAO, 2004). The total number of new childcare places is much higher, but it is estimated that since 1997 about 300 000 childcare places have closed. Many providers close down when start-up funds run out, because their business plans were based on unrealistic expectations about demand or over-optimistic cost assumptions. Fewer than half of providers report that they were always covering their costs (NAO, 2004), while only 52% of providers who had received time-limited funding knew what they were going to do when funding ran out. This puts public investment in childcare funds at risk, and local authorities are now obliged to employ business support officers to help providers understand their costs, price-setting and marketing techniques and long-term business planning.[25] Start-up funding should be made contingent on business plans being in tune with local needs.

Training of staff has not been able to keep pace with the rapid development of the childcare sector. Wages, especially for childcare workers with limited training are not high and there is high staff turnover.[26] The shortage of childcare workers is likely to increase wages and thereby reduce the current high rate of staff turnover that is not beneficial for children. It also increases training costs which together with difficulties in finding suitable locations have been identified as main challenges to sustainability of childcare services (NAO, 2004). Public investment in training of childcare workers is needed to ensure future expansion and quality of childcare services. The Children's Workforce Development Council for England will take the lead in developing career and training frameworks, career pathways and increase the supply of qualified childcare workers.

4.5. Conclusions

Initially female employment growth relies on care by relatives, neighbours and friends, but as these people are increasingly in paid work themselves this source of care dries up. The Swedish experience, which can be documented from the 1960s onwards, suggests there is a limit to the full-time female employment rate of around 60% beyond which female employment will not rise unless there is more public help with childcare. However, public childcare investment is not made for labour supply objectives alone, but address the gamut of policy objectives including on pursuing gender equity, tackling child poverty, enhancing child development and early education and, in some countries, the build up of a society where having and raising children is not at odds with pursuing a career.

Both in the province of Québec and the UK public investment in childcare has increased rapidly since the late 1990s to 0.8% GDP in the province of Québec, and 0.4% of GDP in the United Kingdom. The long-established municipal day-care systems in Nordic countries (including OSH-care) are more costly: 1.1% of GDP in Finland and 2% of GDP in Sweden. Compared with the other countries the Swedish system is expensive because of its intensive use by very young children: almost 85% of 2-year olds use formal childcare in Sweden while this is about half that in Finland, the United Kingdom and the province of Québec, and considerably lower in the rest of Canada. The countries under review are thus at different stages of childcare system development and therefore often face different policy challenges. Nevertheless, there are common concerns such as fostering of quality and childcare services for parents working atypical hours.

The Swedish childcare system is without doubt the most comprehensive. It has developed from "care to facilitate parents working" system in its initial stages in the late 1960s to an "early education and care system" driven by child development and early learning concerns. The ongoing childcare debate focuses on increasing access to the system and further improvement of the already high level of quality. Given the large public subsidy towards childcare costs, it is difficult to improve efficiency in use of the system through price signals: *e.g.*, introducing a fee structure by the hour of use (as exists in half of the municipalities) makes little difference to the overall parental contribution, and thus has a limited impact on marginal childcare use decisions. Maintaining, where possible, the role of (less costly) family day care could contribute to its long-run sustainability, and provide a wider variety of options for parents to choose from.

Prima facie the Finnish system provides parents with very young children with comprehensive choice options. Finland is the only country under review where parents of all young children up to school age have guaranteed access to a subsidised childcare place (even at night if work schedules so require). At the same time, parents who do not use these day-care facilities are entitled to a *Home Care Allowance* payment, which assists them in providing full-time care for their own children under the age of three. However, in practice, central and local government provide parents with strong financial incentives not to use childcare facilities when children are very young. This leads to the proportion of 2-year olds using childcare being much lower in Finland (44%) than in Sweden (85%). In the short term this reduces public outlays, but raises gender equity concerns, and demographic trends point to a need to increase female labour supply. The Finnish system of Home Care Allowances needs to be reformed to address these challenges (Chapter 5).

In many Canadian provinces public childcare support is limited and childcare coverage is patchy, and a further increase in federal spending on childcare has been announced to take a leadership role in childcare development and increase access to childcare among a broader group of Canadians. Ideally, funding needs to follow parental choice and use could be made of a mix of financing tools. For example, there could be direct subsidies to providers towards capital investment, providers in deprived and/or scarcely populated areas or those who provide services to children with special needs. In addition, earmarked childcare (and out-of-school-hours care) support could also be directly awarded to parents, improving market efficiency and choice for parents. Such funding should, however, be strictly tied to providers adhering to pre-set quality standards (*e.g.*, rules on the number of certified staff among personnel, staff-to-child ratios, but also on parental involvement in childcare provision, etc.). To achieve an equitable allocation of public resources, such support can delivered subject to an income test.

Compared to the rest of Canada, childcare policy in the province of Québec is much more developed: 40% of Canadian childcare capacity is in this province, as compared to 22% of very young Canadian children. Since, the second part of the 1990s, Québecois policy opted to develop childcare capacity through increasing subsidised places charging flat-rate fees, which covers more than 80% of the childcare costs. However, access to such subsidised childcare places is not universal, and they are allocated on a "first-come, first-serve" basis. As parents in relatively rich households seem to be either more assertive and/or have better access to information, their children are much more likely to use a subsidised place than children in poorer income groups: and disadvantaged children are more likely to be cared for in poor quality services than are children from more affluent families. Ongoing efforts are underway to extend childcare capacity in Québec; it should be priority to ensure access to high quality childcare for all those low-income families who wish to use it.

Childcare expansion in the United Kingdom has been based on a three-pronged approach: seed funding of private providers to increase supply of childcare facilities in disadvantaged areas (through Sure Start), expansion of the nursery school capacity to all 3 and 4 year olds for 2.5 hours per day (to be extended to thee hours per day) through direct subsidies and earmarked childcare support for (working) parents through the tax system (to be increased in generosity, see Chapter 5). In the past, many British parents cared for children themselves or used informal care because the formal care system was widely regarded as expensive or did not have a good reputation. Surveys also report that location and reputation of providers, the quality of their facilities and the suitability of hours are important factors in determining the hitherto limited use of formal childcare. Parents need to be provided with more information on the range of childcare services available in their area, quality assurance systems need to be more broadly applied, while other initiatives to improve quality (including, for example, quality support to home-based carers through Children's Centres, and the introduction of a comprehensive inspection regime) need to be carried out to increase parental confidence in the system. Policy is increasing access to, and affordability and quality of formal childcare facilities, and when these changes are persisted with, parents will realise that past perceptions of the childcare system (expensive and of low quality) no longer hold. However, building up trust and reputations takes time.

Because the free early education offer for 3 and 4 year-olds in the United Kingdom only covers a few hours per day, working parents have to use additional childcare resources to facilitate finding a suitable match of work and care commitments. British working parents therefore often have complicated lives as they arrange transport of children from one source of care to another. This underscores the importance of childcare facilities being conveniently located. The UK government is aware that this issue also concerns school-going children, and aims to provide by 2010 all parents of 5 to 11 year olds to have access to OSH-care services from 8.00 to 18.00, either at school or elsewhere.

Notes

1. Available data for Finland from the mid-1980s onwards indicates that the proportion of children 0-6 using childcare has since oscillated around 50% (Forssén et al., 2004). OECD (2002) presents historical evidence on the Danish experience.

2. Estimating the returns of public investment in childcare in terms of labour supply, economic growth, and future human capital is fraught with difficulty as generated results are rather sensitive to the assumptions underlying such calculations. Having said that, Cleveland and Krashinky (1998 and 2003) found that public childcare investment in Canada in 1998 for all children between 2 and 5 would have costed about CAD 5.3 billion, but would have generated returns by means of a positive effect on human capital through early learning worth CAD 4.3 billion in 1998, while increased female employment (leading to increased productivity, and economic growth, tax revenue, etc.) would have generated another CAD 6 billion. For the United Kingdom, PriceWaterhouseCoopers (2003) reports a 9% increase in female employment, and ensuing GDP growth, at an initial cost of GBP 3 billion, but this estimate return on childcare investment stands and falls with the assumptions underlying the calculations.

3. In a number of provinces, the Child Study movement of the early 1920s initiated development of nursery schools or preschools as part-day programmes to provide developmental experiences for the children of middle-class families (Doherty et al., 2003).

4. A particularity of the Canadian childcare policy background is the great mobility of Canadians across this vast country. This feature limits the opportunity to rely on relatives or parents for childcare needs. Informal family support networks are often difficult to access, and, for example, certainly not for three hours at short notice to serve the needs of atypical workers.

5. The Finnish Children's Day Care Law was enacted in 1973, obliging municipalities to organise day care for children under school age. According to this Act, each child has an unconditional right to day care provided by the local authority once parental leave expires, regardless of household income or the parental employment status. This also means that municipalities must provide care when it is needed at non-standard hours, e.g., in evenings, week-ends, or for around the clock care.

6. In the province of Québec, regions and municipalities are involved in the decision making process regarding the establishment of childcare centres, but are usually not involved in financing.

7. These so-called Early Years Development and Childcare Partnerships in the United Kingdom were established to plan and co-ordinate early years education and childcare in each local authority area. However, since 2004 local authorities are expected to take on greater responsibility for this role with the EYDCP role being more advisory.

8. Centres pour la Petite Enfance in the province of Québec also provide support for children with specific needs (e.g., children with disabilities) in co-operation with local community service centres "Centre Local de Services Communaux" and other provincial authorities involved in social service provision.

9. Commercial private providers in the province of Québec include chartered and non-chartered garderies: the latter must comply with the same quality standards as the chartered providers but they do not provide CAD 7 per day places.

10. In Sweden, about 8% of children attend a private out-of-school-hours service, while another 8% of children use a private family day care service.

11. Howes and Smith (1995) found that when the number of staff per children was increased, children engaged in more cognitively complex play with objects; showed higher levels of language skills; were more securely attached to their

teachers; and were less aggressive, anxious or hyperactive. At the same time, staff became more responsive and sensitive, and offered more encouragement. In a recent study on the UK experience, Sylva *et al.* (2004) found that an increase in staff-to-child ratios in childcare centres had a significant impact on cognitive child development.

12. The provincial government of Québec sees a key role for local authorities in developing a new approach towards synchronising various services so as to support the parental work-life balance on a daily basis. For example, reduce parental time constraints by streamlining opening hours of childcare facilities, schools and public services, and ensure that these services are located within a relatively short distance of each other.

13. On average children in sole parent families in England use formal childcare for three hours more per week than children in couple families who participate in formal childcare (Woodland *et al.*, 2002).

14. In its "ten year strategy for childcare" as published in December 2004, the UK government announced its intention to increase supply-side funding in England from GBP 3.8 billion in 2004/05 to GBP 4.4 billion by 2007/08 (HM treasury, 2004).

15. For couple families in the United Kingdom to be eligible for Working Tax Credit, both parents must be in employment for at least 16 hours with family earnings up to GBP 14 560 per annum (Chapter 5).

16. The cost of a childcare place can be around EUR 11 000 per annum in Helsinki, so that given a maximum parental fee of EUR 2 400, the costs of a childcare place to the municipal Helsinki budget can be EUR 8 600 at maximum. Given that central government pays 30% of both the childcare costs (and the Home Care Allowance) the municipal costs of a childcare place are EUR 6 020. Municipalities pay 70% of the Home Care Allowance, *i.e.* EUR 2 240, so even when they pay an additional home care payment of EUR 2 600 they save about EUR 1 000 per child.

17. NAER (2004) finds that in Sweden in 2002, 47% of 1 to 5 year olds with one parent on parental leave used formal childcare, while the corresponding figure for 1999 was 26%. The proportion of children with an unemployed parent who used childcare increased from 58% in 1999 to 76% in 2002. However, as unemployment fell during the same period the proportion of children using childcare with unemployed parents in 2002 was not dissimilar from that in 1999.

18. In the province of Québec, childcare programmes were first established in the late 1850s by charitable services which provide basic care and supervision for young children of impoverished working mothers. The first publicly subsidised "garderie" in Québec was opened 1969; the first comprehensive regulation of formal childcare policy was laid down in the Childcare Services Act (Loi sur les services de garde à l'enfance) in 1980.

19. Lefebvre (2004) finds that 58% of children using a subsidised place were from couple families with incomes in excess of CAD 60 000, while children in such families account for only 49% of all children in the province of Québec. Children in families where income is below CAD 40 000 represent 26% of all children but account only for 18% of all children using subsidised childcare services.

20. At introduction in 1997, the objective of the National Childcare Strategy in the United Kingdom was to make childcare available for all who wanted it by 2003 (Bertram and Pascal, 2000). This was to be achieved through four broad groups of measures: i) improvement of the quality of ECEC services through improved training for early childhood staff and the development of quality standards;

ii) establishment of local services to help parents find childcare places; iii) increase of affordability of childcare through providing a childcare-related tax credit for parents; and, iv) increased involvement of employers in childcare policy (which remains very limited.

21. Private sector childcare is a low-margin business with many providers struggling to maintain capacity at a high enough level for operations to be financially viable. This leads to patchy geographic coverage, with relatively few providers in deprived areas – the very areas which the UK government would most like to see covered (NAO, 2004).

22. Woodland et al. (2002) found that a small majority (53%) of parents in England claimed that the childcare tax credit had affected the type of childcare they used, while a much smaller proportion (27%) reported that they had increased the number of hours of formal childcare they used.

23. It is possible that such figures understate an underlying shortfall in provision. For example, parents who choose not to work may also choose not to seek childcare. If the reason why they choose not to work was because they felt that childcare was of insufficient quality to match their needs, or because they "knew" that it would not be convenient for them, then the potential demand for good quality care may be higher.

24. Childcare Partnership Managers (CPMs) are to co-ordinate Jobcentre Plus (the integrated benefit and employment service in the United Kingdom) programmes and strategies with local childcare partnership plans and strategies. Working with Jobcentre Plus colleagues, local authorities, childcare partnerships and Childcare information services, Childcare Partnership Managers help to solve childcare issues for both unemployed individuals and employers; and improve access and co-ordination of information on childcare, keep Jobcentre Plus staff abreast of local childcare issues, and offer career advice regarding childcare work. However, the role of CPMs in the Jobcentre Plus organisation and in local partnerships is not always well-defined, but despite these difficulties many CPMs had been able to get involved local childcare programmes (Barker et al., 2004).

25. In order to support the sustainability of childcare businesses in the United Kingdom, the programme "Business Success for Childcare" launched in April 2004 delivers free business support to childcare providers through a series of workshops and training seminars supported by business guides and videos. The business guides cover a broad range of topics including: business planning; marketing and sales; costing and pricing; and collecting and using relevant information. Business Support Officers are employed by 150 local authorities, who advise potential and existing providers on a range of business issues.

26. In the United Kingdom, care and early education workers can be distinguished in two groups with major implications on training, pay and status. Broadly speaking, pedagogues and teachers have relatively high level of training, and consequently relatively good pay and conditions of employment. Teachers working with children under age 5, have a four year degree at university level, while childcare workers, often employed in day-nurseries, often have a two-year training certificate. Teachers in Nursery classes working on average 40 hours per week earn about 73% of average earnings, while the earnings of workers in childcare services are much lower at 56% of average earnings. In contrast, in Sweden, preschool staff on average earns 94% of average earnings.

Table 4.A.1. Childcare services in the United Kingdom

Service	Nature of provision and hours of operation	Age range catered for	Type of provider	Charge made to parents	Subject to regulation and inspection
Day nursery	Provide full or part-time day care, education and play for children below compulsory school age (5 years). Nurseries can be profit-making or non-profit-making. Generally open 8 a.m. to 7 p.m.	0 to 5 years	Public, private or voluntary	Yes, usually except for children in need.	Yes
Nursery school	Educate pre-school aged children. Staffed with a high ratio of qualified teachers. Work in partnership with other trained professionals. Many staff has special qualifications for the age group. Generally open school hours (9 a.m. to 3.30 p.m.) during term time, sometimes mornings only. Children usually attend for half a day.	3 to 4 years	Public or private (or voluntary in Scotland)	Public sector no charge; private sector sometimes residual charges (no charge at all in Scotland for pre-school education element)	Yes
Nursery class (England)	Can be attended either full time or part-time for six terms before child starts school (same as nursery school). Generally open school hours (9 a.m. to 3.30 p.m.) during term time.	3 to 4 years	Public	No	Yes
Pre-school playgroup	Playgroups are usually part-time or "sessional", and operate for two to three hours per session during school terms.	2½ to 5 years	Private or voluntary	Yes, for children under 3; may be nominal charge where costs not covered by EEG	Yes
Childminder	A self-employed person who provides day care for more than two hours per day. Usually in the childminder's own home. Hours tend to be flexible.	Usually up to 12 years	Private	Yes	Yes for children aged up to 8 years in England, up to 16 years in Scotland
Reception class in a primary or infant school (England)	Children in a reception class are usually in the last year before entering "Year One" of the primary or infant school on reaching statutory school age.	4 to 5 years	Public or private	No	No

Table 4.A.1. **Childcare services in the United Kingdom** (cont.)

Service	Nature of provision and hours of operation	Age range catered for	Type of provider	Charge made to parents	Subject to regulation and inspection
After school, out of school care, breakfast clubs and holiday schemes	Cater for children of school age and to help meet the needs of working parents. A range of activities is offered including sports, drama, arts and crafts, and music. Usually operate 3.30 p.m. to 6 p.m. during term time and 9 a.m. to 6 p.m. during holidays. Less commonly open 8 a.m.-9 a.m. during term time.	Compulsory school age (occasionally includes 3 or 4 year olds)	Public, private or voluntary	Yes	Yes for children up to 8 years in England, up to 16 years in Scotland.
Crèches	Offer short-term childcare for young children, while parents are unable to look after them, for example, if they go on a residential course, training or leisure activities. Crèches may operate all week on a "sessional" basis, but will usually cater for different children at each session.	0 to 5 years	Private or voluntary	Yes, usually.	Only if children attend for more than two hours at a time (In Scotland, if provision operates for more than two hours per day or six days per year)
Nannies or au pairs	Directly employed by parents and working in parents' own home. Flexible hours.	0-12 years	Private	Yes	No
Home childcarers or sitters	Experimental scheme in England, established and provided via childcare agencies in Scotland. Registered childminders (in England) or childcarers (in Scotland) who visit the parents' home rather than take children into their homes. Flexible hours from early morning to late evening.	0-14 years (older if special needs)	Private (England) Public, private or voluntary (Scotland)	Yes	Yes for children up to 8 years and for all agencies in Scotland
Family and friends	Informal care provided either in carer's home or in parents' home. Flexible hours.	0-12 years	Private	Usually unpaid although some nominal payments made.	No

ISBN 92-64-00928-0
Babies and Bosses: Reconciling Work and Family Life
Canada, Finland, Sweden and the United Kingdom
© OECD 2005

Chapter 5

Tax/Benefit Policies and Parental Work and Care Decisions

Tax/benefit systems influence the standard of living of working families and of families temporarily or permanently without income from work. In doing so, they also influence the choice parents make regarding working and caring for their children. This chapter first gives a concise summary of the prevailing tax/benefit systems in Canada and the province of Québec, Finland, Sweden and the United Kingdom. It then discusses policy issues with a focus on financial incentives to work for second earners in couples and sole parent families. In all countries under review, work pays for most parents, but the financial returns to work can differ for different groups of parents in line with the age of a child or family status.

In all four countries under review public policy aims to provide choice to parents in making their work and care decisions. However, the means of providing choice differs across countries and existing policies do not all have a neutral impact on the relative attractiveness of care *vis-à-vis* paid employment. Childcare systems (Chapter 4), workplace practices (Chapter 6), and tax/benefit systems determine whether it pays for parents to work, work more hours, or, alternatively, encourage parents to care for (very young) children on a full-time basis. With typical average effective tax rates for low- and middle-income families at around 15% in the province of Québec, 20% in the United Kingdom, and 31% in Finland and Sweden, work appears to pay for most parents. However, the financial returns to work can differ for different groups of parents in line with the age of a child or family status. Working more hours may also not always lead to marked financial gains.

This chapter discusses the role tax/benefit policies play in the parental work-family balance. The next section illustrates how parental and maternal employment in particular reduces the risk of child poverty. Section 5.2 contains a summary of tax/benefit systems in the four jurisdictions under review, and Section 5.3 discusses how these policies affect the financial incentive structure to enter work (and work more) of second earners in couple families at different earnings levels, when accounting for childcare costs and the age of children. Section 5.4 presents evidence on the impact of tax/benefit policy on parental labour market behaviour. Before concluding this chapter, Section 5.5 considers the financial incentives to work facing sole parents and more generally discusses the public policy approach towards helping sole parents reconcile work and care commitments.

5.1. Maternal employment reduces child poverty

Child poverty has a significant effect on child development (Kamerman *et al.*, 2003) and reducing child poverty is a primary objective of policy in all four countries under review. Policy formulation is perhaps most explicit in the United Kingdom, where government policy aims to half child poverty by 2010 and eradicate it by 2020. To this end, a two-fold strategy is being followed: an expansion of child-related benefits targeted at low-income families and promoting parental employment by reducing barriers to paid work such as childcare (Chapter 4).

Chapter 2 showed that compared to households without children, families in Canada and the United Kingdom have an elevated poverty-risk, while in Finland and Sweden families with children are less likely to live in Poverty. In Finland and Sweden, child poverty rates are at about 3% below those for households headed by an adult of working age. Poverty rates for such working-age households are much higher in Canada (11%) and the United Kingdom at 13-14% (Chapter 2). Child poverty can be related to many factors, including maternal employment.

Table 5.1 shows that in all four countries under review, dual- and single-earner couples with children represent close to 50% of all households, of which many are in paid employment. Joblessness affects 2 to 3% of all families with children in Canada, Finland and the United Kingdom, and its incidence is highest in the United Kingdom at 7% of families with children.

In all four countries, parental employment reduces the poverty risk considerably.[1] Poverty rates of families with children are highest among jobless families and jobless sole parent families in particular. The poverty rate for non-employed sole parent families in Canada was 90% and 63% in the United Kingdom in 2000, compared with poverty rates of 28% and 21%, respectively, for working sole parent families.

Compared with the high poverty rates for jobless sole parent families in Canada and the United Kingdom, poverty rates among non-employed sole parent families in Finland and Sweden are much lower at 25% in Finland and 34% for Sweden. Being in work further reduces the poverty risk for sole parent families to a low 7% in Finland and 6% in Sweden. However, as is apparent from the lower poverty rates Finnish and Swedish benefits are paid at higher rates than in Canada and the United Kingdom, so poverty rates are lower.[2] For example, the share of jobless sole parent families is similar in Canada, Finland and Sweden, but the poverty risk for these families in Finland and Sweden is one-third of the risk in Canada.

Compared with jobless families, poverty rates are much lower for families where parents are in employment. Nevertheless, the poverty risk for single-earner families remains substantial and is highest in Canada at more than 20%. Indeed, the poverty risk for dual-earner families is low in all countries and around 3.5% in Canada and the United Kingdom, and just more than 1% in Finland and Sweden. Ensuring that both parents in couple families work thus plays a key role in reducing the risk of children growing up in poverty, and maternal employment is even more critical to reducing poverty among sole parent families.

Available historical evidence for Canada illustrates trends in earnings position of couple families (Chart 5.1). Average annual earnings of Canadian couple families with relatively limited hours in employment (less than the

Table 5.1. **Poverty rates are very high for jobless families**

Share of individuals and poverty rates by household type, latest available year[a]

	Share of individuals in each household type				Poverty rate (below 50% of median income)			
	Canada	Finland	Sweden	United Kingdom	Canada	Finland	Sweden	United Kingdom
	Percentage				Percentage			
Jobless households								
Single adult[b]	1.4	3.3	3.1	2.5	79.3	43.4	24.5	25.5
Sole parent	1.2	1.0	1.2	4.5	89.7	..	34.2	62.5
Childless couple	1.7	1.8	0.8	4.0	39.9	..	7.4	19.2
Couple with children	1.1	1.2	1.0	2.5	75.3	..	13.7	37.4
Working households								
Single adult[b]	6.1	10.4	18.0	5.8	17.0	15.3	10.2	9.5
Sole parent	3.8	4.4	8.4	4.9	27.7	7.2	5.6	20.6
Childless single-earner couple	6.3	7.9	3.0	5.5	13.7	4.8	3.8	6.1
Childless dual-earner couple	27.5	22.9	18.9	20.9	2.5	1.3	1.0	1.3
Single-earner couple with children	9.3	7.6	4.1	12.9	22.9	5.4	8.2	17.6
Dual-earner couple with children	41.6	39.6	41.6	36.5	3.5	1.3	1.1	3.6
All households with a working-age head	100.0	100.0	100.0	100.0	10.9	5.5	4.7	10.9

.. Data not available.

a) The income measure for relative poverty used here is 50% of the median "equivalised" disposable income of all individuals, where household disposable income is equivalised using the square root of household size. Date sources are: Canada, Survey of Labour and Income Dynamics; Finland, Finnish Income Distribution Survey; Sweden, Income Distribution Survey; and United Kingdom, Family Expenditure Survey. For full detail, see Förster and Mira d'Ercole (2005), Annexes I and II.

b) The high proportion of single adults in Finland and Sweden is related to person who is at least 18 years old being counted as adults with a separate household even when they live with their parents.

Source: Förster, M. and M. Mira d'Ercole (2005), "Income Distribution and Poverty in OECD Countries in the Second Half of the 1990s", *Social, Employment and Migration Working Paper*, OECD, Paris.

Chart 5.1. **Canadian couple families with two full-time earners strengthened their income position since the early 1970s**

Average annual earnings couple families in constant CAD 1997, by full-time equivalent weeks of employment, Canada, 1973-97

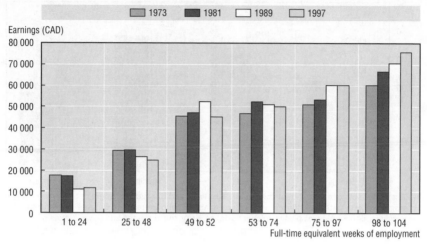

Source: Lochhead, C. (2000), *Factors Associated with Time Stress among Mothers and Fathers in Two Parent Families*, DataQuest Consulting, Ottawa.

equivalent of 24 weeks in full-time employment during the year) fell substantially since the early 1970s, while average earnings of couple families with just below 52 weeks of employment in 1997 was comparable with that of 1973. Families with at least one full-time earner and a part-time worker of 24 hours on an annual basis (75 to 97 weeks in Chart 5.1) have made significant income gains in the early 1980s, but the biggest gains were made by couple families where both parents worked full-time (Lochhead, 2000).

5.2. An overview of tax/benefit systems

As discussed in Chapter 2, gross public social expenditure is highest in Sweden at close to 30% of GDP, compared with 25% in Finland, 22% in the United Kingdom and 17% in Canada. However, as benefit income in Finland and Sweden is generally subject to relatively high income taxation and indirect taxation of consumption (out of benefit) income, net (after tax) public social spending in Sweden is only about 3 to 4 percentage points higher than in Finland and the United Kingdom (see Chapter 2). Net (after tax) spending on family benefits (child allowances and credits and childcare support) is highest in Sweden at almost 3.5% of GDP, compared with 3% in Finland, 2.5% in the United Kingdom and 1% in Canada (data on Canada do not reflect provincial spending on family support, as such information is not available on a comprehensive basis).[3] The differences in gross public social spending are

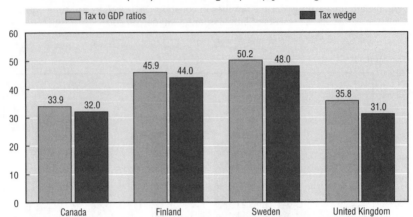

Chart 5.2. **A high tax burden in Sweden**

Tax-to-GDP ratios (2002) and tax wedges[a] (2003), percentages of GDP

a) Tax wedge between total labour costs to the employer and the corresponding net take-home pay to single workers without children at average earnings. Labour costs are defined as equal to gross wages paid to employees plus employer social security contributions and payroll taxes.

Source: OECD (2004), *Revenue Statistics*, OECD, Paris; OECD (2005), *Taxing Wages 2004-2005*, OECD, Paris.

mirrored in tax burdens across countries. In 2002, tax-to-GDP ratios in Sweden and Finland were 50% and 46%, respectively, compared with 34% in Canada and 36% in the United Kingdom (OECD, 2004). The tax wedge on labour at average earnings in Finland (44%) and Sweden (58%) is also much higher than in Canada and the United Kingdom: social security contributions paid by employers are especially high in both Nordic countries at more than 20% compared with 7% to 8% in Canada and the United Kingdom (OECD, 2004j and 2005b).

In all four countries the tax system is individually based, but in Canada and the United Kingdom most tax credits take into account family circumstances. Some child benefits are universal, while other child payments, and/or other social support for families with children, as for example, housing assistance, are targeted at low-and medium-income families. Eligibility to such income-tested support is generally family-based and includes cash transfers, as well as "wastable" and "refundable" tax credits whose role in delivering financial support to families in Canada and the United Kingdom has increased in recent years.[4] Such unconditional financial assistance increases family resources and can thus play an important role in the public pursuit of adequacy objectives. However, as such income-tested support is non-earmarked (*e.g.* receipt is not contingent on using formal childcare), it may also reduce the financial incentives to work for second earners in couple families and affect labour supply both in whether someone works and also how many hours they work.

5.2.1. *Canada and the province of Québec*

The individual federal and provincial income tax systems are progressive (income tax rates rise with income): tax rates range from 16% to 29% at the federal level and from 16% to 24% in the province of Québec, where depending on household status those with earnings below CAD 27 000 generally do not have to pay provincial income tax.[5] Both systems include tax credits for dependent spouses. Taxpayers in Québec receive a tax abatement of 16.5% of basic federal tax in calculating federal tax payable. Québec is the only province that collects its own taxes; in other jurisdictions, the federal government administers provincial income tax systems.

There are two main social insurance programmes in Canada, Employment Insurance (EI), which includes parental leave arrangements (Chapter 6) and the Canada/Québec Pension Plan (CPP/QPP). Three national programmes provide support to families with children through the tax system. The Canada Child Tax Benefit (CCTB), worth a maximum CAD 1 208 per child per annum, and the National Child Benefit (NCB) Supplement, at an annual maximum of CAD 1 511 per child, are income-tested supports available to low- and middle-income families (see Background Annex to the review). The federal Child Care Expense Deduction (CCED) is available to all working families in Canada, in which case an additional CCTB benefit of CAD 238 per year for children under 7 years is reduced by 25% of childcare cost claimed (see Background Annex to the review). Families in Québec with access to a subsidised childcare place at CAD 7 per day can claim the CCED, but not the provincial refundable tax credit for childcare expenses, which can refund up to 76% of childcare costs depending on family income (Chapter 4). The province of Québec also has non-refundable tax credits for dependent children in low-income families and a tax reduction for families, which for couple families is phased out when family income reaches 185% of Average earnings.[6] In addition, the provincial in-work payment for working parents (the Parental Wage Assistance programme as replaced in January 2005, see below) provides financial support for working low-income families (annual family income less than CAD 15 000 for sole parents and CAD 22 000 for couples).[7] Provinces are responsible for social service provision and social assistance benefits, for which they receive federal support through the Canada Social transfer (Chapter 2). In all, public spending on family benefits in the province of Québec increased modestly from CAD 2.6 billion in 1995 to CAD 3.0 billion in 2004, but there has been a marked change in nature towards a greater emphasis on supporting families in work. For example, the proportion of spending on childcare services in spending on Family benefits increased from 14.6% to 51.8% over the same period (Lefebvre and Merrigan, 2003; and MESSF, 2003).

5.2.2. Finland

The central government income tax schedule in Finland is progressive over five bands, ranging from 12% to 35% (those earning less than EUR 11 600 are not subject to central government income tax). Municipal tax is flat-rate (and varies between 15.5% and 20.0% across municipalities) although, since 1997, the earned income allowance (EIA) introduced an element of progressivity in municipal taxation, while increased tax deductions further reduced the tax burden on working low and medium income families.[8]

Statutory earnings-based social insurance systems provide income-support in case of, for example, unemployment, sickness, and parental leave (Chapters 2 and 6). Family allowances are universal (EUR 100 per month, and increasing with the number of children), but payment rates are higher for sole parent families (an additional EUR 37 per month), who are also entitled to maintenance support (EUR 118 per month) in case of default by the absent parent (see Background Annex to the review). Housing benefits and social assistance are means-tested benefits that are withdrawn on a euro-for-euro basis. The 444 municipalities in Finland are responsible for the provision of social services, health and education, including childcare support. There also are considerable cash transfers such as the Home Care Allowance for parents with children not yet 3 years of age who do not use municipal childcare services. The impact of these payments on financial incentives to work for parents with very young children is discussed below.

5.2.3. Sweden

The Swedish income tax system also consists of two parts: a municipal (including county taxes) system and a national personal income tax scheme. Spouses are taxed individually and there are no tax reliefs for marital status or for children. The national income tax scheme is progressive, but only those with earnings above SEK 291 800 (117% of average earnings, see below) are liable to tax, and are taxed at a rate of 20% (income above SEK 441 300 is taxed at 25%). Municipal income tax is proportional and differs across the 290 municipalities: the average rate was 31.2% in 2004 (ranging from 28.9% to 33.7%).

Apart from municipal social services and childcare (Chapter 4), Sweden has universal family benefits, insurance-based family support, and income and means-tested allowances (see Background Annex to the review). The general child allowances are flat-rate monthly payments (SEK 950 or EUR 105 per month), with significant supplements for large families (an additional EUR 28 for the third child, EUR 84 for the fourth child, and an additional EUR 105 (SEK 950) for the fifth and any further child. Social insurance programmes for families with children include income-related parental and temporary parental cash benefits, child pension, pregnancy cash benefits and pension rights for childcare years (see Background Annex to the review). The means-tested allowances include maintenance support (at maximum EUR 130 per month), housing allowance and social assistance payments.

5.2.4. United Kingdom

Since the introduction of independent taxation in 1990-91 the basic unit of taxation in the UK tax system has been the individual (prior to this, the tax system tended to treat married couples as one unit for income tax purposes). In recent years, tax credits have been added to the tax system as awards to families' income. In the United Kingdom, income tax is administered centrally (the local Council Tax is property-related). UK income tax is progressive but only those with earnings above GBP 4 745 (around 25% of median UK earnings) are liable to tax. There are three rates of income taxation: a tax rate of 10% applies to the next GBP 2020 of income, a tax rate of 22% applies to the next GBP 29 380 of earnings, beyond which an income tax rate of 40% applies.

Increasingly the tax system is being used to provide income support to families. Since April 2003, there are two new refundable or non-wastable tax credits, Child Tax Credit (CTC) and Working Tax Credit (WTC). Families are eligible for CTC regardless of employment status, if there is at least one child under 16 present in the family. CTC consists of several elements: a "family payment" (GBP 545 per year, about EUR 800), received by about 90% of families in the United Kingdom; a "baby payment" (an additional GBP 545 per annum) payable for the first year of a child's life and a "child payment" (GBP 1 625 per child). All these amounts are paid in full to families with an income up to GBP 58 000, at which point the amount paid falls on a sliding scale. The working tax credit (WTC) provides in-work support for low-paid working adults and families with children are eligible provided at least one adult works 16 or more hours per week. WTC consists of a basic element worth GBP 1 525 per year with an extra GBP 1 500 for couples and sole parents and an extra GBP 620 for those working at least 30 hours a week (in total if a couple). As discussed in Chapter 4, the WTC includes a "childcare credit" for parents working at least 16 hours, which is worth 70% of registered childcare costs of up to a maximum of GBP 135 per week for families with one child or GBP 200 for two or more children. In addition, all families can receive a child benefit worth GBP 16.5 per week. Means-tested income support and a housing benefit are also available; most of those claimants are jobless families (Bingley and Walker, 2001; Gibbons and Manning, 2003).

With recent reforms, spending on child benefit and tax credits will have increased by more than GBP 10 billion (EUR 15 billion) since 1997: a 75% increase in real terms. The UK government estimates that a typical family will have received GBP 1 300 (EUR 2 000) in extra income per annum, while families in the bottom quintile of the income distribution are about GBP 3 000 (EUR 4 500) per year better off on average in real terms.

5.3. Financial incentives to work for couple families

Tax/benefit systems play a key role in parental work and care decisions. One way of looking at the financial incentive structure that parents face (on a comparable basis across countries) is to consider "family budgets" for couple families at different earnings levels on the basis of the tax/benefit rules as applied in April-May 2004. In this manner, the financial incentive structure to enter work (and work more) of second earners can be considered in view of different family situations regarding the age of children, spousal earnings and access to subsidised childcare. Tax/benefit systems are also considered on their possible bias towards one parent in couple families earning more than the other.

5.3.1. Incentives to work for second earners in couple families without childcare costs

Table 5.2 shows gross and net incomes for couple families with two children ages 4 and 6 at different earnings level of the second earner. The costs of childcare are not accounted for (see below), so it is implicitly assumed that parents who need it have access to free informal childcare. Table 5.2 compares how family benefits[9] and net incomes change when a second adult starts earning one-third of average earnings (which might be interpreted as moving into part-time work) in a couple with two children where the other parent has average earnings. All numbers are expressed as a percentage of average earnings.

For single earner families with average earnings, family benefits are highest in the United Kingdom at 11% of gross income (Table 5.2). When mothers enter work and family incomes increase, the proportion of family benefits in gross family income naturally declines (by about half if mothers have average earnings in Finland, Sweden and the United Kingdom), but the element of income testing in non-conditional financial assistance to households with children is most pronounced in the province of Québec (see Background Annex to the review).

The average total tax wedge on gross family income for single earner families in the province of Québec (11%) and the United Kingdom (20%) is well below that in Finland and Sweden (both 31%). When second earners start to work at one-third of average earnings, marginal effective tax rates (METRs) are very low in the United Kingdom and Finland (respectively at 15% and 17%), suggesting that part-time work pays most in these two countries. Further

Table 5.2. **Work pays for second earners in low- and middle-income families, particularly in Canada/Québec and the United Kingdom**

Net income before childcare for couple families with two children (age 4 and 6); primary earnings at average earnings, while earnings of the second earner vary

	Canada/Québec				Finland				Sweden				United Kingdom			
Wage level (first adult – second adult)	100-0	100-33	100-67	100-100	100-0	100-33	100-67	100-100	100-0	100-33	100-67	100-100	100-0	100-33	100-67	100-100
Gross wage earnings (in % of average earnings)[a]	100	133.3	166.7	200	100	133.3	166.7	200	100	133.3	166.7	200	100	133.3	166.7	200
Family benefits in % of gross earnings	10%	3%	2%	2%	8%	6%	5%	4%	9%	7%	5%	4%	11%	7%	5%	5%
Net income in % of gross earnings	89%	82%	77%	73%	78%	79%	77%	74%	78%	77%	75%	74%	87%	86%	82%	80%
Net income in % of average earnings	89%	109%	128%	146%	78%	105%	128%	147%	78%	103%	126%	147%	87%	115%	137%	160%
Average family tax rate (total tax wedge)	11%	18%	23%	27%	31%	27%	28%	31%	31%	29%	30%	31%	20%	19%	22%	23%
Marginal effective tax rates on additional earnings[b]																
When entering the labour market	–	41%	41%	43%	–	17%	25%	31%	–	25%	28%	31%	–	15%	24%	27%
When increasing hours of work	–	41%	42%	47%	–	17%	32%	43%	–	25%	32%	36%	–	15%	33%	33%

– Not applicable.
a) "Average earnings" refer to the annual earnings of the "average production worker" in the manufacturing sector (OECD, 2005, *Taxing Wages 2004-2005*, OECD, Paris). In 2004, these were USD 34 358 (CAD 41 574) in Canada; USD 29 966 (EUR 29 779) in Finland; USD 26 313 (SEK 254 544) in Sweden; and, USD 33 210 (GBP 21 359) in the United Kingdom.
b) Marginal effective tax rates on additional earnings are calculated as the difference between the increase in gross earnings and the increase in net income when a second earner enters the labour market, and when increasing the hours of work and earnings from 0 to 33%, from 33% to 67%, and from 67% to 100% of average earnings, expressed as a proportion of the change in gross earnings.

Source: OECD tax/benefit models.

earnings increments lead to higher tax rates on second earner returns (due to income-tax progressivity and income-testing of transfers), but working more hours continues to pay as marginal tax rates remain below 50% in all countries.

5.3.2. Financial incentives to work for second earners in low-income couples

In couple families where the primary earner has relatively limited earnings, say, two-thirds of average earnings, there is a greater financial need for spouses to engage in paid work. However, because of the lower family income, seconds earners are more likely to have to consider the loss of income-tested benefits (and the phase-in) of earnings disregards when coming to decision to work more hours. Work for second earners in two-income households pays in all four counties, but financial incentives to work more hours are weak at certain earnings ranges (as measured by high marginal effective tax rates (METRs) which indicate a small financial return on an increment of individual labour supply).

With earnings of the partners at two-thirds of average earnings, second earners in couple families in Finland have few incentives to engage in paid employment for limited hours as at this family earnings range (from 67% to 87% of average earnings) housing support is phased out (Chart 5.3). In Sweden too, the phase-out of housing benefit generates very high METRs (see right-hand axis of Chart 5.3) at family earnings just above two-thirds of average earnings, but otherwise METRs for second earners in low-income families are below 50% in Finland and 40% in Sweden. In the United Kingdom, marginal effective tax rates increase when income tax and national insurance contributions start to rise with increased earnings, to drop off again when income-tested child support is phased out. Therefore, second earners in low-income families have financial incentives to either work and earn very little or to earn at least 45% of average earnings. The combined impact of federal and provincial income tax and benefit systems in Québec means that second earners in low-income families face METRs generally below 50% across the earnings range.[10] The income position of couple families with young children in the province of Québec has significantly improved in January 2005, when child support for the first child was increased threefold to CAD 2000 at maximum, while at the same time, the system of in-work benefits was reformed to increase coverage sixfold to 200 000 households with children (Box 5.1).

Chart 5.3. **Second earners in low-income couple families
have financial incentives to work full-time**

Net income before childcare for couple families with two children (age 1 and 4);
"primary earnings" at two-thirds of average earnings,
while earnings of second earner vary

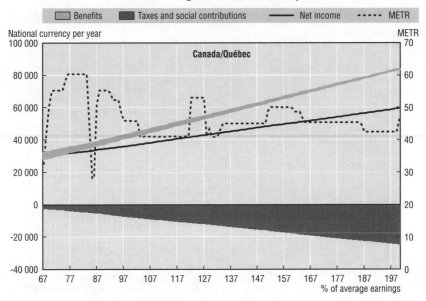

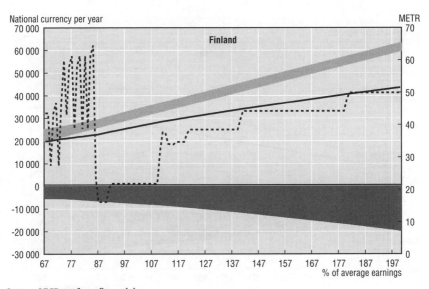

Source: OECD tax/benefit models.

Chart 5.3. **Second earners in low-income couple families
have financial incentives to work full-time** (cont.)

Net income before childcare for couple families with two children (age 1 and 4);
"primary earnings" at two-thirds of average earnings,
while earnings of second earner vary

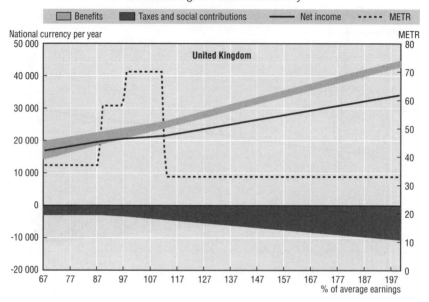

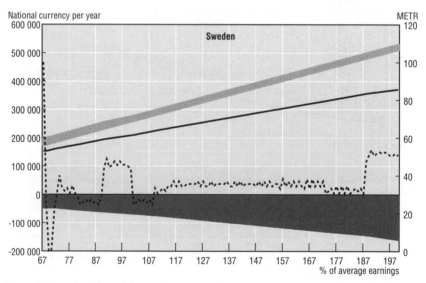

Source: OECD tax/benefit models.

Box 5.1. **Anti-poverty policy in Québec**

In April 2004, the provincial government of Québec launched a new package of policy measures, effective 1st January 2005, in its fight against poverty (MESSF, 2004 and 2004a). The package strengthens in particular the income position of low-income working families with children by increasing both unconditional child support and in-work benefit payments. Because of the reform package, a single person with earnings at minimum wage level gains 3% in disposable income, sole parents with two children about 11.5% and 23% for couple families with two children. The package is worth CAD 2.5 billion over five years (by comparison, spending on social assistance including for elderly clients is about CAD 2.7 billion per year) and involves the following broad groups of measures that constitute the core of the new policy initiative (for detail on spending on the difference components of the plan, see the Background Annex to the review):

● A new income-tested quarterly family assistance programme payment "Soutien aux enfants", replaces the family allowance and children tax credits, with rates that range from CAD 553 to CAD 2 000 for one child, with at the maximum level increments for additional children of CAD 1 000 after the first child and CAD 1 500 after the third child (Panel B in chart next page). Spending on the new family benefits will amount to about CAD 2 billion, a net increase of CAD 500 million per year over the previous measures.

● The "Work-premium" or "Prime au travail" supersedes the PWA or APPORT in-work benefit, whose programme rules linked entitlements to an asset test. PWA reached about 33 000 families, while the Work-premium (a refundable tax credit) is expected to reach about 535 000 households, of which 200 000 have children. Coverage of the programme is much wider due to inclusion of families without children and the level of earnings where support is phased out: about twice as high as under PWA. For couple families, the payment is phased out at CAD 42 800 (about average earnings) and for sole parents at CAD 31 600 (previously CAD 16 000). The maximum Work-premium payment to individual families is lower than under the PWA-rules (compare Panels A and B of Chart Box 5.1): for couple families CAD 2 780 (was CAD 3 782), and CAD 2 190 for sole parent families (was CAD 2 382). For a couple family with earnings of CAD 14 900 per annum (equal to 2 000 working hours at the minimum wage, which was increased to CAD 7.45 per hour per 1st May 2004), the prime au travail pays CAD 2 780 per annum, while at the same earnings level sole parents receive a payment of CAD 1 670 and this is CAD 764 for single persons.

Box 5.1. **Anti-poverty policy in Québec** (cont.)

● Increased housing support, especially in the 2004-07 period: construction of social housing (habitations à loyer modéré, HLM) for 16 000 households (in 2004 there were about 65 000 HLMs operated by municipalities, and another 8 200 operated by housing associations and NGOs), adaptation of 6 010 dwellings for the disabled and extend rent subsidies (paid to the landlord) to another 5 276 households (tax authorities operate financial support towards single persons aged 55 and over).

● Social assistance reform introducing indexation of social assistance payments and streamlining of benefit design to make sure that work pays. Social assistance clients can have earnings up to CAD 200 per month (CAD 300 for couple families), with additional earnings being off-set against benefit income on a dollar-for-dollar basis. Because of the prime au travail, clients can now always keep some of their additional earnings. Reform also increased the "Prime à la participation" from CAD 130 to CAD 150 per month paid towards travel cost, new clothes, and so on for clients who are not in work but who participate in an active labour market measure. In all, about CAD 50 million is available for intensifying labour market supports for clients.

Changes in family assistance in the province of Québec

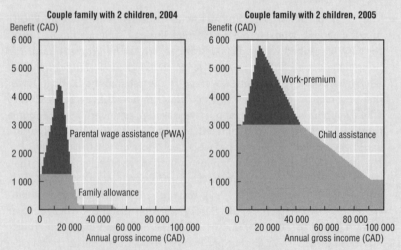

Source: Information provided by the provincial government of Québec.

5.3.3. Incentives to work for second earners in couple families with childcare costs

As discussed in the previous chapter, there are marked cross-country differences in public subsidisation of childcare. This contributes to cross-country differences in the fees that parents have to pay for the use of formal childcare as reflected in Table 5.3. In both Finland and Sweden childcare fees are income-tested and subject to a maximum: in Finland about EUR 200 per month for the first child and EUR 180 for the second child; in Sweden, about EUR 140 per month for the first child and EUR 93 for the second child (Chapter 4). Table 5.3 assumes that parents in Québec have access to a subsidised childcare place and pay a flat rate of CAD 7 per day, or CAD 1 827 per annum. For the United Kingdom it is assumed that 4-year olds have access to free part-time nursery schools of two-and-a- half hours per day, so that childcare costs amount to GBP 140 per week.

Table 5.3 shows the effect of childcare costs on family budgets of couple families with two children ages 1 and 4. Because of the extensive public subsidies towards the cost of parental childcare, parental fees are below 10% of gross family earnings in Finland, Sweden (lowest at 3%) and the province of Québec, even for couple families with an income equivalent to twice average earnings. Parental childcare costs in the United Kingdom increase with earnings levels and hours worked, so that they reach 14% for couples with earnings equivalent to 167% of average earnings.[11] In all, Table 5.3 suggests that in all four countries under review, when public childcare fee support is available, the cost of childcare does not establish barriers to employment of mothers with very young children, particularly in Sweden and Québec.

Once in work, marginal tax rates for second earners in Sweden after accounting for childcare costs are not very different from those for parents with free access to childcare (Table 5.2): generous childcare support is available to all working families regardless of earnings and hours. In Finland (see below) and the province of Québec, family income increases proportional if the working mother works full-time rather than part-time, which in Québec is related to subsidised childcare being supported on a full-day basis. In the United Kingdom on the other hand, design of childcare support contributes to spouses earning more than two-thirds of average earnings to face relatively high METRs: the UK tax benefit system facilitates part-time labour supply.

The finding that childcare costs do not impede mothers to choose work in the United Kingdom (Table 5.3) is more dependent on the assumptions on childcare fees than in Finland and Sweden. Financial returns to work are obviously much lower if parental fees are not, as assumed, GBP 140 but closer to GBP 300 per week for two children (Chapter 4). Such high fees for full-time care are not entirely unrealistic if living in London, where parental childcare

Table 5.3. **When public childcare support is available, parental fees are not a barrier to employment for mothers with very young children**

Net income after childcare for couple families with two children (age 1 and 4); "primary earnings" at average earnings while earnings of the second earner vary

	Canada/Québec				Finland				Sweden				United Kingdom			
Wage level (first adult – second adult)	100-0	100-33	100-67	100-100	100-0	100-33	100-67	100-100	100-0	100-33	100-67	100-100	100-0	100-33	100-67	100-100
Gross wage earnings (in % of average earnings)[a]	100	133.3	166.7	200	100	133.3	166.7	200	100	133.3	166.7	200	100	133.3	166.7	200
Family benefits in % of gross earnings	10%	3%	2%	1%	29%	6%	5%	4%	9%	7%	5%	4%	12%	7%	6%	5%
Childcare fees in % of gross earnings	..	7%	5%	4%	..	9%	8%	7%	..	3%	3%	3%	..	9%	14%	17%
Net income in % of gross earnings	86%	73%	70%	67%	98%	70%	68%	66%	78%	74%	73%	71%	87%	78%	69%	63%
Net income in % of average earnings	86%	98%	117%	135%	98%	94%	114%	133%	78%	99%	121%	141%	87%	104%	115%	126%
Average family tax rate (total tax wedge)	14%	20%	25%	28%	35%	27%	28%	31%	31%	29%	30%	31%	20%	19%	22%	23%
Marginal effective tax rates on additional earnings[b]																
When entering the labour market	–	65%	54%	51%	–	113%	76%	65%	–	36%	36%	37%	–	49%	58%	61%
When increasing hours of work	–	65%	43%	46%	–	113%	40%	43%	–	36%	35%	38%	–	49%	67%	67%

.. Not applicable.
–
a) "Average earnings" refer to the annual earnings of the "average production worker" in the manufacturing sector (OECD, 2005, Taxing Wages 2004 2005, OECD, Paris). In 2004, these were USD 34 358 (CAD 41 574) in Canada; USD 29 966 (EUR 29 779) in Finland; USD 26 313 (SEK 254 544) in Sweden; and, USD 33 210 (GBP 21 359) in the United Kingdom.
b) Marginal effective tax rates on additional earnings are calculated as the difference between the increase in gross earnings and the increase in net income when a second earner enters the labour market, and when increasing the hours of work and earnings from 0 to 33%, from 33% to 67%, and from 67% to 100% of average earnings, expressed as a proportion of the change in gross earnings.

Source: OECD tax/benefit models.

costs are closer to around one-third of gross earnings. This leads some parents to decide to not engage in paid work, to work part-time or to work full-time and making greater use of informal childcare. Indeed, some parents, especially sole parents, choose to use informal care in any case as even with public childcare support, as out-of-pocket costs can be significant (Chapter 4).

From April 2005 onwards, the childcare element of the Working Tax Credit covers childcare costs up to GBP 175 per week for one child and GBP 300 for two children (up from GBP 135 and GBP 200, respectively). This is equivalent to a reduction of the parental contribution to childcare fees of 41% to 16% of the total cost for a couple with earnings of GBP 24 000 per annum (equivalent to 112% of average earnings), and from 70% to 46% of the total cost for a couple with earnings at 175% of average earnings (assuming parents use childcare on a full-time basis at a cost of GBP 4 per hour; HM Treasury, 2004). This significant reduction in the parental contribution to childcare costs reduces barriers to employment for many (sole) mothers.

On the other hand, reform of the WFTC also meant that childcare support is almost immediately cut off when parents lose their job or when they are forced to work less than 16 hours per week. The loss of childcare support may act as a barrier to work (or work more hours) for low-income parents who are moving between jobs, or who are forced to reduce hours with one employer and are looking to work additional hours elsewhere. Reform should be initiated to introduce more flexibility in WTC-delivery, for example, by extending the period upon which childcare support through the WTC upon job-loss (or reduced working hours to below 16 hours per week) is available from the current seven days to three months after job loss.

5.3.4. *The age of the child and parental work incentives in Finland*

Parents of children aged 4 and 6 generally do not face financial disincentives to paid work in Finland as shown in Table 5.2. By contrast, potential second earners in couple families with very young children in Finland face strong financial disincentives to engage in paid work, because of the substantial income transfers to such families. Table 5.3 shows that for families with children ages 1 and 4 with one parent in work at average earnings, family benefits amount to 29% of gross family income (the equivalent figure for parents with older children was 8%), which drops to 6% when the second earner is in work and earns one-third of average earnings.

Finnish parents with young children have a choice: either use childcare support or receive a Home Care Allowance (HCA) until the child turns 3 years of age. Chapter 4 showed that, from a municipal budgetary perspective, it makes sense to pay parents to stay at home and care for toddlers as providing family- or centre-based childcare for very young children is more expensive. From the parental perspective, the HCA establishes clear disincentives to work for potential second earners in couple families in which very young children are present. Table 5.3 shows that a second earner in a family with very young children who enters work and earns about one-third of average earnings would actually leave the family worse off (net family income declines from 98% to 94% of average earnings). The METR faced by a second earner is greater than 100%, since childcare fees (although not high in themselves) now have to be paid and the home care allowance is lost in its entirety (worth about EUR 650 per month at maximum, including income-tested and municipal supplements, before taxation, see Box 5.2). If municipal home care supplements were ignored, METRs for second earners would still be around 80%, while, in the absence of the basic HCA, METRs would be around 44%. Through the HCA, policy encourages potential second earners, usually mothers, in families with very young children to provide care on a full-time basis.

Box 5.2. **Paying parents for not using formal childcare in Finland**

Municipalities in Finland are responsible for organising care for children under school age. Broadly speaking there are three forms of such support: provision of municipal childcare services to parents and subsidising parental fees; providing parents who use private centres with fee support, or making a cash transfer to parents when they choose not to make use of public or private day-care facilities (Chapter 4). Such parents who do not use childcare and who have at least one child not yet 3 years of age are entitled to the Home Care Allowance (HCA) as paid by the Social Security Institution (KELA): in 2004, payment rates were EUR 252 per month for one child and EUR 84 for each additional child under 3 years of age (for siblings between ages 3 and 7 who also do not use municipal childcare, another EUR 50 is paid). In addition, KELA pays income-tested monthly supplements worth up to EUR 168 per month. Furthermore, some (often larger) municipalities make supplementary payments worth on average about EUR 190 per child per month (in Helsinki this payment was EUR 219 per month in 2004). In September 2004, some 49 000 families received HCA, of which about one-quarter received supplementary municipal payments.

As neither the basic HCA payment nor the municipal supplements are gradually phased out, starting to use formal childcare, involves an immediate income loss of EUR 500 per month, with childcare fees (for one child) at around EUR 200 per month: total family income loss is about one-third of average earnings. Finnish mothers who are paid less than their spouses must have either high potential earnings or a very strong career commitment to decide to go to work under these circumstances.

5.3.5. Cost of care when children are at school

There is considerable public support towards the costs of out-of-school-hours care (OSH-care) in all four jurisdictions under review. In Finland, the monthly parental fee of OSH-care is about EUR 60 and in Sweden this is EUR 93 (subject to variation across municipalities in both countries).[12] In the province of Québec, OSH-care is financed as CAD 7 per day places, which given the relatively limited hours of care is thus relatively expensive compared to day-care. Childcare tax support for low-income parents in the United Kingdom also covers OSH-care reducing the costs to parents. Because financial support to parents for both childcare and out-of-school-hours care (OSH-care) is considerable in all four jurisdictions work continues to pay when children enter primary school (see Table 5.A.1 at the end of this chapter). The issue in the United Kingdom is not so much the price as the availability of OSH-care places that has led to the expansion of OSH-care capacity emerging as a policy priority in the UK childcare debate (Chapter 4).

5.3.6. Gender neutrality in tax/benefit systems

So far, the discussion of financial incentives to work for adults in couple families is based on considering different earnings levels of the second earner, while assuming constant earnings (and hours) for the primary earner. However, couple families can choose a range of possible labour supply options to procure a desired level of disposable family income: the single-breadwinner approach, a combination of full-time and part-time work, or by both partners earning equal amounts. If tax/benefit systems are largely neutral between these choices, then public policy has little effect on how paid work is distributed within couple families.

The tax systems in the jurisdictions under review, all have the individual as the tax unit: of the level of taxation of taxable income is independent of family status. However, tax reliefs and credits are frequently related to family composition, as indeed, are most income-tested cash benefits. Because of this, when the second adult in a couple family starts earning, these earnings first off-set the value of the tax allowance and lead to a (often equivalent) loss of benefit income (e.g. housing benefit). Hence, such income-tested benefits, family-based tax credits and transferable tax allowances introduce a certain bias towards single earner couples in tax/benefit systems (e.g. Dingeldey, 2001). On the other hand, as all income tax systems under review have progressive income tax schedules, they all include a certain bias towards spreading earnings across different household members: tax payments to government are highest when a single earner provides for all family income.

Tax/benefit systems in Canada, Finland, Sweden and the United Kingdom, favour dual earner couples over single earner families (except for

Finnish couple families with very young children, see above). At the chosen level of family income (133% of average earnings), the UK tax/benefit system appears to be the most gender equitable of the systems under review: net payments (taxes minus family benefits) for a family in which both spouses earn two-thirds of average earnings pay 9% (15 percentage points) less of gross family income to the government than single earner families (Table 5.4). This result is related to the design of the childcare payment in the Working Tax Credit that favours working hours falling short of a full-time working week. Choosing another family-earnings level would produce a less pronounced effect.

5.4. Evidence of incentive effects

5.4.1. Benefit traps in Finland and Sweden

The economic crisis in the early 1990s in Finland and Sweden led to demand-side reduction of (female) employment, while subsequent tightening of public budgets altered supply-side factors. For example, the larger role for HCA payments in Finland (relatively cheap to public budgets, Chapter 4) and in the mid-1990s increments in parental childcare fees in Sweden weakened financial incentives for second earners to engage in paid work. The relative importance of such supply-side effects in determining parental employment trends is difficult to gauge, but they play a considerable role in ongoing policy reform to make work pay for workers in all four countries.

In Finland, despite reform to make work pay (e.g. the introduction of the Earned Income Allowance during the 1990s), income traps exist for benefit recipients in certain circumstances. For example, Kurjenoja (2004) found that financial incentives to increase hours for sole mothers who work part-time are frequently weak, because of the loss of benefit income. Similarly, in couple families with one parent in work, disposable family income may well decrease if the spouse who is in receipt of unemployment benefit starts to work, due to the reduction in housing benefit. In general, labour supply elasticties for women in Finland are very small, especially for married women (Bargain and Orsini, 2004).[13]

Since 1997, Swedish policy reform has reduced average marginal tax rates from 53% in 1997 to 46% in 2003 through a variety of measures including reduced income tax rates, extended tax allowances and the introduction of maximum childcare fees, (SOU, 2004). Nevertheless, 10% of working age individuals face METRs of more than 80% and, when leaving unemployment benefits for work, the average METR is 84% (ibid.). The labour supply of sole parents in Sweden is relatively elastic and thus more sensitive than that of mothers in couple families to variations in marginal tax rates (Flood et al., 2003 and 2004). Because of the reforms since 1997, the average marginal tax

Table 5.4. **Tax/benefit systems favour dual earnership over single-earner couples**

Average payments to governments as a percentage of gross earnings, at different earning distributions of a couple with two children age 1 and 4 and family income equal to 133% of average earnings

Wage level (first earner-second earner)	Canada/Québec			Finland			Sweden			United Kingdom		
	133-0	100-33	67-67	133-0	100-33	67-67	133-0	100-33	67-67	133-0	100-33	67-67
1. Payments to government												
a) Income tax	17.5%	14.8%	12.6%	28.5%	22.3%	19.7%	33.1%	29.2%	28.4%	15.7%	11.3%	6.9%
b) social security contributions	4.7%	6.1%	6.3%	5.5%	6.0%	6.0%	7.0%	7.0%	7.0%	10.7%	8.6%	8.6%
2. Family benefits												
a) for children aged 1 and 4	2.5%	2.1%	1.8%	20.3%	6.4%	6.4%	6.7%	6.7%	6.7%	6.8%	6.8%	11.3%
b) for children aged 7 and 9	1.9%	2.1%	1.8%	6.4%	6.4%	6.4%	6.7%	6.7%	6.7%	7.0%	7.0%	7.0%
3. Total payments to government less family benefits (1-2)												
a) for children aged 1 and 4	19.6%	18.9%	17.2%	13.8%	21.9%	19.4%	33.4%	29.4%	28.7%	19.6%	13.1%	4.2%
b) for children aged 7 and 9	20.3%	18.8%	17.1%	27.6%	21.9%	19.4%	33.4%	29.5%	28.7%	19.4%	12.9%	8.5%

Source: OECD tax/benefit models.

rate that sole parents face dropped from 70% to 62%, but remains well above METRs (46%) faced by mothers in couple families (SOU, 2004). The combined effect of income taxation, social assistance payments and housing benefit may in particular cases leave some sole mothers better off when they do not work at all. Sole parent employment rates in Sweden are higher than in the other three countries, and indeed most other OECD countries, but despite general childcare coverage provided at low parental cost, employment rates for sole parents with children who do not yet go to school are lower than for sole parents with school-age children (Chapter 3).

5.4.2. Individualisation of income taxation and introducing in-work benefits in Canada and the United Kingdom

Both Canada and the United Kingdom have experienced substantial pronounced female employment growth since the 1980s, although experiences differ with household status. Tax/benefit reform has contributed to changing female employment patterns during the 1990s in both countries. The Canadian tax reform of 1988 reduced the number of tax brackets and involved the replacement of various family-related tax deductions (for spouses and children) with non-refundable tax credits, which were less dependent on the primary spouse's earnings. Because of this reform, the incentive structure faced by individuals married to low-income earners changed little; but for those women with high-earning husbands, increasing their labour supply became much more financially attractive. Jeon (2004) found that this latter group of women increased their labour force participation by 7.3%, while their annual labour supply increased by almost 200 hours compared to women with a low-earning husband.

Individual taxation in the United Kingdom was introduced in 1990 and was accompanied by a "married couples allowance" (to limit the immediate negative impact of tax reform on the income position of single-earner couples), which was gradually phased out and abolished by 2000. Reform improved financial incentives to work for second earners in couple families, while the relative attractiveness of part-time employment was enhanced by successive reforms of the national insurance contribution schedule that reduced incentives to employers to hire workers for a limited number of hours only (Chapter 6 and Gregg et al., 2003). Moreover, the design of in-work payments to working families (WFTC, WTC) embodies incentives to mothers to engage in paid work for just over 16 hours per week.

By now, both Canada and the United Kingdom have, established a tradition in trying to increase employment and income among working families through in-work benefits that make work pay.[14] In-work benefits can both increase the likelihood to accept employment (or increase hours) and redistribute resources towards working families, in particular when such measures are non-wastable (Pearson and Scarpetta, 2000). Critical to family policy, in-work benefit payments can be very effective in improving the financial incentive structure for households in which no one is employed, but can provide disincentives to paid work among potential second earners in couple families.

Each province in Canada has its own in-work benefit scheme for low-income families (for an overview see Jenson, 2003). The APPORT programme in the province of Québec (see above) failed to reach more families than it did because of stringent eligibility criteria and convoluted administration and benefit calculation procedures. This contributed to the programme being ineffective in reducing dependency on social assistance income, except for some positive effect observed in the employment status of sole parents and claimants not yet 30 years of age (Eaton *et al.*, 2000, and Box 5.1).

Although not an employment-conditional benefit, the National Child benefit (CCTB and the income-tested supplement) has made moving from welfare rolls into work more financially attractive for (sole parent) families across Canada. Milligan and Stabile (2004) found that the introduction of the NCB has reduced social assistance take-up in Canada by as much as about one-third. Prior to NCB-introduction, sole parents with two children starting to work at minimum wage levels would make made few financial gains and were better off on welfare if they had three children. In the aftermath of the reform, gains in disposable incomes for such families exceeded 10%. Because of the introduction of the NCB there were 55 000 children (of which almost one-third in sole parent families) less living in low-income families, and the incidence of low income among families with children declined with 0.6% (Government of Canada, 2003). The Canadian Self-Sufficiency Project has clearly shown how financial incentives can help stimulate employment and reduce poverty in sole parent households at little cost to public budgets, particularly when such clients require little employment support to return to paid work (Box 5.3).

There is an extensive and growing body of research in the United Kingdom, which shows the effect policy changes since 1997 have had on employment and poverty outcomes (an overview of tax/benefit reforms since 1997 that increase returns to work for low-income families can be found in Table A.4 in the Background Annex to the review, also Bennett and Millar, 2005). Reforms have increased the redistribution of resources among households without children to families and among families themselves: the incomes of the poorest fifth of families have increased by more than 20% (Brewer and Shephard, 2004). Because of the importance of reducing child poverty as a policy objective, the increase in child-related payments improved the income position of jobless families with children by almost as much as that of low-earning families. Reduced joblessness and increased child benefit and employment conditional tax credits (Sutherland *et al.*, 2003) have reduced

Box 5.3. **Lessons from the Canadian self-sufficiency project**

The Self-Sufficiency Project (SSP) showed that improving the financial incentives to work for sole parents limits benefit dependency by increasing employment, thereby reducing the poverty risk for sole parents and their children. The costs to public budgets of introducing such policies are limited when targeted at clients with relatively recent work-history: increased tax revenue and lower transfer payments covers about 90% of the total cost. Only one-third of programme costs are covered when clients have a longer history of social assistance receipt.

The federally funded Self-Sufficiency Project (SSP) involved experimental studies over a 10-year period to establish the effects of financial incentive structures in particular on the labour market behaviour of sole parents in receipt of social assistance. SSP was launched in 1992 and included three main studies: the Recipient SSP study involving about 6 000 sole parents on social assistance in the provinces of New Brunswick and British Columbia who had been on social assistance for at least a year but often longer (Michalopoulos *et al.*, 2002); the SSP Plus study, involving 600 sole parents in New Brunswick (Lei and Michalopoulos, 2001); and, the "Applicant study" concerning 3 300 sole parent claimants of social assistance in the province of British Columbia who had not been in receipt of social assistance six months prior to their most recent claim (Ford *et al.*, 2003). In all three studies half of the selected sole parents were randomly assigned to a programme group and the other half to a control group, with those in the programme group becoming eligible for generous earnings supplements for up to 36 months provided they did not claim social assistance and worked full-time (on average at least 30 hours per week during the reference month). In all three studies, clients lost eligibility for the earnings supplement if they did not claim it within a year of it being offered. Earnings supplements were calculated as half the difference between a participant's earnings and an "earnings benchmark" set by SSP so as to ensure that full-time work paid for most social assistance recipients. Earnings supplements were generous: for example, for most families in British Columbia, in 1996 net family income was CAD 3 000 to CAD 7 000 higher than it otherwise would have been at similar hours of work.

Key SSP findings include:

● *Financial incentive structures affect the speed with which sole parents leave welfare rolls*: Sole parents who were long-term social assistance claimants (the "recipient study") left welfare rolls for full-time employment much faster if they had access to generous earnings supplements, with the biggest effect immediately after the close of the one-year period limit for

Box 5.3. **Lessons from the Canadian self-sufficiency project** (*cont.*)

finding full-time employment. However, the effect was temporary: six years after random assignment, employment rates (full-time) among clients with and without access to earnings supplements were close to 30%.

● *Financial incentives had the largest effect on clients with recent employment experience*: 45% of the clients in the "applicants study" who were eligible for the earnings supplement were in full-time employment six years upon random assignment (compared to 30% for the "recipient group" while this was 41% for those without earnings supplements. A design feature of this "applicant study" was that clients had to wait for 12 months before becoming eligible for the earnings supplement. This delayed exits for those still on social assistance after three months of benefit receipt; with the largest employment effect on those with earnings supplement just two years following the random assignment.

Evidence from the SSP study suggests that the provision of employment supports contributes to clients finding better long-term employment solutions. Participants in the SSP Plus study with access to employment supports (including intensive counselling and individual re-integration plans, information on vacancies and various workshops) had slightly better employment and earnings outcomes than those without such support. Nevertheless, the positive effects of the SSP Plus programme are largely related to the supplement rather than the employment supports, although the programme appears to have helped some SSP Plus clients to find more stable employment than their otherwise similar counterparts in the "recipient study" (Lei and Michalopoulos, 2001). However, the small sample size of this study makes it difficult to establish the exact nature of the relationship between employment assistance and exit rates.

child poverty, especially among sole parent families: 57% of low-paid sole mothers working 16 hours or more avoid poverty through benefit receipts, including in-work benefits and such tax credits lift 40% of these sole parent families above the poverty line (Millar and Gardiner, 2004).

The UK body of evidence (using various sources and estimation techniques) universally finds that policy reform since 1997 in the United Kingdom have increased the employment incidence among sole parents from 45% in 1997 to 54% in 2004 (Chapter 3). Estimates point to an increase of about 4 to 7 percentage points in the sole parent employment rate because of "Make Work Pay" reform depending on the time period (and number of reforms) covered in the analysis (Table 5.5). However, it is much more difficult to find a positive impact of in-work benefits on employment in couple families; if there

Table 5.5. **Has "Make Work Pay" reform in the United Kingdom since 1997 improved parental labour market outcomes?**

Study	Data	Reforms analysed	Estimated impact on lone parents	Estimated impact on couples	Other notes
Difference-in-differences approach					
Gregg and Harkness (2003)	LFS and GHS, 1979-2002	Changes affecting lone parents between 1998 and 2002.	Increased employment by 5 ppts.	n.a.	Estimated that reforms also increased hours worked and weekly earnings.
Francesconi and van der Klaauw (2004)	BHPS, 1991-2001	Policies affecting lone mothers between 1998 and 2001.	Increased employment by 4 ppts in 1998 and 7 ppts by 2001 (lone mothers only).	n.a.	Uses longitudinal (panel) data. Estimated that lone mother's fertility and propensity to cohabit/marry declined after 1998.
Leigh (2004)	LFS, 1999-2000	All changes affecting parents between September and November 1999.	Increased employment by around 1 ppt.	Increased employment by around 1 ppt.	Estimated that reforms also increased hours worked and earnings by parents.
Blundell et al. (2004)	LFS, 1996-2002	All changes affecting parents between 1999 and 2002.	Increased employment by 3.6 ppts (lone mothers) and 4.6 ppts (lone fathers).	No statistically significant impact for mothers. Reduced employment by around 05 ppts for fathers.	
Structural model approach					
Brewer et al. (2003)	FRS, 1995-2002	All changes to taxes and benefits made in October 1999 and April 2000.	Increased employment by 3.4 ppts (lone mothers only).	Reduced employment by 0.4 ppts (men and women).	Estimated that reforms also increased hours worked by lone mothers.
Blundell et al. (2004)	FRS, 1995-2002	All changes to taxes and benefits made in April 2000 and April 2003.	Increased employment by 3.4 ppts (lone mothers only).	Reduced employment by 0.3 ppts (women) ; increased employment by 0.9 ppts (men).	Uses same model of behaviour as Brewer et al. (2003b).

n.a. Not available.
ppts = percentage points.
Note: LFS is Labour Force Survey, FRS is Family Resources Survey, BHPS is British Household Panel Study, GHS is General Household Survey. For more details, see individuals papers.
Source: Brewer, M. and A. Shephard (2004), *Has Labour Made Work Pay?*, Joseph Rowntree Foundation, York.

is an upward effect on employment in couple families it concerns fathers rather than mothers (Brewer *et al.*, 2003).[15]

5.5. Reducing joblessness and poverty among sole parent families

During the past decades, sole parenthood has increased in almost all OECD countries, with many children in all four countries now living in sole parent families, as do 24% of Swedish children compared to 22% of Québécois children, 20% of British and Canadian kids and 17% of dependent children in Finland (Chapter 2). Cross-country differences in sole parent employment rates are more pronounced: more than 70% in Canada and Finland, and 82% in Sweden compared with just more than 50% in the United Kingdom (Chapter 3). As non-employment in sole parent families results in a very high poverty risk (Section 5.1), for "anti child poverty policy" to be effective, it should include a strong focus on keeping and/or re-integrating sole parents in the labour force. Such a policy should involve each of the three following characteristics: 1) provide sufficiently strong financial incentives to work; 2) provide employment supports; and 3) childcare support (Chapter 4). Each of these three policy elements is needed to make any labour market-reintegration strategy towards sole parents a success, with training needs most likely to occur when sole parents have been out of work for a considerable period.

5.5.1. Financial incentives to work for sole parents

Sole parents on means-tested income support in all four countries generally have substantial financial incentives to engage in paid work: comparing benefit income with after tax income from work, net replacement rates for such sole parents (compared with average earnings) are 41%, 51% and 56% in the province of Québec, the United Kingdom and Sweden, respectively. Replacement rates (the value of benefit income relative to earnings) for sole parents in the United Kingdom have increased with the reform of the WFTC into the CTC and the WTC (see above): the child payment in the WFTC that was only paid to those working 16 hours or more is now available to all parents (OECD, 2004n). Net replacement rates for Finnish sole parents are 57% but for sole parents with very young children (ages 1 and 4) these are much higher at 82%, because of the elevated HCA payments to sole parents (with supplements as paid in some municipalities, these could be as high as EUR 8 275 per annum). If, in addition, childcare fees are also considered (Table 5.6, Panel B), then clearly it does not pay for a Finnish sole parent to enter the labour market and work limited hours (sole parents in Finland with two children ages 4 and 6 have much stronger financial incentives to work, see Table 5.A.2 at the end of this chapter).

Table 5.6. **Childcare costs are most likely to be a barrier to employment for sole parents in the United Kingdom**

Net income before and after childcare costs for sole parent families with children age 1 and 4 at different earnings levels (Panel A)
METRs on additional earnings for sole parent families, with and without childcare fees (Panel B)

	Canada/Québec			Finland			Sweden			United Kingdom		
	33.3	66.7	100	33.3	66.7	100	33.3	66.7	100	33.3	66.7	100
Gross wage earnings (in % of average earnings)[a]	33.3	66.7	100	33.3	66.7	100	33.3	66.7	100	33.3	66.7	100
Panel A: Sole parent families having two children aged 1 and 4												
Family benefits in % of gross earnings	66%	21%	8%	106%	40%	21%	93%	40%	20%	130%	42%	12%
Net income in % of gross earnings	167%	107%	83%	189%	115%	90%	168%	112%	89%	221%	121%	87%
Net income in % of average earnings	56%	71%	83%	63%	77%	90%	56%	75%	89%	74%	81%	87%
Marginal effective tax rates on additional earnings[b]	36%	45%	51%	66%	62%	61%	82%	63%	61%	47%	63%	69%
Panel B: The impact of childcare fees for children aged 1 and 4												
Childcare fees in % of gross earnings	26%	13%	9%	0%	7%	10%	3%	3%	3%	34%	34%	34%
Childcare fees in % of average earnings	9%	9%	9%	0%	4%	10%	1%	2%	3%	11%	23%	34%
Marginal effective tax rates on additional earnings												
When entering the labour market	63%	53%	58%	131%	102%	93%	85%	66%	64%	62%	78%	79%
When increasing hours of work	63%	43%	68%	131%	73%	76%	85%	47%	59%	62%	93%	83%

a) "Average earnings" refer to the annual earnings of the "average production worker" in the manufacturing sector (OECD, 2005, *Taxing Wages 2004 2005*, OECD, Paris). In 2004, these were USD 34 358 (CAD 41 574) in Canada; USD 29 966 (EUR 29 779) in Finland; USD 26 313 (SEK 254 544) in Sweden; and, USD 33 210 (GBP 21 359) in the United Kingdom.

b) Marginal effective tax rates on additional earnings are calculated as the difference between the increase in gross earnings and the increase in net income when a sole parent enters the labour market or increases working hours and income from 0 to 33%, from 33% to 67%, and from 67% to 100% of average earnings, expressed as a proportion of the change in gross earnings.

Source: OECD tax/benefit models.

Family benefits are an important source of household income for all sole parent families, even when the sole parent in question is in work. For a sole parent with relatively small earnings (at one-third of average earnings), the proportion of family benefits in gross household income ranges from 62% in the province of Québec to 130% in the United Kingdom (Table 5.6, Panel A).

Chart 5.4 shows the METR structure that sole parents face. It illustrates that Finnish sole parents in general have limited incentives to increase hours up to the point where housing benefits are phased out: given the high METRs, Finnish sole parents are likely to work full-time. High METRs reflect the weak financial incentives to work structure that sole parents in the United Kingdom face. Across the earnings range up to average earnings, work most evidently pays, when earnings are just above the threshold levels associated with the WTC and in particular the thresholds for childcare support: at 16 and 30 hours work per week. Chart 5.3 clearly shows this with the two "negative spikes" at earnings levels around 40% and 75% of average earnings: the UK tax/benefit system facilitates sole parents to work part-time.

Sole parents in the province of Québec face METRs of 100% at the low earnings range, where social assistance income is clawed back on a dollar-for-dollar basis. METRs are lowest just above the level of (low) earnings (22% of average earnings) where APPORT payments are highest. However, for higher earnings, the METR oscillates around 50% (because of the impact of the GST-credit, phase-out of family benefits and becoming liable for provincial income taxation), so that working more hours generally pays for sole parents in the province of Québec. In Sweden, the picture is fairly similar: taking up few hours of part-time work does not pay for sole parents on social assistance (means-tested income support is withdrawn on a kroner-for-kroner basis). But at all earnings above a quarter of average earnings, working more hours pays off handsomely for sole parents in Sweden (Chart 5.4).

Panel B in Table 5.6 shows the impact of childcare fees the financial incentive structure that sole parents face. Sole parents in Finland and in particular Sweden spend a relatively small part of their earnings on childcare compared with the United Kingdom, where childcare costs amount to one-third of gross earnings (this contributes to working sole parents in the United Kingdom often preferring to use informal care, Chapter 4).

So far, the calculations for the province of Québec assume that parents have access to a subsidised childcare place. Under certain circumstances (depending on the fees charged, the number of days per week that childcare is being used, household income and family composition) families, in particular sole parent families, can be financially better off using a private childcare place that is not offered at a flat-rate fee (Laferrière, 2003). For example, if childcare fees are CAD 27 per day and earnings ranging from about 50% to 120% of

Chart 5.4. **Unlike their Finnish and Swedish counterparts it pays for British sole parents to work part-time**

Net income before childcare cost for sole parents with two children (age 1 and 4)
at earnings from 0 to 133% of average earnings

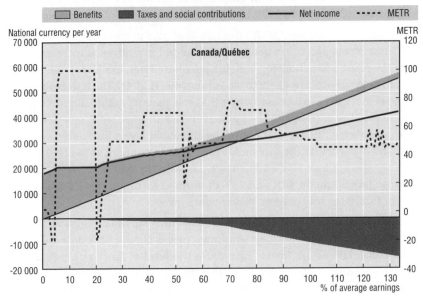

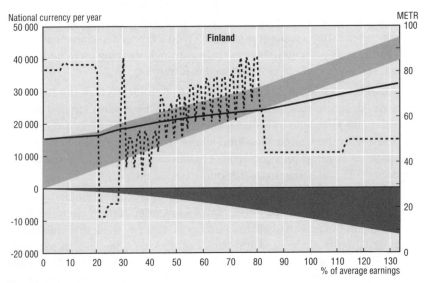

Source: OECD tax/benefit models.

Chart 5.4. **Unlike their Finnish and Swedish counterparts it pays for British sole parents to work part-time** (*cont.*)

Net income before childcare cost for sole parents with two children (age 1 and 4) at earnings from 0 to 133% of average earnings

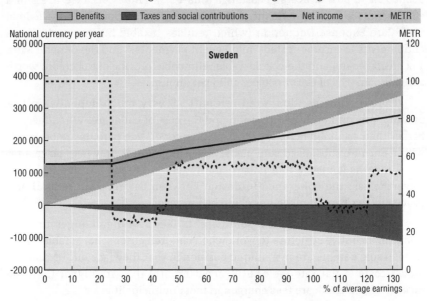

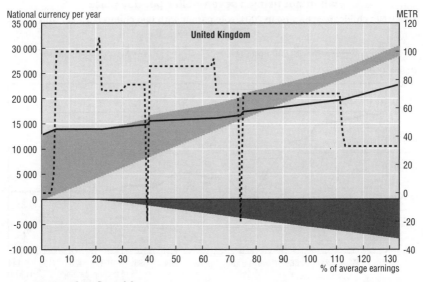

Source: OECD tax/benefit models.

average earnings, sole parent families are financially better off compared to using a CAD 7 dollar per day place. In fact, for this sole parent the financial gains of claiming childcare costs exceed the actual cost when earnings range from about 75% to 90% of average earnings (Chart 5.5). This is because users of a childcare place that is not financed at CAD 7 per day can claim both the federal ChildCare Expense Deduction (which reduces taxable income and affects entitlements to income-tested Child Benefit payments[16] and the General Sales Tax credit rebate) and the considerable refundable provincial tax credit, worth at maximum 75% of CAD 7 000 per child per annum.

The outcome as illustrated in Chart 5.5 very much depends on the assumptions on family composition and the cost of childcare. When fees are higher than assumed here, say, CAD 40 (Chapter 4), sole parents are better off with a flat-rate subsidised care place. Moreover, refunds only take place after a few months (an issue that is particularly relevant to low-income families). Nevertheless, the coherence in design between the relevant federal and provincial tax/benefit measures could be improved.

As with couple families, sole parents face few big changes to their financial incentive structure to work when children enter school (Table 5.A.2). Finnish sole parents are in a unique position in that they face out-of-school – hours costs (a flat-rate fee of EUR 60 per month) that are higher than the income-tested childcare fees charged in most municipalities.

Chart 5.5. **Sole parents in the province of Québec can be better off when not using a seven-dollar-per-day place**

Net childcare spending in 2004, sole parent with two children, CAD 7 and CAD 27 per day

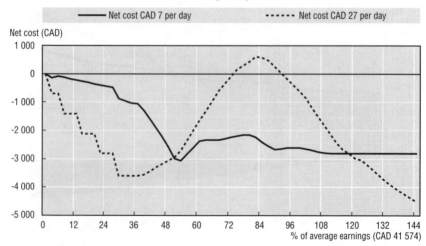

Source: Information provided by the provincial government of Québec.

5.5.2. *The policy approach towards sole parents*

Comprehensive employment and childcare supports for all parents in Finland and Sweden

The policy approach towards sole parents in Finland and Sweden is the same as for any other parent. Parents who are no longer entitled to parental leave (Sweden) or home care allowance (Finland) are work – tested for benefit receipt (either unemployment insurance or social assistance). This policy stance towards sole parents is facilitated by the extensive childcare systems of both countries (Chapter 4) and a comprehensive system of employment supports including job-matching, training and other skill-upgrading programmes, that is made available to clients from an early stage in the unemployment spell. In 2002, public spending on training, subsidised employment and public employment service amounted to 0.8% of GDP in both Finland and Sweden compared with 0.4% of GDP in Canada and 0.2% of GDP in the United Kingdom (OECD, 2004b). In all, the comprehensive employment and childcare support facilitates focusing parents on income support on their labour market (re-)integration from an early age of their youngest child onwards.

Economic growth and benefit reform in Canada

The experience in Canada and in particular the province of Québec is somewhat different in that high sole parent employment rates at 68% in 2001 are a relatively recent feature: in 1981 the sole parent employment rate was 59% for Canada and 47% for the province of Québec (Chapter 3).[17] The increase of sole parent employment rates is related to improved economic conditions and a tightening in the generosity of the provincial social assistance programmes, an effect created by narrowing eligibility criteria and curtailing payment rates (often through non-indexation). For example, by 2000, social assistance payment rates across Canada were on average about 30% of the low-income levels used by Statistics Canada, while this was 40% in 1985 (Sceviour and Finnie, 2004). Furthermore, it is likely that increased childcare support in the province of Québec since 1997 (Chapter 4) also contributed to increased employment among sole parents.

The proportion of the Canadian population in receipt of social assistance support has halved from 10.8% at peak in 1994 to 5.5% in 2003, while this proportion for the province of Québec fell from 11.0% to 7.3% over the same period. As a result, by 2003, one-third of Canadians on social assistance lived in the province of Québec, up from a quarter in the early 1990s (Roy, 2004). The downward trend in benefit dependency is related to policy reform that reduced barriers to employment (*e.g.* childcare support, Chapter 4) and otherwise strengthened financial incentives to work. The trend in benefit recipiency is also related to diverging trends in benefit generosity: social assistance payment rates for single employable clients in Québec are among the highest in the country, while payment rates to sole parent families with one child and couple families with two children are low compared to other provinces (CCSD, 2003; and Jenson, 2003). This payment structure contributes to the province of Québec having a high proportion of single persons on social assistance (21.4%) compared to the Canadian average (15.9%), while as in the rest of Canada about one-third of sole parents in Québec is in receipt of social assistance.[18] Sole mothers in the province of Québec are almost as likely to leave welfare rolls as sole mothers in other provinces, but since 1993 entry rates into social assistance for sole mothers in Québec have fallen relatively strongly from 13% to 4%; together with Ontario the lowest level in Canada (Sceviour and Finnie, 2004).

Sole parents on social assistance in Québec receive an exemption ("contraint temporaire à l'emploi") from a mandatory job search until their youngest child is 5 years of age (this applies to sole parents and one parent in a couple family). However, the provision of employment supports for social assistance clients is not considered to be comprehensive, also when accounting for the measures included in the new anti-poverty strategy (Box 5.1 and Background Annex to the review). Except for a recent pilot programme "Ma Place au Soleil"[19] there is no specific employment support package for sole parents on income support. Moroever, caseworkers can have up to 350 clients, which is too high for employment counselling to be effective; the international norm in this regard is a staff-to-caseload ratio of 1 to 125 (OECD, 1999a).

The philosophy underlying the anti-poverty reform involves a greater emphasis on adequacy of family payments and incentives to work, rather than on policy elements as administrative sanctions that can be regarded as punitive in the absence of a comprehensive employment support strategy. However, abolishing administrative sanctions sends the wrong policy signal to new clients. Instead, the Québecois government may consider suspending administrative sanctions until more investments have been made in active labour market measures that help clients re-enter the labour market.

A gentle push towards the labour market in the United Kingdom

Given the importance of the child poverty concerns in the United Kingdom and the very high levels of child poverty among jobless sole parent families (see above) it is not surprising that the UK government has focussed its attention on increasing the number of sole parents in work, with an explicit policy target of an employment rate for this group of 70% by 2010.

The United Kingdom is the only country in this review without a work-test in the income support system for sole parents and it is no coincidence that it has a much lower employment rate among this group (Chapter 3). The conditions of benefit receipt do not require sole parents on income support in the United Kingdom to participate in activation programmes (e.g. training-course or work-experience placements), go to job-interviews, or accept job-offers under certain conditions. However, UK policy has introduced an element of compulsion in its policy approach towards sole parents on income support with the mandatory Work Focused Interviews (WFIs), which is being extended to cover all clients regardless of the age of their child. During the WFI, personal advisers provide information on the help and support available to clients to prepare for, find and retain employment, emphasise the short- and longer-term financial gains from being in work,[20] and encourage clients to participate in the New Deal for Lone Parents.

The NDLP was launched nationally in 1998 and is available to all sole parents who are not working or working less than 16 hours per week.[21] It is a voluntary programme wherein personal advisers assist in job search, appropriate training and finding suitable childcare to increase the clients' ability to find and enter work. Sole parents who are relatively job-ready are most likely to engage in the programme during which participants continue to draw their benefits and receive additional help with childcare.[22] Since October 2004, some NDLP-participants are also financially encouraged to look for work through a Work Search Premium of GBP 20 per week which is available for six months on a pilot basis in eight areas.

The evidence suggests that the introduction of Work Focused Interviews did not directly generate a detectable change in exit rates from income support for new sole parent claimants, and only led to a small increase of exit rates of clients with older children (Knight and Lissenburgh, 2004; and Thomas and Griffiths, 2004). By contrast, the NDLP has a significant impact on the employment chances of clients: Evans et al. (2003) found that 50% of NDLP-participants found work, compared to 26% of non-participants.[23] However, thus far the impact of the NDLP on the sole parent employment rate has been limited: Lessof et al. (2003) found that over a six month period 1.1% of the eligible client population left income support. This is because many clients have not yet had the opportunity to access the employment and childcare supports that are being made available through the system of mandatory WFIs, the NDLP and Jobcentre Plus (the fully integrated employment and benefit service in the United Kingdom), as this system of employment and childcare supports is still being rolled out.[24]

The recent increase in the generosity of childcare support (Francesconi and van der Klaauw, 2004) and reform of making work pay policies more generally (see above) have contributed to the significant increase of sole parent employment rates from 45% in 1997 to 54% in 2004 (Chapter 3). In view of this success, it is no surprise that UK policy continues to pursue reform in this area. Childcare support for all parents will be enhanced (Chapter 4), while for sole parents back-to-work payments have been being tried out in 12 pilot areas (Millar and Gardiner, 2004). This so-called "In Work Credit", GBP 40 per week paid to sole parents for the first 12 months of work, will be extended from April 2005 to sole parents out of work in all but one of the London districts, and an extension to six further areas in the South East in October 2005 will bring coverage to 40% of sole parents who have been out of work and on income support for a year.

5.6. Conclusions

Child poverty concerns are central to policy development in all countries under review, not least because it has a significant impact on child development. Second earners, usually mothers, thus play a key role in reducing the risk of children growing up in poverty. Maternal employment is even more critical to reduce poverty in sole parent families.

In all four countries, work pays for second earners because public childcare support is widely available to working parents. Average tax rates on family income equivalent to 133% of average earnings (after childcare fees) are highest in Finland and Sweden at just more than 30%, and lowest at about 19% in the United Kingdom and 20% in the province of Québec. However, work does not always pay for Finnish parents with very young children, while housing support in can seriously weaken financial incentives to work for sole parents on income support in all four countries. While tax/benefit systems in Canada and the province of Québec, Finland and Sweden otherwise facilitate full-time work; the UK tax/benefit system involves financial incentives to work on a part-time basis for second earners in couple families as well as sole parents.

Finnish policy offers parents with a child not yet 3 years old a choice: they can either exercise their right to affordable municipal day-care or receive a payment for not using this service, and, generally, provide parental care on a full-time basis. In all, parents with a very young child in Helsinki who do not use municipal day-care will receive transfers which, including non-payment of parental childcare fees, are worth about one-third of net average family income. As a result, about two-thirds of mothers with very young children stay at home for a prolonged period. The Finnish Home Care Allowance payments are at odds with the avowed policy objective to raise female employment rates to 70% by 2010.

The policy approach towards sole parents in Finland and Sweden is the same as for other parents because all parents who are no longer entitled to parental leave are work – tested for benefit receipt. In the province of Québec, however, sole parents on income support are exempt from job-search until their youngest child is 5 years old. This contributes to the employment rates for sole parents in the province of Québec and Finland of around 70%, and 80% in Sweden. The United Kingdom is the only country in this review that has no tradition of work-testing sole parents on income support and it is no coincidence that it has a much lower employment rate and a relatively high incidence of poverty among this group.

To reduce the risk of long-term benefit dependency and poverty among sole parents and their children a strategy of active and early interventions in labour market re-integration is required. This involves improving financial incentives to work, and investment in employment supports and childcare support. The UK policy approach has moved in this direction. With the introduction of the mandatory Work Focussed Interviews (WFI) and the New Deal for Lone Parents (NDLP), sole parents in the United Kingdom are increasingly made aware of the financial gains employment brings them, while public authorities have started to put in place a system of employment and childcare supports to reduce barriers to work. However, the system of WFI, NDLP and Jobcentre Plus is still being rolled out, and many clients have not yet had the opportunity to access the employment and childcare supports that are being made available. It takes time to build the necessarily capacity for a comprehensive support system of case-management, work-experience placements, appropriate training and job-search assistance; it also takes time to change attitudes among clients and staff. However, once such a comprehensive childcare and employment support system has been put in place, then it is reasonable to oblige clients to make use of the opportunities a rolled-out support system offers them. Further down the line, some form of compulsory work-related activity, beyond the Work Focused Interview, could be introduced.

The general policy thrust of recent reform in the province of Québec is welcome, as it strengthened the financial position of working families and greatly extended coverage of in-work benefit support. Reform should be extended to include additional investments in employment supports for sole parents on benefit, and until then, work-testing could be suspended. Indeed, for many of the existing (long-term) income support clients, in both the United Kingdom and the province of Québec, additional medium-term investment in skills upgrading is necessary before a work-test can be meaningfully applied.

Notes

1. Förster and Mira d'Ercole (2005) find that on average across the OECD, higher employment-rates, particularly among women reduce poverty rates. The poverty risk is higher in economies with relatively high incidences of low pay among full-time workers and a higher degree of literacy underachievement among the working age population.

2. Chapter 2 showed that tax/benefit systems contribute significantly to poverty reductions among families with children. Pre-tax/transfer poverty rates of 25% for families with children in 2000 in the United Kingdom were almost reduced by half after accounting for taxes and transfers, while in Canada poverty rates were reduced from 18% to 12%. Finnish and Swedish tax/benefit systems involve significant re-distribution of resources towards families with children: pre-tax/transfer poverty rates for families with children of about 14% are reduced to below 4% upon accounting for tax/benefit system.

3. Public spending data on family benefits do not reflect this, but in all four countries, the calculation of pension entitlements takes account of parents providing personal childcare, see Background Annex of the review and Queisser and Whitehouse (2005, *forthcoming*).

4. In case of a "wastable" (or "non-refundable") tax credit, entitlements only accrue to the extent that they are off-set against tax liabilities, while "non-wastable" or "refundable" tax credits involve cash transfers to people (*e.g.* low income workers) whose tax liabilities are not large enough to make (full) use from a particular entitlement (tax credit). Non-wastable tax credits thus reinforce the re-distributional nature of a tax/benefit system.

5. In the province of Québec, a tax rate of 16% is applied to all personal income up to CAD 27 637 per annum; however, because of various tax credits, personal income subject to provincial income tax depends on household composition and is, for example, CAD 37 000 for a couple with two children CAD 25 500 for a sole parent with one child, CAD 23 000 for a childless couple and CAD 13 000 for a single person.

6. "Average earnings" refer to the annual earnings of an average production worker in the manufacturing sector. In 2004, these were USD 34 359 (CAD 41 574) in Canada, USD 29 959 (EUR 29 779) in Finland, USD 26 323 (SEK 254 544) in Sweden and USD 33 218 (GBP 21 359) in the United Kingdom (see Background Annex to the review). OECD (2004a) includes a special feature, which discusses whether the earnings of a manual production worker are a sufficiently representative measure of average earnings of a "typical taxpayer". OECD (2005b) uses earnings data that reflect a broadened income definition.

7. The Parental Wage Assistance programme (PWA) which is better known by its French acronym "APPORT" (Aide aux parents pour leurs revenus de travail or parental wage assistance) in the province of Québec has stringent eligibility criteria (it includes an asset test), involves two provincial government departments in its administration, while the calculation method of benefit payments is not very transparent to clients (Eaton *et al.*, 2000).

8. The Finnish earned income allowance (EIA) is EUR 3 550 at maximum (with annual earnings just below EUR 20 000), and covers all individuals with earnings below EUR 100 000 per annum.

9. As discussed in the previous section the four countries differ substantially in the importance of the role of tax allowances or tax credits (especially Canada and the

United Kingdom), local taxation (Canada, Finland and Sweden) and social security contributions (particularly Finland and Sweden). Therefore the discussion should not merely focus on *one* aspect of the system (*e.g.* family benefits), but rather on changes in net family income.

10. METRs at relatively low earnings of the second earner in a Québecois family in Chart 5.3 vary with, respectively, the beginning of phase out of the Goods and Service tax credit, National Child Benefit, the refund of 16.5% of federal tax, while the GST phase-out is complete at a family income just above average earnings. In the 2004 tax/benefit system, the Québec family payment was rapidly phased out around family income of about 125% of average earnings, while at family earnings of 155% the second earner exhausted provincial tax and social security deductions.

11. For the calculations in Table 5.3 it is assumed that a UK family with earnings at 167% of average earnings uses childcare on a partial basis (for two-thirds of the week at GBP 97 per week). If full-time childcare use had been assumed at GBP 140 per week, childcare costs would increase from 14 to 19% of gross family income. In case the second earner in a couple earns at one-third of average earnings, the parental fee is assumed to amount to GBP 47 per week.

12. In Sweden the maximum parental fee for OSH-care diminishes with the ranking of the child. For the first child a fee of EUR 93 per month is charged; for second and third children the maximum monthly fee is EUR 46, while no parental fee is charged for fourth and subsequent children.

13. Bargain and Orsini (2004) find that the introduction of a working tax credit for families in Finland would reduce labour force participation among married women, and increase employment among single women. However, effects would be very small, and policy intervention towards increasing employment in Finland is likely to be most successful when focusing on reducing the cost of low-skilled labour.

14. Making work pay policies include employment-conditional benefits and tax credits or employment subsidies and tax rebates given to employers. For an in-work benefit payment to have a desired effect on the behaviour of recipients, it has to be substantial enough in size to alter replacement rates and this is obviously cheaper in economies with relatively wide earnings distributions. Moreover, to avoid very high METRs when recipients gradually reduce benefit receipt, the phase-out range has to be sufficiently wide. For both these reasons, in-work benefits are very costly to public budgets in economies (as Finland and Sweden) with relatively condensed earnings distributions.

15. The effect of the WTC on couple families is limited as not many couples with children qualify for receipt. This is because both partners have to be in work for at least 16 hours, and have earnings at a low level. For example, a couple family in the United Kingdom wherein the primary earner works full time (40 hours) and the secondary earner work 16 hours at minimum wage (GBP 4.5 per hour) has annual family earnings worth GBP 12 600 (which would involve benefit payment of GBP 270 per year). The maximum earnings at which WTC can be received is GBP 14 560 per annum. In all, there will not be many couple families who qualify for WTC, and if they do, benefit payments are small.

16. Since both the CCTB and the associated income-tested supplement are calculated on the basis of net family income (*i.e.* income after accounting for the childcare expense deduction), a family claiming childcare costs will receive higher child

benefits than an otherwise similar family in Canada who does not claim childcare expenses.

17. Increase of sole parent employment rates were particularly pronounced over the 1996-2001 period: an increase of 10 percentage points for Canada as a whole and 12 percentage points for the province of Québec.

18. Among the provinces, Québec is the only one which provides advance maintenance payments to sole parents, and then only in certain cases (Jenson, 2003).

19. The "Ma Place au Soleil" programme helps sole mothers on income support complete high school. For the duration of one year, clients can attend school with other clients in a similar situation and receive intensive counselling and childcare support. Clients without access to a subsidised childcare place who use private care can be reimbursed up to CAD 20 per hour. There is also support for transport costs and other work-related costs.

20. Recipients of housing benefit still face weak financial incentives to work (Brewer and Shephard, 2004). In addition, a state of household joblessness helps to obtain access to social housing. Without reform of such rules, the system of housing support contributes to hesitancy among sole parents to actively look for work.

21. The New Deal for Partners was launched in April 1999. However, because of the failure to generate an adequate response among the target group of clients (partners of jobseekers), the programme was scaled back in 2002 (Bonjour and Dorsett, 2002). It is, however, being revitalised since April 2004 and Work Focus Interviews (covering similar ground as under the NDLP) are being extended to partners of benefit claimants. It is, however, too early to assess whether the initiative is successful this time.

22. Compared to the sole parents who have to attend the WFI, those who participate in the NDLP are better qualified and more job-ready (Lessof *et al.*, 2003.).

23. Evans *et al.* (2003) estimate that the NDLP is a cost-effective way of providing employment support to benefit recipients: the costs of NDLP-provision per job are estimated to be just over one-third of the economic gains to society.

24. Since the launch of sole parent Work Focused Interviews in April 2001 and the end of September 2004, over 1.1 million WFIs had been attended by a sole parent on income support, and 215 100 (or 19%) of these sole parents had joined the NDLP caseload (information provided by the UK authorities).

Table 5.A.1. **Financial incentives to work for second earners in couple families with two children of school age**

Family benefits and net income for couple families at different earnings levels with two children and a primary earner with average earnings, and resulting average effective tax rates on second earners

	Canada/Québec				Finland				Sweden				United Kingdom			
Wage level (first adult – second adult)	100-0	100-33	100-67	100-100	100-0	100-33	100-67	100-100	100-0	100-33	100-67	100-100	100-0	100-33	100-67	100-100
Gross wage earnings (in % of average earnings)[a]	100	133.3	166.7	200	100	133.3	166.7	200	100	133.3	166.7	200	100	133.3	166.7	200
Family benefits in % of gross earnings	10%	3%	2%	1%	8%	6%	5%	4%	9%	7%	5%	4%	12%	7%	6%	5%
OSH-care fees in % of gross earnings	..	7%	5%	4%	..	3%	2%	2%	..	2%	2%	2%	..	4%	7%	9%
Net income in % of gross earnings	85%	73%	70%	67%	78%	76%	75%	72%	78%	75%	74%	72%	87%	82%	76%	71%
Net income in % of average earnings	85%	98%	117%	135%	78%	102%	124%	143%	78%	101%	123%	143%	87%	109%	126%	143%
Average family tax rate (total tax wedge)	15%	20%	25%	28%	31%	27%	28%	31%	31%	29%	30%	31%	20%	19%	22%	23%
Marginal effective tax rates on additional earnings[b]																
When entering the labour market	–	61%	54%	51%	–	28%	30%	34%	–	32%	33%	35%	–	32%	41%	44%
When increasing hours of work	–	61%	43%	46%	–	28%	32%	43%	–	32%	34%	37%	–	32%	50%	50%

.. Data not available.
– Not applicable.
a) "Average earnings" refer to the annual earnings of the "average production worker" in the manufacturing sector (OECD, 2005, *Taxing Wages 2004-2005*, OECD, Paris). In 2004, these were USD 34 358 (CAD 41 574) in Canada; USD 29 966 (EUR 29 779) in Finland; USD 26 313 (SEK 254 544) in Sweden; and, USD 33 210 (GBP 21 359) in the United Kingdom.
b) Marginal effective tax rates on additional earnings are calculated as the difference between the increase in gross earnings and the increase in net income when a second earner enters the labour market, and when increasing the hours of work and earnings from 0 to 33%, from 33% to 67%, and from 67% to 100% of average earnings, expressed as a proportion of the change in gross earnings.

Source: OECD tax/benefit models.

Table 5.A.2. **Financial incentives to work for sole parents with two children of school age**

Family benefits and net income for sole parent families at different earnings levels, and resulting effective tax rates on additional earnings
(Panel A)
Marginal effective tax rates on additional earnings for sole parent families, with OSH-care fees (Panel B)

	Canada/Québec			Finland			Sweden			United Kingdom		
	33.3	66.7	100	33.3	66.7	100	33.3	66.7	100	33.3	66.7	100
Gross wage earnings (in % of average earnings)[a]												
Panel A: Sole parent families having two children aged 7 and 9												
Family benefits in % of gross earnings	62%	19%	7%	106%	40%	21%	93%	40%	20%	130%	42%	12%
Net income in % of gross earnings	164%	105%	82%	189%	115%	90%	168%	112%	89%	221%	121%	87%
Net income in % of average earnings	55%	70%	82%	63%	77%	90%	56%	75%	89%	74%	81%	87%
Marginal effective tax rates on additional earnings[b]	36%	45%	51%	66%	62%	61%	82%	63%	61%	47%	63%	69%
Panel B: The impact of OSH-care fees for children aged 7 and 9												
OSH-care fees in % of gross earnings	26%	13%	9%	11%	5%	4%	2%	2%	2%	17%	17%	17%
OSH-care fees in % of average earnings	9%	9%	9%	4%	4%	4%	1%	1%	2%	6%	11%	17%
Net income in % of gross earnings	137%	97%	76%	178%	110%	87%	166%	110%	87%	212%	112%	82%
Marginal effective tax rates on additional earnings												
When entering the labour market	63%	53%	58%	78%	68%	65%	84%	65%	63%	57%	73%	74%
When increasing hours of work	63%	43%	67%	78%	59%	59%	84%	46%	58%	57%	88%	78%

a) "Average earnings" refer to the annual earnings of the "average production worker" in the manufacturing sector (OECD, 2005, *Taxing Wages 2004-2005*, OECD, Paris). In 2004, these were USD 34 358 (CAD 41 574) in Canada; USD 29 966 (EUR 29 779) in Finland; USD 26 313 (SEK 254 544) in Sweden; and, USD 33 210 (GBP 21 359) in the United Kingdom.

b) Marginal effective tax rates on additional earnings are calculated as the difference between the increase in gross earnings and the increase in net income when a sole parent enters the labour market or increases working hours and income from 0 to 33%, from 33% to 67%, and from 67% to 100% of average earnings, expressed as a proportion of the change in gross earnings.

Source: OECD tax/benefit models.

ISBN 92-64-00928-0
Babies and Bosses: Reconciling Work and Family Life
Canada, Finland, Sweden and the United Kingdom
© OECD 2005

Chapter 6

Time-related Workplace Supports for Parents

Many people manage to achieve their preferred work/life balance, but there are many others who find it very difficult. Workplace practices as flexi-time, and part-time work, can play a major role key role in determining to what extend parents can reconcile their work and care commitments. This chapter takes a closer look at why and how public policy might intervene to procure time-related family-friendly workplace support. The chapter then goes on exploring why employers might be interested in providing family-friendly policy measures, and why some parents (especially fathers) may not always use them, even when available. The chapter ends by illustrating that future labour supply concerns related to demographic trends could be addressed by making better use of female labour force potential, the case for family-friendly policies is getting stronger every day.

There is great variation in the work and care solutions that families find. Many parents in Canada, Finland, Sweden and the United Kingdom are satisfied with the number of hours they work and the level of family income this generates. Many others, however, feel that they face a poor set of choices in working time and, lacking in good alternatives, are overwhelmed by a time crunch. Many parents feel they do not spend enough time with their families, but are constrained by inflexible and long working hours. Parents who are sufficiently wealthy may be able to afford quality childcare or reduce working hours, but for many other parents these options are not financially feasible. Yet, the number of hours parents engage in paid work depends on many factors, including their preferences, career attachment (of both parents, if a couple), household income, the age of children, the availability of quality childcare (Chapter 4) and access to public family benefits (Chapter 5). Furthermore, much depends on the prevailing workplace practices and the extent to which public and private supports help parents in the four countries under review to find the time to combine of employment and parenthood.

Time-related policy development (e.g. flexible working arrangements, parental leave, part-time employment) for working parents depends on the general public policy stance toward family-friendly policies, industrial bargaining outcomes and the relationship between the two. In Finland and Sweden, comprehensive social and family support models have been developed in close co-operation with employers and unions: time-related workplace support for parents is provided collectively. By contrast, parents in Canada and the United Kingdom rely to a much greater extent on support made available in individual workplaces.

This chapter looks at parental working hours and the time-related support policies in the countries under review. It sets the framework by presenting some outcomes on the time that employed parents generally spend in the workplace and how this may affect workplace stress levels. The chapter then considers these outcomes in terms of the cross-country differences in the way policy is being developed (Section 6.2), design of child-related leave programmes (Section 6.3) and support for parents in work (Section 6.4). The chapter then discusses why some parents, in particular fathers, do not take greater advantage of workplace opportunities. The final section of the chapter explores possible avenues for policy development.

6.1. Working time outcomes

Time-related support can be distinguished in two broad categories: support for parents around childbirth and support for parents who are in work. To start with the former, there are considerable differences in maternal labour force behaviour around childbirth. In Sweden mothers with very young children are most likely to be in employment (either on employment-protected leave or at work, see Chapter 3), compared with less than 50% of such mothers in the United Kingdom. Chart 6.1 shows that a significant number of mothers with very young children in the United Kingdom are not in the labour force, compared with more than 44% in Finland (a significant number of these mothers are on home care leave with employment protection, Chapter 3) and 34% and 24% in Canada and Sweden, respectively.

Chart 6.1. **British and Finnish mothers of very young children are most likely not to be in the labour force**

Distribution of all mothers with children not yet 3 years old who are in employment, unemployed or not in the labour force, percentage[a]

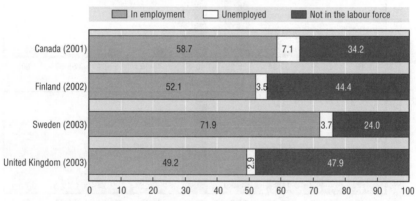

Note: Percentages do not always add to 100 due to rounding.

a) See definition of "in employment" in Table Box ; unemployment rates are based on labour force survey standards of countries; not in the labour force consists of inactive women, which in Finland also includes mothers on job-protected home care leave.

Source: For Finland, Labour Force Survey; for Canadian and Swedish maternity/parental leave rate, OECD Secretariat calculations; other data, national authorities.

There is considerable variation in working hours in the four countries under review. Chart 6.2 suggests that working hours in Finland are more concentrated into a standard pattern than in other countries. In the United Kingdom, there is considerable diversity in working hours, particularly among female employees. The majority of women in Canada (65%), Finland (71%) and Sweden (62%) work between 35 and 44 hours per week. In the United Kingdom, nearly one-third of employed women work either less than 20 hours per week (17%) or more than 45 hours per week (14%). In the province of

Chart 6.2. **The United Kingdom has the least
concentrated working hours**

Incidence of weekly hours of work among prime-age (20-54)
workers, 2002 percentages[a]

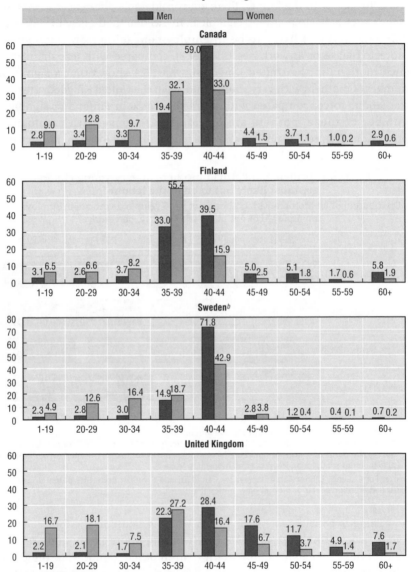

a) Hours worked are defined as usual hours in all countries except Finland, where data is based on
actual hours worked.

b) Note the scale change for the vertical axis.

Source: OECD (2004), Database on Usual Weekly Hours of Work.

Québec, more women keep their weekly working hours work under 40 hours than in Canada as a whole.[1] By contrast, 42% of British males work more than 45 hours per week, much more than their Finnish (18%), Canadian (12%), and Swedish (5%) counterparts. Recent trends suggest, however, that the incidence of long hours has declined slightly since 1998 in the United Kingdom and since 1996 in Canada (OECD, 2004g).[2]

Information on parental working hours is not available on a comparable cross-country basis, but existing evidence suggests that paternal working hours are similar to those for men generally, except in the United Kingdom, where fathers on average work three more hours per week (Stevens *et al.*, 2004).[3] Mothers are most likely to reduce their working hours in Sweden and the United Kingdom (Chapter 3). Little if no difference in working hours between mothers and non-mothers exists in Finland, where part-time employment primarily involves students and older workers. While gender differences in working hours are most pronounced in the United Kingdom, mothers rather than fathers remain the primary caregiver in all four countries under review (see below).

Chart 6.3 suggests that most workers (80%) do not perceive their working hours as a considerable source of conflict with their personal life. Directly comparable information is not available for Canada, but Duxbury and Higgins (2003) suggest that about 40% of the Canadian labour force experiences at least moderate levels of conflict in balancing their professional and personal lives (see Section 6.4.4). Yet, even though differences in work-life conflict levels do not differ much between part-time and full-time employment, those employees who work more than 55 hours per week experience medium to high levels of work-life conflict most frequently. Cross-country comparisons show that the perception of poor work-life balance for these workers decreases with the prevalence of long working hours generally. For example, in the United Kingdom and Finland, where long working hours are more common than the other two countries, employees working more than 55 hours per week are much less likely to feel that they are in an exceptional position compared to similar workers in Sweden (where long hours are less common).

Reducing working hours can sometimes ease the stress parents feel when balancing work and family life (Box 6.1). Surveys suggest that many parents would like to reduce their working hours, although it is less clear whether they would choose to do so if it also meant reducing family income (Bielenski *et al.*, 2002). A survey of parents in the province of Québec suggests they would like to decrease their working hours by nearly 20% (SOM Recherche et Sondages, 2003). Mothers often work part-time in the United Kingdom, but not in Finland, where part-time work is not often available and full-time employment is considered the norm for all workers (Paull *et al.*, 2002). Part-time employment is uncommon

Chart 6.3. **The majority of workers do not face considerable conflict
in their work-life balance**

Degree of conflict between working hours and family or social commitments,
by weekly hours of work, 2000/01

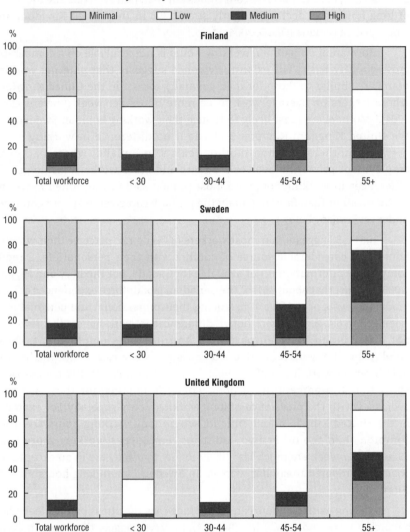

Note: The classification by degree of conflict is based on question 20 which asks workers to assess how well their work hours "fit" with their family or social commitments outside work, with the responses "not at all well", "not very well", "fairly well" and "very well" being interpreted as indicating minimal, low, medium and high conflict, respectively.

Source: OECD Secretariat calculations based on data from the European Foundation for the Improvement of Living and Working Conditions, Third European Working Conditions Survey 2000/01.

Box 6.1. **Stress and health in workplaces**

Although most working parents do not perceive that work-life conflict on its own is a major issue, many recognise that the *stress* related to work-life balance can be overwhelming. High levels of role overload (*i.e.* not having enough time to do everything) and role interference (*i.e.* incompatibility of responsibilities) in parents' daily schedules are strongly indicative of workers with very significant job stress (Duxbury *et al.*, 1999). In Canada, this affects about one-third of the labour force (Duxbury and Higgins, 2003). Although information is not directly comparable with Canada, in Finland and Sweden, workers perceive higher stress in their work (respectively 35% and 37%), than their British counterparts (23%, see EFILWC, 2000). Stressors (sources of stress) in the work and home environments have been found to negatively affect an individual's physical and psychological health and may, for example, lead to substance abuse, depression and gastrointestinal disorders, or, at the organisational level, increased employee absenteeism, high turnover, poor work performance, job dissatisfaction and low firm loyalty.

Stress frequently occurs due to the high psychological job demands (*i.e.* high output required) combined with low job decision latitudes or low perception of control (Karasek, 1979). Non-professional and non-managerial workers with high demand/low control jobs (*e.g.* restaurant/hospitality work, data entry, assembly line, clerks, administrative support staff) are most likely to have a relatively high work life conflict (Duxbury *et al.*, 1999). In Canada, women reporting high work life conflict are much more likely to be unsatisfied with their jobs, have a higher rate of absenteeism, and have a higher level of perceived stress and experience burnout and depression (Duxbury and Higgins, 1998). In the United Kingdom, nearly half of all long-term sick absences from work for non-manual workers is due to stress (CIPD, 2004).

Available estimates suggest that, in 1995, stress-related absenteeism costs companies more than GBP 3.7 billion per year, but workers' perceived stress levels have more than doubled since that study was conducted (HSE, 1999; Hewitt, 2004). Canadian estimates of the direct and indirect costs of workers with high work-life conflict (*e.g.* absenteeism, inability to meet deadlines, temporary worker replacement of worker, reduced productivity) are between CAD 4.5 billion and CAD 10 billion per year (Duxbury and Higgins, 2003). Employers thus have a financial case for considering workload intensity of workers and management practices (Reynolds *et al.*, 2003), Although policy development is in its infancy, Health Canada and the Health and Safety Executive (United Kingdom) are beginning to respond by trying to raise awareness among employers and employees on the benefits of a work environment without unwarranted stress.

in Finland despite parents being entitled to reduce their working hours until the youngest child finishes the second year of primary school. More than half of Swedish parents believe a better work-family balance can be found by working fewer or more flexible working hours, but evidence suggests that workloads often do not decrease when parents reduce their working hours (RFV, 2003). Some parents are likely to have more control and flexibility over their working hours and arrangements than others: in the United Kingdom, for example, these workers are generally in professional or managerial occupations, female or employed in the public sector (Stevens et al., 2004; DTI, 2000). At the same time, though, managers are more likely to work longer hours, even though nearly 75% of them find that it negatively affects the relationship with their partner and children (Worrall and Cooper, 1999). Hence, parental labour market outcomes frequently do not reflect household labour supply considerations, but rather the family response to various systemic pressures.

Some families might choose to work more hours to increase their household income. About one-third of British employees (including those who work part-time) would choose to work longer hours than usual for increased pay (Stevens et al., 2004). By contrast, in Canada, only 15% of fathers and 10% of mothers in full-time employment would choose to work more hours with a proportional increase in pay (Lochhead, 2000). Moreover, more than one-third of Finnish parents and 18% of British mothers would be willing to take a pay cut to reduce their weekly hours (Lilja, 2003; Stevens et al., 2004).

6.2. Public policy approaches to time-related workplace supports

The extent to which time-related support for working parents (e.g. parental leave, flexible working hours, part-time employment) is available depends in large part on how important the work-life balance issue is to public policy, employers and unions and on the nature of their relationship. The public case for family-friendly workplaces hinges on health concerns (for pregnant mothers, unborn children and infants, but also for workers in general, see above); child development issues (Chapter 4); non-discrimination, gender equity and labour supply concerns (see below). In addition, public policy in Sweden regards time-related workplace support for parents to be an integral part of a comprehensive strategy to help parents have as many children as they desire (Batljan, 2001).

The emphasis in Finland and Sweden on universality of social support and equity for different income groups, family types and genders, combined with the close involvement of employers and unions in public policy development and operations, has led to the development of a comprehensive collective model of family-friendly policy support for parents throughout a large part of childhood (Box 6.2). By contrast, in Canada and the United

Box 6.2. **Industrial bargaining systems**

Employment-oriented policy development in both Finland and Sweden involves trade unions and employer federations to the extent that relevant parliamentary bills have been agreed upon previously with unions and employers and, thus, are rarely subject to change. Since the 1980s central wage negotiations no longer exist in Sweden, but trade unions co-ordinate their bargaining position at the national level. In Finland, sectoral agreements can be administratively extended to cover the whole sector, while relevant stipulations may also be supplemented through enterprise bargaining. By contrast, industrial bargaining may take place at sectoral level in the United Kingdom or involve province-wide negotiations in Canada, but industrial bargaining often concerns single employers and/or individual bargaining.

The role of Finnish and Swedish unions in policy development and operation (*e.g.* unions administer unemployment insurance) contributes to high membership rates including three-quarters of the labour force and more than 90% of the working population covered by collective bargaining agreements (see table next page). By contrast, union membership and collective bargaining coverage is less prevalent in Canada and the UK. Union membership has been falling somewhat in Canada from 37% in 1980 to 32% in 2000. The decline in union power in the United Kingdom was far more significant. Industrial reforms initiated by the Thatcher government and the changing structure of the British economy led to a decline of union membership from 51% in 1980 to about 31% in 2000 (coverage of collective bargaining dropped from around 70% to around 30% over the same period). Except for Canada and the province of Québec, women now are as or more likely to be union members than men. This is related to the high proportion of female employees in the public sector, which has a significantly higher unionisation rate than the private sector in all four countries in this review. The high rate of female membership contributes to public sector union prioritisation of demands for family-friendly policies. Recent collective bargaining outcomes in Sweden reduced working hours and extended parental leave provisions for central government and public sector employees.

Examples of family-friendly measures that have become available through many collective agreements in Finland and Sweden deal with both child-related leave and working time: full pay during maternity leave, shorter working hours, working time flexibility and the introduction of working time saving banks in 20 Swedish sectoral agreements (EIRO, 2004; EFILWC, 2002).

Box 6.2. **Industrial bargaining systems** (cont.)

Industrial bargaining coverage rates are high in Finland and Sweden

Collective bargaining coverage and unionisation rates by gender and sector, latest year available[a]

	Canada[b]	Province of Québec[b]	Finland	Sweden	United Kingdom
Collective bargaining coverage	32.2	40.4	90+	90+	30+
Unionisation rates					
All employees	32.4	41.2	73.4	78.0	29.1
Women	31.9	39.1	77.8	80.0	29.2
Men	32.9	43.1	69.0	75.9	29.0
Public sector	75.6	78.3	88.0	90.7	59.1
Private sector	19.9	28.4	66.6	75.3	18.1

a) Collective bargaining coverage: 2000 for Finland, Sweden and the United Kingdom; 2001 for Canada and the province of Québec. Data for unionisation rates are for 2003, except for Finland, where they are for 2002.

b) Data refer to union coverage, not union membership.

Source: Collective bargaining data from OECD (2004), Employment Outlook, OECD, Paris, and Statistics Canada for Canada and the province of Québec; unionisation rates from national and provincial authorities.

Kingdom, concerns on public budgets and labour costs have always constrained the scope for public family-friendly policy support (although less so in the province of Québec). In Canada, certain employees are under the jurisdiction of federal labour legislation (i.e. inter-provincial and international-related sectors), while other employees rely on provincial policy preferences.[4] Hence, current public policy in these two countries is probably best described as encouraging greater partnership between unions and employers and increasing employers' awareness of their reasons for implementing family-friendly policy measures (Section 6.5.3).

6.3. Scope and impact of time-related measures out of work

Time-related support in Finland and Sweden is an integral piece of the policy frameworks which provide parents with a continuum of support from birth into primary school: substantial income support during long periods of employment-protected leave; high financial support with childcare and out-of-school-hours care costs; broad-based application of collectively-agreed standard working hours at around 40 weekly hours; and, entitlements for parents to reduce hours of work until the youngest child goes to primary school. The British and Canadian policy models are very different in that while they include provisions for maternity and/or parental leave, these provisions do not necessarily connect with childcare support when it becomes widely available. In the United Kingdom, paid leave is available for six months (and unpaid leave is available for another six months). Moreover, early nursery education is free for two-and-a-half hours per day for 3 and 4 year olds, and at other ages is subsidised through tax credits and in-kind benefits to low-income parents. In the province of Québec eligible parents have access to 12 months of child-related leave, but not all parents have access to a subsidised childcare place afterwards (Chapter 4).

6.3.1. Leave from work around childbirth

Regarding the review of leave arrangements around childbirth, the four countries vary in their support to working parents during a period in their lives when their infants need intensive personal care. Among the countries' policies, the Swedish leave system provides the most options for parents with young children in terms of eligibility, payment rates and flexibility, while the duration of income support during child-related leave is longest at 3 years in Finland (Table 6.1 and Background Annex to the review). From 1 January 2006, residents of the province of Québec will have access to maternity and parental leave benefits under a new Quebec parental insurance programme).[5]

- *Eligibility*: all Finnish and Swedish parents, regardless of their employment status, are entitled to income support following the birth of their child. Depending on the validity of their employment contract, parents are also entitled to employment-protected leave. By contrast, all working mothers in the United Kingdom are entitled to a leave period, but parental payments are based on work history. About 60% of British mothers qualify for some form of maternity payments (Hudson *et al.*, 2004). Working mothers in Canada must meet separate eligibility requirements for provincial employment-protected leave and income support provided through the federal Employment Insurance programme (EI). Legislation in the province of Québec, for example, employment-protected leave is after one day of employment, which, however, does not involve a sufficient quantity of contributable hours to receive EI payments (assuming no previous employment in the year). Self-employed mothers in Canada tend to be ineligible for payments, while in the United Kingdom the basic leave payment (maternity allowance) is accessible by the self-employed, low-income workers or recent job changers.[6]

- *Payment rates*: minimum guaranteed income support for non-working parents in Finland and Sweden (respectively 12% and 23% of average earnings) encourages parents – and young women in particular – to secure employment before having children (Table 6.1). Payment rates for Swedish working parents are capped at 80% of gross income for the first 390 days

Table 6.1. **Finnish and Swedish parents are entitled
to generous leave benefits**

Parental paid leave benefits

	Canada	Finland	Sweden	United Kingdom
Maximum length of combined paid leave periods (weeks)[a]	Mothers: 50 Fathers: 35	Mothers: 156 Fathers: 156	Mothers: 60 Fathers: 61.4	Mothers: 26 Fathers: 2
Father quota/paternity leave (weeks)[b]	–	3 to 5	10	2
Beginning and end of paid leave periods (child's age)[c]	–8 weeks; 50 weeks	–8 weeks; 3 years	–8 weeks; 8 years	–11 weeks; 26 weeks
Leave payment (% of average earnings)[d]	52%	65%	80%; 0.09%	90%; 25%
Minimum leave payment (% of annual average earnings)[e]	–	–	23%	–
Public spending on combined leave allowances (% GDP)[f]	0.24%	0.62%	0.90%	0.11%

– Not applicable.
a) Combined paid leave periods include maternity (Canada, Finland, UK), parental (Canada, Finland, Sweden), paternity (Finland, Sweden, UK) and home care leave (Finland). Each calculation is based on the selected parent taking the full allocation, which often means that the other parent cannot take the maximum leave period. In Sweden, calculations are based on a seven-day week for payment (parents also can choose five- or six-day weeks). The United Kingdom has a parental leave, but it is unpaid (see Section 6.4).
b) Non-transferable paid leave allocated to the father. Employment is a pre-requisite for payment eligibility in the United Kingdom, but not for Finland and Sweden.
c) Dates indicate the earliest and last date at which the paid leave can be taken by law. They do not necessarily indicate the length of the benefit period because, in some countries, leave periods can be taken in parts or non-consecutively.
d) Calculations are defined as maximum benefit allowed per year for an eligible person with average annual earnings (2004). In Canada and Finland, payments are the same level regardless of the particular leave period (maternity or parental). In Sweden, calculation of benefits for the first 390 days (income-based) and the universal last 90 days are presented. In the United Kingdom, eligible parents receive two levels of Statutory Maternity Pay, one for the first six weeks and one for the remaining 20 weeks.
e) Minimum leave payment for all parents who are not otherwise eligible for income-related benefit exists in Finland and in Sweden.
f) Canada benefits include maternity and parental leaves for 2002-2003. Finnish spending for 2002 includes maternity and parental benefits, child home care allowance and maternity grant. Swedish spending consists of all parental benefits (parental benefit, temporary parental benefit and pregnancy benefit) for 2003. The calculation for the UK includes only maternity allowance for 2003. See Background Annex to the review for more detail on leave and related benefits.

Source: National authorities; OECD Secretariat calculations.

and fall to less than 9% of average earnings for the last 90 days. In Finland, maternity and parental payment rates are determined through a regressive formula, such that there is no maximum rate and the replacement rate for average workers is around 65%.[7] In addition, for Finnish parents caring for children under age 3 at home, a home care allowance provides significant income support per child (Chapter 5). In Canada and the United Kingdom, payment rates are much lower, as average workers receive respectively 52% or 25% of their wages during most of their child-related leave. Low-income parents in Canada are eligible for the EI family supplement which can raise the replacement rate up to 80% of previous earnings.

- *Duration*: the combination of maternity/parental allowances in Finland followed by the receipt of home care allowance, if chosen, effectively extends the duration of income support beyond Sweden's combined 480 days for both parents. Moreover, if the duration of the employment contract is long enough, home care leave can provide Finnish parents with employment-protection and income to care for children at home until they reach age 3 (and beyond, if there is another child in the household below age 3). In contrast, paid leave options for Canadian and British parents are strictly limited to the child's first year, but eligible Canadian mothers qualify for nearly twice as much paid leave (50 weeks) compared to British mothers (26 weeks).[8] The majority of women eligible for this first paid leave in the United Kingdom are likely to have access to an additional 26 weeks of unpaid job-protected leave (Hudson *et al.*, 2004).[9] All fathers in the four countries receive a limited number of non-transferable weeks (ranging from two to ten weeks), except in Canada, where entitlement to paid parental leave is family-based.[10] In Finland, Sweden and the United Kingdom, regulations influence the beginning of the leave period by prohibiting mothers from working immediately around the birth. Women are granted reprieve from work for two weeks (Finland) or seven weeks (Sweden) both before and after birth, while British women are not allowed to work two weeks preceding the birth (four weeks if working in a factory).

- *Flexibility*: by and large, leave regulations in Sweden provide parents with flexibility through two means. First, parents can choose when to allocate their 480 leave days until the child is 8 years old and, second, they can decide how much of the work day is attributed to leave (in increments as small as one-eight of a day). By comparison, systems in Canada, Finland and the United Kingdom have rigid regulations on the timing of leave, which are mostly limited to sequential periods taken after the birth of the child.

Public provision of income support during leave can be complemented by employer provision of supplementary payments. The Swedish central government has a generous policy of providing parents with 90% of their salary during the entire parental leave, while many private sector employees receive an employer supplement up to 80% to 90% of their last earnings for a three- to six-month period. Most sectors in Finland provide full pay during most of the maternity leave. In Canada and the United Kingdom, estimates of top-ups by individual employers (available only through surveys of collective agreements and workplaces) suggest that employers are more likely to provide unpaid than paid leave to mothers (Table 6.2). Additional maternity pay is limited to only 17% of collective agreements in Canada and

Table 6.2. **Some employers provide extra-statutory provisions for parents**

Employer-provided leave provisions in British and Canadian workplaces

	Canada (2001) % of collective agreements	United Kingdom (2003) % of workplaces
Mother		
Additional maternity leave[a]	37.8	27.0
Extended right to return[b]	–	59.0
Additional maternity pay	17.0	22.0
Accumulate seniority during leave	40.9	..
Keep in touch schemes	..	35.0
Retraining schemes	..	24.0
Father		
Paternity leave[c]	39.4	62.0
Paid paternity leave	35.0	42.0

.. Not available.
– Not applicable.

a) In Canada, this indicates leave allowed beyond the statutory 17 weeks; in the United Kingdom, beyond 18 weeks. Provision of this extension can be either paid or unpaid.

b) Allows mothers to return beyond 29 weeks after birth, that is, extending the range of time during which leave can be taken, but not necessarily extending the total duration of leave.

c) In Canada, this includes one day leave for celebration reasons. In the United Kingdom, this is any form of policy applied to the birth of a child for the father (e.g., written policy or discretionary time off); paternity leave was not yet an entitlement at the time of the survey.

Source: For Canada: HRDC (2000), *Work and Family Provisions in Canadian Collective Agreements*, Labour Program, Human Resources Development Canada, Ottawa/Hull.; for the UK: Woodland, S., N. Simmonds, M. Thornby, R. Fitzgerald and A. McGee (2003), *The Second Work Life Balance Study: Results from the Employers' Survey*, National Centre for Social Research, Department of Trade and Industry, Employment Relations Research Report, No. 22, London.

22% of British workplaces. Most Canadian public sector employers offer an income supplement to EI allowances: eligible employees in the federal government can receive 93% of their usual salary for the duration of the maternity and parental leave (CAALL, 2002). Employer top-ups in Canada usually last two weeks to close the gap created by the waiting period for EI payments (HRDC, 2000).[11]

6.3.2. Parental use of leave and benefits

Effective time on child-related leave is much shorter in Canada and the United Kingdom do than in Finland and Sweden. Individual circumstances vary, but considered from a narrow labour supply perspective there is evidence that suggest the optimal period of maternity leave to be around five months (Jaumotte, 2003). Estimates suggest that at least 69% of British mothers on leave return to work within 10 to 11 months of childbirth (Hudson et al., 2004).[12] Many British mothers who return to work before the end of their unpaid leave entitlement do so because of financial considerations (Stevens et al., 2004). In Canada, 63% of all new mothers receive maternity/parental allowances and more than 70% of claimants used at least 11 months of leave (CEIC, 2004). In Canada, one in three self-employed mothers return to work within two months, compared to 5% of paid workers (Statistics Canada, 2004a).

In contrast, most mothers in Sweden stay at home with their child from birth to 16 months, while many mothers in Finland take at least 18 months of combined leave. Nearly all Finnish mothers (99%) receive parenthood allowances and the majority (80%) extend their parental leave (average of 32 weeks used out of maximum 38 weeks) with some receipt of home care allowance (data provided by the Social Insurance Institution of Finland, KELA). Of these mothers, about half stop receiving home care allowance by the time their child is 18 months old and one-third remain on leave for nearly three full years (Chart 6.4). The share of women who are unemployed (18%) rather than homemakers among these mothers without work has grown steadily since 1990 (Salmi, 2000).

Chart 6.4. **Finnish parents maximise time with their child after birth**

Distribution of amount of leave taken by parents, based on the child's age (months), percentage of maximum duration, latest available year[a, b]

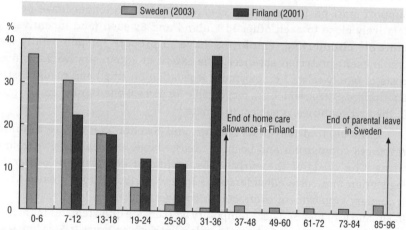

a) In Finland, home care allowance payments immediately follow the parental leave period, which generally ends when the child is about 9 months old.
b) Data for Sweden concerns the number of full parental benefit days used by mothers.
Source: National authorities.

Chart 6.4 suggests that, in Sweden, two-thirds of available parental leave days are used before children are 18 months and 90% by age 2. Swedish fathers, who account for 17% of all parental days, restrict most of their leave to when the child is between 6 and 18 months old. Also, most Swedish parents gravitate towards using entire days rather than the smaller denominations: 80% of all parental days are full day leaves and only 11% are half-day leaves.

The Swedish leave system has a fertility-related feature which encourages some working mothers to dedicate consecutive periods of the leave to childbearing. Sweden's speed premium guarantees parents the same daily payment rate (despite not re-fulfilling employment length and contribution requirements) if the mother is pregnant again before the previous child reaches the age of 21 months. Finnish mothers who have another child while on home care leave and with a valid ongoing employment contract retain their right to return to work and can go back on maternity leave, albeit at a reduced payment rate.

6.3.3. *Employer behaviour in response to leave systems*

To a certain degree, how an employer decides to manage temporary absences due to child-related leaves depends on the length of the expected leave period and the employee notice requirement (Background Annex to the review). In countries such as Canada and the United Kingdom with less than a year of paid parental leave, employers usually redistribute the workload internally on a temporary basis and limit hiring replacement workers to support staff positions (Bevan et al., 2004). Due to longer leave periods relatively close to each other in Finland and Sweden (and incentives for multiple childbirths), employers have to prepare for potentially long employment-protected absences. The extent of administrative adjustment costs of family-related employment legislation on small and medium-sized enterprises (SMEs), which are responsible for at least one-third of employment in the four countries, is subject to debate.[13]

Child-related leaves in Finland and Sweden can create a human resources conundrum and become unaffordable, especially for very small firms. The crisis of the early 1990s, stringent employment protection legislation and costs considerations have contributed to a greater use of temporary employment contracts for younger workers by local governments in Finland (Chapter 3). These temporary workers are often females in their 20s and 30s (Chapter 3) and frequently replace workers on leave. In Sweden, some employers hire temporary replacement workers, while others reportedly use a relatively short top-up period to incite parents to reduce their period on leave.

In the United Kingdom, employers carry a heavy administrative burden related to pregnancy and maternity rights, which are the subject of a government committee review. In addition to managing the temporary absence of an employee, employers oversee administrative issues related to the identification of notice periods, the calculation of eligible maternity leave and disbursement of maternity payments. Legislation around these rights is relatively complex and less than straightforward: very small firms (less than 20 employees), which employ about one-fifth of British workers, are less likely to experience a pregnancy than larger firms (Bonjour and Lissenburg, 2004).[14] Some employers might respond to these difficulties by being hesitant to employ women of childbearing age (Leighton and Evans, 2004).

A notice period for the beginning and end dates of leave periods give employers some degree of commitment from their employees and, generally with duration of about a year, two to three months notice provide employers with sufficient planning capacity for their human resources (Alewell and Pull, 2001). In Finland and Sweden, parents can change the return date from leave by giving their employers two months' notice, but only one month's notice is required in Canada and the United Kingdom. Given the short notice period in Canada and the United Kingdom, employees can change their mind close to the return date and leave employers unprepared for the vacancy. Some British employers reportedly offer a bonus (up to 25% of annual salary) designed to encourage parents to return to the same employer. Nevertheless, about one-third of mothers do not return to their employer, costing employers a cumulative GBP 35 million in recruiting and training costs (DTI, 2001).

6.4. Time at work

6.4.1. The long hours culture in the United Kingdom

Long working hours are not necessarily compatible with family responsibilities: the direct (e.g. child care) and indirect (e.g. emotional strain, stress) cost of working rises for parents, especially for mothers (Duxbury and Higgins, 2003). Increasing concerns about the decreasing quality of work conditions related to long working hours, also among non-manual labour, led the countries in this review to respond with legislation limiting the average duration of working time. In 1996 and 2002, respectively, Finland and Sweden passed legislation to reduce the maximum statutory working week to 40 hours. In Canada, federal employees are restricted to 48 hours of work per week employment, while legislation in the province of Québec mandates overtime payment above a 40-hour standard working week.

In contrast, British men work relatively long hours (Chart 6.2). The EU-directive on working hours was legislated in the United Kingdom with a 48-hour working week limit in 1998, and provided employees with a voluntary opt-out clause. Opting out is most likely to occur in large private companies and in seasonal industries with traditionally long hours (e.g. agriculture, hotels, restaurant, transport).[15] Whether employees are pressured into signing opt-outs to preserve their job/career is subject to debate (Woodland et al., 2003; TUC, 2003). Relatively few workers have signed opt-out agreements and average working hours in the United Kingdom have decreased slightly since the introduction of the legislation.

6.4.2. Creating flexibility in working time arrangements

Flexibility in working time allows parents to adjust their schedules to co-ordinate with school or childcare centre hours, which are usually not in line with workplace practices. Parents in Canada and the United Kingdom rely mostly on individual workplaces to establish working hours flexibility, in contrast to Finland and Sweden where working hours are, by and large, determined by collective intervention. Many Canadian and UK firms are likely to provide a host of time-related features to ease parental working time, with the most common option being part-time work (respectively 74% and 57% of employers), followed by flexible hours (Tables 6.3 and 6.4). Large employers in the United Kingdom, especially those within the public sector, are most likely to offer alternative family-friendly policies such as term time employment (i.e. schedule in parallel with school calendars) and job sharing. In contrast, small companies in Canada appear more amenable than large employers to creating flexibility in working hours for their employees (Table 6.4). Since the late 1980s, a growing number of collective agreements covering large Canadian companies include flexible work arrangements such as job-sharing (10%) and compressed working time (20%) and about a quarter of large employers offer child care services to working parents (HRDC, 2000). Teleworking and compressed working weeks are not offered in many workplaces, but British workers are nearly three times more likely to work at home (5.1%) for more than half their working hours compared to their Finnish (1.8%) and Swedish (1.4%) counterparts (EFILWC, 2000).

In Canada, 36% and 44% of all female and male employees used flexible working hours respectively. Yet, not all employees make use of policies available to them and matching employee/employer data in the United Kingdom suggests that mothers appear to have greater knowledge of the existence of some policies (part-time work, term time, job sharing) than other workers (Table 6.3).

Employment legislation in Finland and the United Kingdom also provide parents with specific rights to request changes in their working hours. In Finland, all employees have the right to reach an agreement on flexible working hours with their employer, although the law imposes that new working hours do not deviate by more than three hours from their regular working hours. Since 2003, British parents with children under age 6 have had the right to request flexible working arrangements, including flexible or reduced working hours and teleworking; in the first year, 90% of the 1 million requests were accepted (granted in whole or in part) by employers. Early indications suggest that nearly one-quarter of all eligible employees used

Table 6.3. **Very large employers offer the greatest variety of family-friendly workplaces in the United Kingdom**

Percentage of British workplaces and employees with access to flexible time policies, 2002-03

	Part-time work	Flexible hours	Compressed week	Reduced hours	Term time	Job share	Teleworking
Employer responses[a, b]							
All workplaces	74	24	7	15	16	14	15
Company size							
Less than 100	69	23	6	11	11	9	17
100-999	74	26	9	16	11	15	20
1 000-9 999	75	23	9	18	17	12	9
10 000 +	91	30	11	23	26	20	11
Ownership							
Public	83	37	8	18	41	35	14
Private	72	21	7	14	10	8	15
Employee responses[b]							
Availability[c]							
All employees	57	48	30	62	32	41	20
Mothers	74	43	30	66	42	55	16
Fathers	47	48	29	62	23	30	24
Recent take-up[d]							
All employees	11	55	36	20	46	15	54
Parents	12	57	38	19	46	16	60
Non-parents	10	53	34	21	0	14	49

Definitions:

Part-time: Less than 30 working hours per week.

Flexible hours: Employee has no set start or finish time but a required number of hours per week. In some cases, specific core hours might be required.

Compressed week: Employees work full-time hours over four days or a nine-day fortnight.

Reduced hours: Hours are reduced from original working hours for a limited amount of time (usually several months).

Term time: Employees work in accordance with school terms and not during summer holidays.

Job share: A full-time job is divided between two people, who normally work at different times and receive full-time benefits pro rata.

Teleworking: Arrangement to work at home for all or part of working hours.

a) Employer observations based on provision that the policy exists and has been used at least once in past 12 months.

b) Employer and employee observations are not matched by workplace.

c) Employee observations consist of answers to the question: If you personally needed any of the following arrangements, would they be available at your workplace?

d) Employee observations consist of answers to the question: Do you currently work, or have worked, in any of these ways over the last year and with your current employer?

Source: For employers: Woodland, S., N. Simmonds, M. Thornby, R. Fitzgerald and A. McGee (2003), *The Second Work Life Balance Study: Results from the Employers' Survey*, National Centre for Social Research, Department of Trade and Industry, *Employment Relations Research Report*, No. 22, London; for employees: Stevens, J., J. Brown and C. Lee (2004), *The Second Work Life Balance Study: Results from the Employees' Survey*, Department of Trade and Industry, *Employment Relations Research Report*, No. 27, London.

Table 6.4. **Canadian workers in small companies are most likely
to have access to flexitime**

Percentage of Canadian employer provision and percentage of employee take-up
of selected family-friendly policies, 1998-99

	Employer provision			Employee take-up[a]			
	Part-time work[b]	Child care services[c]		Flexible hours		Teleworking	
	Total	Women	Men	Women	Men	Women	Men
All workplaces	57	6	6	36	44	5	5
Company size							
Less than 10	53	2	1	42	53	7	6
10-49	68	3	2	35	48	4	5
50-99	74	3	3	41	39	5	4
100-499	72	4	4	34	37	4	4
500-999	86	9	12	34	39	5	6
1 000 +	91	23	24	30	39	4	7
Collective bargaining status							
No coverage in workplace	57	3	3	38	48	6	6
Some coverage in workplace	57	12	11	32	36	3	4
Employment status							
Full-time				35	44	5	6
Part-time				41	42	6	3
Permanent				36	43	5	5
Non-permanent				37	54	8	4

Definitions:
Part-time: Less than 30 working hours per week.
Childcare services: Category includes a variety of support services, such as information and referral services and assistance with external suppliers or on-site centres.
Flexible hours: Employee has no set start or finish time but a required number of hours per week. In some cases, specific core hours might be required.
Teleworking: Arrangement to work at home for some of regularly scheduled hours.
a) The proportion refers to employees who have used the policy.
b) Denotes percentage of workplaces employing part-time workers.
c) The proportion refers to employees who have knowledge of employer offering policy.

Source: Comfort, D., K. Johnson and D. Wallace (2003), *Part Time Work and Family Friendly Practices in Canadian Workplaces*, The Evolving Workplace Series, Human Resources Development Canada and Statistics Canada, *www11.sdc.gc.ca/en/cs/sp/arb/publications/research/2003 000183/page01.*

this right, but it is used significantly more by eligible mothers (37%) than fathers (10%). Fathers' preferences for flexibility relate mostly to part-time work (31%), flexitime (30%) and teleworking (17%), while nearly half of all maternal requests are for part-time work and one-quarter for flexible hours (Palmer, 2004).

Workplace flexibility also depends on legislated vacation time, which is short in Canada and the United Kingdom with respectively 10 and 20 days.[16] Some employers, though, do compensate for the short vacation time by allowing employees to concentrate their holiday time, for example, using annualised hours or working only during school terms. Collective agreements in Finland and Sweden have extended vacation time by an extra one to five days from the statutory 24 days and 25 days, respectively.

6.4.3. Reducing working hours

Legislation in Finland and Sweden encourages parents to reduce working hours. Swedish parents are entitled to reduce working hours by up to 25% until their children are 8 years old (Nyberg, 2000). Chapter 3 showed that many Swedish mothers with young children reduce working hours, but this is less common in Finland. Finnish policy tries to support part-time work by paying parents a limited amount (EUR 70 per month) if they reduce working hours when their children are below age 3 and during their children's first two years in school. In addition, parents have the right to request – and employers must seek to arrange – a reduction in working hours for social or health reasons, but the part-time work must take the form of a six-month fixed-term contract. In all, 18% of mothers and 4% of fathers worked part-time for family reasons in 1998 (Salmi et al., 2000).

Part-time employment is most widespread in the United Kingdom and many mothers choose to work part-time to spend more time with their family and caring for their children (Stevens et al., 2004).[17] Mothers with very young children (under age 3) are slightly more likely to work part-time than women with older children (Chapter 3). Half of British mothers returning to work reduce their working hours either temporary or, more likely, on a permanent basis (Brooker, 2002). Yet, moving to part-time work is linked to downward occupational mobility and a wage penalty (compared to full-time work), especially in the United Kingdom (Manning and Petrongolo, 2004).

In Finland, Sweden and the United Kingdom, part-time employees were relatively cheap until recently when they became covered by legislation stipulating the *pro-rata* remuneration of workers with reduced working hours.[18] Reform has remedied this in all three European countries under review, but employers in the United Kingdom continue to have a financial incentive to employ workers on a low-wage and short-hour basis, as there is a threshold below which no national insurance contributions are due over wage payments.[19] In 1997, Canada reformed EI to remove a similar incentive which encouraged employers to hire workers for less than 15 hours per week. The Canadian Pay Equity Act provides part-time workers with equal wage protection for equal value. Only provincial legislation in Québec and Saskatchewan grants part-time workers an entitlement to some pro-rating of benefits.

Providing women with a transitional period of part-time work might help them to remain with their current employer. In a British survey, 60% of workplaces, and especially large firms, would accept that a mother move from full-time to part-time work on return from maternity leave (Woodland *et al.*, 2003). Some collective agreements in Canada offer similar support, while in the province of Québec, half of the collective agreements for female-dominated sectors (*i.e.* health, public sector, social services and education) include a clause on the reduction of working time (HRDC, 2000; Rochette, 2002).

6.4.4. Choosing hours of work: shift parenting

One option to manage work/life balance for parents in dual-earner families is to organise their individual work schedules in tandem to ensure continuous parental care (shift parenting). In Canada, nearly half of all dual-earner couples with children are organised such that both parents are working in shifts (Marshall, 1998). Even though husbands are more likely to be employed in shifts overall, nearly half of all women working in services and the health professions are employed in shifts (Table 6.5). Night work and work during Saturdays and Sunday, for example, are also more common in the United Kingdom compared with Finland and Sweden.

In the United Kingdom, 53% of employed mothers and 79% of employed fathers are working non-standard hours and this often limits time for interaction with children as well as with partners (La Valle *et al.*, 2002). Nearly half of all British fathers work before and after school hours, while mothers who work atypical hours are more likely to be working on weekends, presumably when spouses care for children (Table 6.6). Although working atypical hours may be necessary to square work and care commitment, the majority of British women would prefer to work standard hours (La Valle *et al.*, 2002).

6.4.5. Emergency time off

Legislation in the reviewed countries grants workers the ability to take time off from work for emergency dependent care of family relatives as well as children. Compassionate care legislation in Canada, Finland and Sweden guarantees working parents paid emergency leave rights (see Background Annex to the review). British legislation provides eligible employees with the right to 13 weeks of unpaid parental leave to care for a child under age 5. The reasons for the leave are flexible (*e.g.* arrange for childcare, child's first day of school) and parents must confer with their employer to find a mutually agreeable solution on the time division. British employees can also take off a "reasonable" amount of unpaid leave to deal with emergencies or other unexpected family situations involving a dependent relative. Finland gives employees the right to take unpaid leave for non-care related family emergencies (*e.g.* in the aftermath of a household fire).

Table 6.5. **Many Finnish and Swedish women engage in shift work**
Panel A. Shift work and atypical working hours in Finland, Sweden and the United Kingdom
Share of workers in atypical working hours by total employment and by gender, 2003[a]

	Shift work[b]	Night work	Saturday	Sunday
Finland				
Total	24.1	9.5	18.8	13.5
Women	26.4	8.4	20.4	14.7
Men	21.7	10.5	17.1	12.3
Sweden				
Total	22.0	4.6	12.0	10.8
Women	25.1	4.2	14.8	13.1
Men	18.8	4.9	9.2	8.5
United Kingdom				
Total	17.9	11.1	20.3	11.7
Women	15.3	8.3	19.7	12.2
Men	20.2	13.7	20.8	11.2

Panel B. Frequency and distribution of shift work in Canada
Employees in shift work by gender, % of dual-earner couples[c]

	Women	Men
All workplaces	20	26
Sector		
Public	10	22
Private	23	27
Union coverage		
Unionised[d]	23	32
Non-unionised	18	20
Selected occupations		
Managers and administrative	10	11
Medicine and health	48	56
Other professional[e]	10	13
Clerical	9	22
Services	47	56
Processing and machinery	26	33

a) Responses of salaried employees ages 15+ stating conditions under which they are usually employed.
b) Shift work is defined here as employees who work in two or more distinct periods of work within a 24-hour day over a given four-week period (that is, shifts between which employees are regularly rotated). Persons whose working hours do not vary significantly are not considered as shift workers.
c) Shift work for Canada is defined here as working regularly on the evening, night or graveyard shift (12 a.m. to 8 a.m.); rotating or split shift; being on-call; or any other form of irregular work arrangement.
d) Includes both union members and non-union members who are covered by a collective agreement.
e) Includes natural sciences, social sciences, religion, teaching and artistic and literary professions.
Source: Panel A: Eurostat New Cronos (2004); Panel B: Marshall, K. (1998), "Couples Working Shift", Perspectives on Labour and Income, Catalogue No. 75 001 XPE, Statistics Canada, Ottawa, Autumn, pp. 9-14.

Table 6.6. **British parents often work non-standard hours**

Percentage of employed parents who report to work at atypical hours, 2001

	Mother	Father
6 a.m.-8.30 a.m. several times a week	21	41
5.30 p.m.-8.30 p.m. several times a week	25	45
Saturday at least once a month	38	54
Sunday at least once a month	25	31
Saturdays *and* Sundays two to three times every month	14	17
On call outside normal working hours	18	36
Regularly works more than 40 hours a week	13	50
Regularly works more than 48 hours a week	6	30

This sample of working parents is nationally representative of parents of children aged 0 to 14 years old, but does not include first-time parents with children under age 2.

Source: La Valle, I. et al. (2002), "The Influence of Atypical Working Hours on Family Life", Findings, No. 982, Joseph Rowntree Foundation, York.

6.5. Finding time to care and work

The development of family-friendly policies reviewed thus far (i.e. leave periods, time-related workplace supports) aim to lessen the impact of multiple constraints faced by parents seeking work-life balance. Yet, parents and, in particular, fathers do not always take advantage of all family-friendly policies available to them and, conversely, many employers do not always provide time-related support.

6.5.1. Mothers as carers

Despite significant increases in female employment rates in the past 30 years and increased paternal engagement in care provision, women allocate much more time to caring than men and working women are therefore more likely to perceive a time crunch (Smith, 2004).[20] In all four countries (including the province of Québec), women who work full-time spend less time in paid work and allocate more time to childcare and other unpaid housework than the average man (Table 6.7). The ratio of time spent on paid to unpaid work is highest for fathers in the United Kingdom, which suggests that long working hours preclude men from engaging in household chores. Although Finnish and Swedish parents strive for more equality in dividing household responsibilities, women working full-time spend nearly twice as much time caring for a young child than the average male. In Canada, and especially in the province of Québec, the female/male ratio of time spent in childcare appears slightly more balanced.

Parental attitudes also factor into maintaining mothers in traditional caring roles. Generally, British men are equally divided on whether they think that family life suffers when a woman works full-time (40% in agreement

Table 6.7. **Mothers remain the main carer in all countries**

Average hours per day spent by parents on paid work, childcare and unpaid work at home[a]

	Couple families												Men (average for all men)			
	Women in full-time (paid) work				Women in part-time (paid) work				Women mainly at home[b]							
	Paid work	Child care	Other unpaid	Ratio paid/total unpaid work[c]	Paid work	Child care	Other unpaid	Ratio paid/total unpaid work[c]	Paid work	Child care	Other unpaid	Ratio paid/total unpaid work[c]	Paid work	Child care	Other unpaid	Ratio paid/total unpaid work[c]
Canada (1998)																
With at least one child[d]	5.1	1.3	3.5	1.06	2.5	1.9	4.5	0.39	0.2	2.6	5.7	0.02	5.6	1.0	2.5	1.60
With youngest child under age 6	4.6	2.3	3.2	0.84	2.2	2.7	4.4	0.31	0.2	3.8	5.0	0.02	5.4	1.5	2.4	1.38
Province of Québec (1998)																
With at least one child[d]	5.2	1.2	3.3	1.16	3.2	1.6	4.0	0.57	0.3	2.4	5.7	0.04	5.1	0.9	2.6	1.46
With youngest child under age 6	4.9	2.2	2.7	1.00	2.3	2.3	4.3	0.35	0.2	2.7	4.1	0.03	5.0	1.4	2.5	1.28
Finland (1999-2000)																
With at least one child[d]	4.3	0.9	3.1	1.08	1.8	1.3	4.3	0.32	0.1	2.6	4.3	0.01	5.1	0.6	2.0	1.96
With youngest child under age 7	4.0	1.9	2.9	0.83	..	..	..	..	0.1	3.2	4.1	0.01	5.2	1.0	1.8	1.86
Sweden (1991)[e]																
With at least one child[d]	..	..	..	..	..	..	..	..	..	..	..	..	5.7	0.4	2.8	1.82
With youngest child under age 5[f]	3.9	2.2	3.9	0.64	3.2	2.0	4.9	0.46	0.3	4.4	5.1	0.03	5.5	1.1	2.7	1.45
United Kingdom (2003)																
With at least one child[d]	5.1	1.0	2.5	1.46	2.6	1.4	3.3	0.55	..	2.3	4.3	..	5.8	0.6	1.6	2.64
With youngest child under age 6	5.1	1.6	2.4	1.28	2.5	1.8	3.1	0.51	..	2.6	4.3	..	5.8	0.9	1.5	2.42

Table 6.7. **Mothers remain the main carer in all countries** (cont.)

Average hours per day spent by parents on paid work, childcare and unpaid work at home[a]

| | Sole parents | | | | | | | |
| | Female sole parent | | | | Male sole parent | | | |
	Paid work	Child care	Other unpaid	Ratio paid/total unpaid work[c]	Paid work	Child care	Other unpaid	Ratio paid/total unpaid work[c]
Canada (1998)								
With at least one child[d]	1.9	2.9	3.6	0.29	5.9	1.1	2.9	9.9
Province of Québec (1998)								
With at least one child[d]	1.7	2.6	3.9	0.26	6.7	0.8	3.0	10.5
Sweden (2003)[e]								
With at least one child[d]	3.9	1.5	3.5	0.78	..	..	..	..
United Kingdom (2003)								
With youngest child under age 6	3.5	1.4	2.6	0.88	4.5	0.2	0.9	5.6

.. Not available.

a) Time use data is not always comparable among countries (or sometimes within them) for many reasons, including the different forms of definitions and questionnaires used to determine each category. Generally, here, paid work includes working in a family enterprise (which explains why housewives report some paid work) and is averaged over the year, including weekends and paid leave (this explains why the figures may appear low). Childcare is defined strictly as requiring parental physical involvement and includes, for example, feeding, bathing and dressing children. Other unpaid work is broadly defined and includes for example, travel to school with children, cooking, washing dishes, house cleaning and shopping.

b) In Finland, women mainly at home are not employed, that is, they are out of the labour force, unemployed or on home care leave. See notes to Table Box .

c) For this ratio, total unpaid work includes time used for child care and for other unpaid household work.

d) In Canada and the province of Québec, child is under age 17; in Finland, under age 18; in Sweden, from age 7 to 17; in United Kingdom, age is under 15, except for paid work data which is under 17.

e) Data for Swedish men and female sole parents are from Statistics Sweden (2003) and other data for women from (OECD, 2001, Employment Outlook, OECD, Paris). Sampling of male sole parents is too small for this categorisation.

f) For men, youngest child is under age 7.

Source: For Canada, Finland and the province of Québec, national and provincial authorities; for Sweden, see note e) of this table; and, for the United Kingdom, estimates for paid work and other unpaid work are from the Labour Force Survey (2002-03) and estimates for childcare time are derived from the UK Time Use Survey (2000-01).

compared to 41% in disagreement); in contrast, only 27% and 23% of Swedish and Finnish men, respectively, find full-time employment of women problematic (GESIS, 2004). When the child is below school age, however, British men (61%)and, to a lesser extent, British women (55%), Finnish men and women (43% and 37%, respectively) believe that women should stay at home, while attitudes in Sweden lean to part-time work for mothers of young children (GESIS, 2004).[21] In contrast, Canadian fathers appear to be narrowing the gap in the gender division for both unpaid housework and childcare since the late 1980s (Zuzanek, 2001).

6.5.2. Why do some parents not take more time off work?

The parental decision on whether or not to reduce working hours after childbirth depends on a great many factors, including individual parental preferences (on providing personal care and engaging in work), spousal earnings, other sources of family income, and the cost of alternative care solutions (which often varies with the age of children).[22] Families' decisions about which, if any, parent will take time out of work in order to look after children are influenced by the amount of earnings which they will forgo.[23] Since paternal earnings are generally higher than maternal earnings (Chapter 3) it is more likely that mothers rather than fathers take leave or work part-time after childbirth.

Are these maternal labour market decisions a response to work-life imbalance or is it also that employers assume that women's caring responsibilities overshadow their work, and reduce their productivity? Available evidence is not clear on the direction of the relationship between the parental time crunch and female labour market behaviour. However, it appears that for mothers, more than for fathers, being in employment induces stress through role overload and role interference: among Canadian parents working full-time, for example, 70% more mothers than fathers experience severe time stress. This also contributes to mothers adjusting working hours and/or gravitating towards working for family-friendly enterprises (or sectors). Evidence of women self-selecting into the public sector which has more favourable family-friendly working conditions and a lower wage penalty for having children (Nielsen et al., 2004).

Despite gender equity legislation and workplace equality measures (Box 6.3) women face more difficulties in their career progression than men. Female labour market behaviour is influenced by concern that taking paid or unpaid time off from work to care for children inevitably signals reduced commitment and productivity to employers (Spence, 1973). About 40% of British parents believe that taking dependent care-related leave on a regular basis has a negative impact on one's career (Stevens et al., 2004).[24] The longer the absence, the higher the chance the employer will infer low employee

Box 6.3. **Gender equity measures for working mothers**

All countries in this review have legislation protecting mothers against direct and indirect discrimination using gender and/or employment legislation. Additional health and safety measures protect pregnant women: for example in the United Kingdom, some of these measures are extended to the first few months after birth and during breastfeeding. In the province of Québec, doctors are responsible for assessing the safety of a workplace for pregnant and breastfeeding women and can demand the woman's reassignment or paid leave if the employer cannot guarantee safe conditions. In addition, Finland and Sweden have instituted several policies to reduce gender inequity in the labour market, although their effect in this regard seems to have been limited. Employers in both countries must prepare gender equity plans that provide for equity in pay and working conditions, and in Sweden employers must also conduct an annual wage survey, which is monitored by the Equal Opportunities Ombudsman. The process imposes administrative costs on employers, while the benefits from this approach are unclear: the annual gender equity reports assessing workplace progress are largely reflective in nature and do not seem to lead to structural changes in behaviour, of, for example, fathers taking longer leaves.

To reduce gender wage differences (which ranges from 3.5% for blue-collar to 6% for white-collar workers in industry), in Finland for employees within the same company with the same position and work intensity, sectoral agreements provide for a wage bonus to reduce wage disparities reflecting the sectoral distribution of women (Kuusisto, 2004). The bonus is calculated based on the proportion of women employed in the sector (the higher the proportion, the higher the bonus), but it has had little impact on reducing the overall gender wage gap.

It is impossible to be precise on the proportion of pregnant workers who feel harassed. Evidence is weak, not least because many women who may potentially lodge a complaint do not do so because of the associated costs, or because they wish to avoid further deterioration of the employment relationship or have otherwise little faith in the recourse process. Nevertheless, research by equal opportunity commissions suggests the issue persists. For example, Sweden's Equal Opportunities Ombudsman (EOO) recently observed a sharp rise in the number of pregnancy discrimination complaints, some of which could be explained by a recent EOO information campaign on women's rights. In England and Wales, about 1 000 women per year file cases regarding unlawful dismissal during pregnancy (Carvel, 2004). These estimates are considered the tip of the iceberg, since most cases are resolved through out-of-court mediation (EOC, 2004). In the province of Québec, nearly two-thirds of all cases are mediated out of court and cases of discrimination against pregnant women accounted for 14% of these complaints (Ministère du Travail, Québec, 2003).

commitment. Because few men take leave, or reduce working hours after childbirth, those fathers who do are more likely to pay a very high career penalty for this (Jansson *et al.*, 2003; Albrecht *et al.*, 1999).

Signalling has the potential of reducing maternal career advancement and earnings progression (Flexecutive, 2002), but evidence on the magnitude of this effect is hard to find. What is clear is that gender wage gaps at the top earnings decile are above OECD average in all four countries and national studies often refer to many women having difficulty getting through the glass ceiling (Chapter 3). In Finland and Sweden, this feature is sometimes also related to the high costs of domestic services. Hence, rather than working long hours and pursue their career, women in these countries return home after standard hours and engage in household chores, while women in countries where domestic services are relatively cheap, such as in the United States, find it easier (less costly) to pursue their career (Datta Gupta *et al.*, 2001). To assist working women, a large Swedish insurance firm arranged a personal assistant "butler" service for its employees to compensate for the expensive domestic work market. The company-subsidised butler performs employees' household chores such as laundry, running errands, fixing household appliances and buying birthday presents.

In the United Kingdom, most fathers' attitudes for greater gender equity in domestic roles are negatively related to the amount of time spent they spend caring for their children: fathers in professional positions and those working longer hours are least likely to get involved with their children or sacrifice their career (Dex, 2003). To encourage men to take more time off from work for caring, Finnish and Swedish parental leave systems reserve specific leave periods for exclusive use by fathers (Table 6.1). Yet, Finnish and Swedish fathers use only 4% and 17%, respectively, of the total parental allowance days available. The Finnish system strictly regulates when fathers can take paid leave and about 80% of new fathers take time off right around the birth of their child. In Sweden, fathers take more leave, but there has not been a fundamental change in behaviour among Swedish men despite the non-transferable leave entitlements and high income support payment rates: fathers tend to combine parental leave with Christmas or summer holidays. Increasing take up among fathers is also hampered by mothers who do not wish to reduce the duration of their leave period, and workplace practices: collective agreements may provide for top-ups to leave payments for mothers, but not always for fathers.

Proposed policy reform in Sweden involves increasing public income support during leave on the argument that this increased generosity will increase the likelihood that fathers take leave. However, this reform is more likely to further increase the effective duration of leave among women, which may be counterproductive. One way forward is to gradually extend individualisation of paid parental leave entitlements, which may increase maternal labour supply (Pylkkänen and Smith, 2003). A fully-individualised leave system does not yet exist in the OECD area, but Iceland's system goes furthest: each parent has the right to a non-transferable three-month leave period and a shared three-month period until the child turns 18 months old. The current set-up is relatively new, but already working fathers take about 30% of total available leave days.[25]

6.5.3. Why do employers not provide more time-related support?

Employers have a case for making their workplaces more family friendly. Such policies help motivate and retain existing staff (and increase the likelihood that mothers return to work upon expiry of maternity leave) and attract new workers, while reducing workplace stress and absenteeism and improving worker loyalty (Bevan et al., 1999; Comfort et al., 2003; Duxbury et al., 1999; Johnson, 1995; Gray, 2002; and Nelson et al., 2004). Moreover, some employee control in the implementation of family-friendly policies (e.g. choosing a work schedule) is also linked to a reduction of work-life interference (Sparks et al., 2001). Policies that enable women to reach management positions will help these employers access a greater pool of skilled workers (Catalyst, 2004), while the cost of not having family-friendly policy measures is highest for sectors with a high proportion of female employees (Wortsman and Lochhead, 2002).

Against the benefits are costs. Introducing flexible work schedules may be prohibitively expensive compared to existing shift production schedules. Hiring additional workers to maintain productivity and output levels creates additional training costs. Both enterprise costs and benefits related to family-friendly policies are increasingly a function of i) the difficulty with which (skilled) workers can be replaced and ii) how important it is to these workers that they have access to family-friendly policy support. The latter also determines the intensity with which unions are likely to negotiate for family-friendly policies (Box 6.2 above). Policymakers in Canada, for example, are hesitant to pass additional costs to Canadian employers in face of competition with the United States.

When asked on the (quantifiable) positive effects of introducing family-friendly workplace measures, companies often refer to significant reductions in staff turnover, recruitment and training costs, and absenteeism. Emerging research corroborates this picture, but evidence is often based on individual enterprises.[26] In general, it is difficult to identify separately the exact effect of introducing flexible work-hours schedules on worker performance and/or profits. Moreover, there is no panacea: different measures will suit better in different workplaces.[27]

Supply of family-friendly workplace support, nevertheless, seems to be well below potential, and this is particularly important to British and Canadian parents who are much more dependent on individual workplace support, than their Finnish and Swedish counterparts. In part, limited workplace support is related to the limited financial and organisational capacity of many small and medium-sized enterprises to implement family-friendly workplaces. Moreover, entrepreneurs may not be fully aware of the benefits of introducing family-friendly policies and have exaggerated perceptions of the associated costs. This is important, as the decision to introduce family-friendly measures is often the result of a personal decision by someone (or small group of people) in the leadership of an organisation about how the company should behave as an employer. A lack of commitment among senior and middle management to the introduction of family-friendly support also limits the wider application of family-friendly policies.

Theory suggests that firms would be more likely to invest in family-friendly measures in a tight labour market. However, present labour markets are relatively tight in all four countries, perhaps least so in Finland (Chapter 3). Nevertheless, demographic trends are likely to add impetus to the case for family-friendly polices, with firms increasingly competing for workers, of whom many would like to have access to family-friendly policy support (Fortin, 2004).

Potential gains from increasing female labour force attachment are most significant in Canada and the United Kingdom: changing female participation (in terms of person and hours) would increase effective labour supply in both countries by about 20% in 2050 (Chart 6.5). Such effects are smaller in Finland and Sweden (smaller gender employment gaps for older cohorts), but nevertheless are vital to both economies in the long-run, as an increase in female employment rates to current male levels will increase labour supply by about 10%. This is particularly important to the Finnish labour force, because if current employment rates do not change, the labour force will shrink by almost 20% over the next 50 years. This is yet another reason to reconsider policies that encourage mothers to interrupt their careers for prolonged periods of time.

6.5.4. How can policy help making workplace more family-friendly?

In Finland and Sweden, there seems little need for further policy intervention concerning time-related workplace practices, except, perhaps, with respect to part-time employment in Finland. There is some support to encourage parents working part-time (see above) but this is hardly used. Incentives for mothers with very young children not to engage in paid work are strong (Chapter 5) and, without relevant reform, it is difficult to increase

Chart 6.5. **More workplace family friendly policies can limit the projected decline in the Finnish labour supply**

Total weekly hours from 2000 projected to 2050, index 2000 = 100

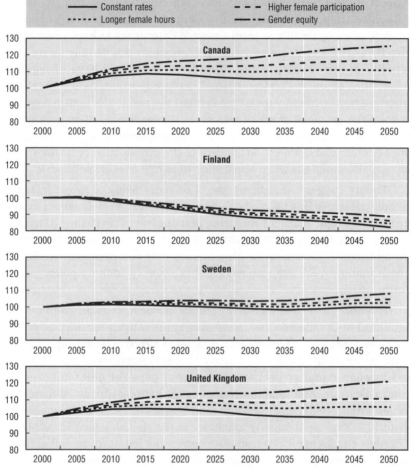

"1-Constant rates": assumes constant labour force participation rates and constant weekly hours for men and women from 2000 to 2050.

"2-Higher female participation": assumes that female participation rates reach current male participation rates in each country in 2050, and constant weekly hours.

"3-Longer female hours„: assumes constant participation rates and female weekly hours to reach male weekly hours in each country in 2050.

"4-Gender equity": assumes that female participation rates reach current male participation rates and female weekly hours to reach male weekly hours in each country in 2050.

Source: OECD (2004), Database on Population and Labour Force Projections and Database on Usual Weekly Hours of Work.

female labour force attachment of mothers with young children, on a part-time or full-time basis.

Directive legislation is not always effective in flexible labour markets with considerable resistance from small and medium-sized firms to any public intervention that increases labour costs. Direct intervention in workplace practices is much less comprehensive in Canada and the United Kingdom. Policy intervention towards more family-friendly workplace support often concerns initiatives to increase awareness of the merits of such support and/ or provide some financial assistance to enterprises which make family-friendly support available. In the United Kingdom, the Work-Life Challenge Fund, a component of the government's Work-Life Balance Campaign, does both. Between 2000 and 2003, the Challenge Fund provided GBP 11 million in financial assistance to more than 400 public and private companies for the employment of private human resources consultancies to develop and implement tailored work-life balance measures. In an early evaluation, employers stated that the presence of specialist consultants facilitated acceptance and implementation of family-friendly policies in the workplace (Nelson et al., 2004). The province of Québec supports companies by connecting them with Emploi Québec, a public service where employers can find assistance with employment, vocational training on human resources management concerns, including work-life balance; up to half of the costs can be paid by Emploi Québec. The sustainability of newly established family-friendly policies is based on support from all relevant stakeholders, including unions and middle management, as well as a continued re-assessment of the effectiveness and take-up of implemented policies. In contrast to the province of Québec, the element of re-assessment is absent from the UK initiative which should be broadened to include it, thereby fostering long-term enterprise commitment to family-friendly workplaces.

In between "exhortation" and "direct legislation of entitlements" lies the recent UK policy approach that grants British parents with children under age six the legislated *right to request* flexible working hours. Legislation does not grant parents an *entitlement* to part-time work (as in Sweden), but there are nevertheless costs associated with the legislation as employers have to justify why they may not wish to grant a specific request. At present, though, case law does not yet indicate "how strong" the right to ask for flexible working hours in the United Kingdom really is (and thus how high are employer costs).

6.6. Conclusions

The design of time-related support measures for parents around childbirth differs markedly in the countries under review. In Finland and Sweden, paid leave with relatively high replacements rates is an integral part of the family-friendly policy model that provides a continuum of support from birth until young adolescence. By contrast, in Canada and the United Kingdom, income support during leave is relatively limited in amount and duration, and there is a gap between the date of leave expiry and the moment that childcare support becomes universally available (Chapter 4). In addition, not all working mothers are eligible for leave payments, which, in Canada, has led to increased discussion on extending leave coverage to atypical workers. Once back in work, mothers in Finland and Canada are most likely to work full-time, around 38 to 40 hours. In Sweden, legislation entitles parents to reduce working hours until children go to school, and almost half the mothers in Swedish dual-earner couple families work less than 35 hours per week. Mothers in the United Kingdom are most likely to work on a part-time basis or, more recently, might request a right to flexible working hours per their entitlement. Rather than reducing hours, British men work long hours, and almost one-third of fathers work more than 48 hours a week, and raises concerns on the time that fathers are able to spend with their children.

Collective agreements cover about 90% of the employees in Finland and Sweden, while working parents in Canada and the United Kingdom rely to a much greater extent on support made available in *individual* workplaces. Flexible work schedules (without reducing weekly hours) are much more likely to be used in Canada (especially among men) than in the United Kingdom, where mothers often use part-time work options. Other forms of flexible working arrangements remain quite rare (*e.g.* teleworking, compressed hours, temporarily reducing hours) in the United Kingdom, but a quarter of very large British workplaces (mostly in the public sector) offer term-time employment options to workers. Shift-parenting seems to be widespread in Canada, where parents in almost half of the dual-earner couples use atypical hours to synchronise their full-time work and care commitments.

There is a "business case" for family-friendly workplace support, and companies that introduced such measures often refer to significant reductions in staff turnover, recruitment and training costs, absenteeism, while the likelihood that mothers return to work upon expiry of maternity leave increases. However, hard evidence for this business case is difficult to find, as it is not easy to identify separately the exact effect of, say, introducing flexible work-hours schedules on worker performance and/or profits.

The question arises what mix of policy tools, legislative stipulation (as in Finland and Sweden), encouragement and tailored advice, or a greater use of tax incentives is the most likely to generate greater access to family-friendly workplace support? Generally, directive legislation is not always effective in flexible labour markets with considerable resistance from small and medium-sized firms to any public intervention that increases labour costs. One way to overcome such opposition is to financially support "consultancy" initiatives that provide tailored advice to companies, as happens in the United Kingdom, but for such initiatives to be effective, they should include re-assessment, as they do in Québec, to ensure long-term enterprise commitment. The recent initiative to grant British parents the right to request flexible working hours gives a clear policy signal on the desirability of family-friendly support, but does incur costs on employers, although it is not clear how much, since case law has yet to establish the extent of the entitlements that accrue from the right to ask for flexible working hours.

In all four countries, women spend more time providing care for children than men, overwhelmingly take more parental leave then men and are most likely to reduce working hours after childbirth. Since husbands, on average, earn more than their spouses, they contribute most to family income. Compared to Canada and the United Kingdom, there is a traditionally strong emphasis on gender equity concerns in policy development in both Finland and Sweden. Nevertheless, many Finnish women find it hard to find employment security before establishing a family. With so many Finnish mothers using the Home Care Allowance, employers are understandably reluctant to hire someone who may take a leave of absence for three years. The long leave periods in Sweden also contribute to mothers being absent from work for more than a year, which is unlikely to advance career prospects.

In order to reduce the penalty on women for taking leave, Finnish and Swedish policies try to get more fathers to take parental leave for longer by reserving some generously paid weeks of leave exclusively for their use. These policies have had some success as, for example, in Sweden the fathers' share of total parental leave days taken increased from 11% in 1994 to 17% in 2003. However, this does not reflect a fundamental behavioural change, as mothers almost exclusively take long periods of leave. Suggested policy reform involves increasing public income support during leave, but this is more likely to further increase the effective duration of leave among women, which may be counterproductive. Paternal attitudes are not the only issue, as mothers frequently seem reluctant to give up leave to their partner's benefit. A Swedish government committee is reviewing different aspects of the parental leave system, and it could consider different options to achieve a more gender equitable use of parental leave, including, for example, granting a bonus to parents who equally share parental leave entitlements, increasing the duration of leave periods that are non-transferable between the parents, and/or increasing information to both parents about fathers rights to parental leave. In Sweden, as in most other OECD countries, the policy debate about a more equal sharing of the care burden during the early months has yet to start in earnest.

Notes

1. Although data is available to compare the distribution of working hours in Canada and the province of Québec, the same data is not fully comparable with data on the other countries in this review (as presented in Chart 6.2). The division of working hours for women between part-time and full-time work in Canada and the province of Québec is similar (27% and 28%, respectively, work less than 30 hours per week), but slightly more Canadian women (36%) work more than 40 hours per week compared to Québécois women (30%).

2. Although the general trend among most OECD countries has been towards a decline of annual working hours (except for Sweden, see Chapter 3), working hours in both Canada and the United Kingdom became more polarised between the beginning of the 1980s and the late 1990s: a growing number of employees worked long hours, while over the same period the incidence of part-time work increased. Since the late 1990s the incidence of part-time work has been stable, while the prevalence of long working hours declined since 1996 in Canada and 1998 in the United Kingdom (OECD, 2004g).

3. According to a longitudinal study of early childhood in Québec, only one-third of mothers, but 70% of fathers with two-and-a-half year olds work more than 40-hour weeks (Rochette and Deslauriers, 2003).

4. Employees who fall under federal labour legislation in Canada work in the following sectors: federal government; interprovincial and international transport (air, land, sea); physical communication systems; radio and television broadcasting; banking; fishing; food-related warehouses; and uranium mining and processing.

5. Until 1940, social and employment policy was within the jurisdiction of Canadian provinces, but a constitutional amendment made unemployment insurance payments fall under federal direction. Originally developed for unemployment insurance, the superseding Employment Insurance (EI) scheme now includes four special income support areas: maternity, parental leave, compassionate care and sickness. The governments of Canada and Quebec have agreed on reform to be introduced 1 January 2006, that will give residents of Quebec access to maternity and parental leave benefits under the Quebec parental insurance programme (SDC, 2005). The new Québec benefit rules on payment rates and time periods differ from the existing rules, while coverage of the new programme in the province of Québec will be extended to the self-employed (MESSF, 2005a).

6. Changes in the Canadian EI scheme increased the eligibility of workers. EI eligibility shifted from a weeks-based to an hours-based system on 30 June 1996 and, on 31 December 2000, the number of required insurable employment hours fell from 700 hours to 600 hours. After the first change, the percentage of maternity claims per birth increased by 3 percentage points, but decreased by 2 percentage points in 1998. The introduction of a lower number of required hours increased maternity claims per birth by 7 percentage points after 2001.

7. In Finland, workers with average earnings are in one of the categories with the highest income replacement level. On average, though, the average wage replacement rate in Finland in 2002 was 66% of previous earnings for all workers (Gornick and Meyers, 2003).

8. In Canada, under certain circumstances, mothers are eligible for 65 weeks of combined maternity, parental and sickness benefits. See Background Annex to the review.

9. In fall 2004, the UK government proposed to extend paid maternity leave to nine months as of 2007 (and subsequently to a full year) in addition to childcare measures.

10. Some provinces in Canada provide each parent, on an individual basis, with the full duration of unpaid job-protected parental leave.

11. This is not always necessary in the province of Québec which has the PRALMA programme to cover the waiting period for EI benefits (see Background Annex to the review).

12. The survey data used by Hudson et al. (2004) include a high rate of female workers in the United Kingdom (85%) who are eligible for additional maternity leave. Survey respondents were mothers who had worked for at least 26 weeks before the birth of their baby and, therefore, were more likely of meeting employment conditions for additional maternity leave (one year of continuous employment with employer by the beginning of the 11th week before the expected week of childbirth).

13. Studies in the United States and the United Kingdom, where maternity leave is relatively short (respectively 12 weeks and 18 weeks long at the time of the analysis) suggest that employers do not incur significant direct costs due to leave policies (Hofferth and Curtin, 2003; Edwards et al., 2003). Furthermore, evidence on employers' attitudes is not always reliable in survey data: small and medium-sized businesses tend to have a low awareness of maternity-related employment regulations and attempt to learn them only when necessary. Yet, small businesses in the United Kingdom receive a preferential reimbursement rate compared to larger firms of up to 104% on maternity payments.

14. To provide an example of confusion, if an employer in the United Kingdom provides a mother with a similar job that is less favourable than her previous position upon her return from a full year leave (additional maternity leave), because her previous position is now occupied by a replacement worker, the employer could be held liable for discrimination under the Sex Discrimination Act 1975 but not under the Employment Rights Act (which governs maternity leave).

15. In 2003, respectively 6% and 7% of workplaces in the United Kingdom had managerial and non-managerial employees opt out of the Working Time Regulations (Woodland et al., 2003). Of those employees working more than 48 contractual hours, only 25% have signed opt-out agreements (Stevens et al., 2004).

16. In the United Kingdom, employers are allowed by law to incorporate the eight public (bank) holidays into the employees' right to four weeks holiday.

17. Involuntary part-time work is most common among part-time female workers in Finland (36%), followed by Canada (27%) and Sweden (22%), and is almost negligible in the United Kingdom (5%). To reduce involuntary part-time work Swedish authorities fund (SEK 100 million over a three-year period ending in 2004) the HELA (full-time) project, which supports public and private initiatives that involve full-time participation. An evaluation of programme results has not yet been made.

18. To protect the rights of part-time and fixed-term workers Finland (2001) and Sweden (2002) amended employment legislation, while the United Kingdom introduced new regulations in 2000 (for part-time workers) and 2002 (for fixed-term workers). Workers are protected against discrimination in terms of pay and

working conditions: they are entitled to *pro rata* remuneration, access to the employer's pension scheme, sick pay, maternity leave, parental leave and training opportunities.

19. Until 1999, British employers did not pay national insurance contributions for workers earning below GBP 64 per week in 1999, thereby providing an incentive for low-paying part-time jobs. Although that incentive has been abolished and replaced with a more gradual system, employers can still keep earnings of some of their workforce below the earnings threshold (around GBP 91 per week in 2004) to avoid the cost and paperwork. In addition, a new incentive for the creation of part-time work emanated in October 2001 with the regulation requiring employers with at least five employees to offer a pension scheme or pay pension contributions. Workers who earn less than the National Insurance lower earnings limit (GBP 79 per week in 2004) for at least one week during a three-month period are not counted as eligible employees (Kingsmill, 2001).

20. In Canada, though, the ratio in the time spent on childcare by women and men who work full-time has declined slightly from 1.82 to 1.72 between 1992 and 1998 (Clark, 2001).

21. Evidence on attitudes towards mothers in work in GESIS (2004) does not include results on Canada. Evidence on attitudes needs to be interpreted with great care, as survey results are not independent of circumstances and policy. To explore the issue, Antecol (2000) examined the employment behaviour of first and later generation immigrants in the United States in view of the situation in their country of origin. After controlling for exogenous and endogenous variables, it appears that gender labour force participation of British, Canadian, Finnish and Swedish immigrants are in fact rather similar. This supports the notion that policy is crucial to explaining existing cross-country differences in attitudes.

22. The cost of childcare sometimes acts as a barrier to female employment, as is the case for many sole parents on Income Support in the United Kingdom (Herrington and Cattell, 2004).

23. Similarly, the amount of earnings foregone also influences parental decision on how much leave is taken, or for how long one engages in part-time work. In general, the smaller the loss of income, the longer part-time work arrangements and leave periods are likely to last (see Section 6.3.2).

24. The Equal Opportunities Commission (EOC) in the United Kingdom has received reports from employed mothers who are not able to obtain flexible working hours upon their return from parental leave. In some cases, employers suggest that female employees accept a downgrade of their job responsibilities in order to have access to flexible working time (Womack, 2004).

25. In Iceland, eligible working parents receive uncapped leave-related benefits equivalent to 80% of average earnings and non-working parents receive a guaranteed minimum payment ranging from 18% to 40% of average earnings. The current set-up applies since 1 January 2001 and, although it is too early to make a full assessment of the policy change, initial data shows an increase in men's relative use of leave compared to women: fathers take an average of 83 days leave or 30% of the total leave days available (Einarsdóttir and Pétursdóttir, 2004). Public spending on leave benefits was estimated to be around 0.75% of GDP in 2003 (OECD, 2003b).

26. For example, implementing a flexible benefits package (*e.g.*, added vacation days, unpaid time off) in a medium-sized consulting company may have contributed to halving staff turnover and bringing recruitment costs down 38%. A large British

avionics company developed a human resources package consisting of home working, career breaks, part-time working, term-time working and job share was able to decrease stress-related absences by 15% and increase the number of mothers retuning from maternity leave by 35% (DTI, 2004).

27. Meyer *et al.* (2001) found that paid care days or teleworking (which only suits a certain number of employers) to deal with sick family members, are worth introducing because they are relatively cheap if and they assure workers they can deal with child-related contingencies. On the other hand, job-sharing is found to have a negative effect on profits because of the associated diseconomies of scale. By contrast, Gray (2002) finds that job-sharing may have a positive impact on enterprise productivity, but less so than measures (flexi-time) which support a more visible (full-time) workplace engagement of the worker.

Bibliography

Adema, W. and M. Ladaique (2005), "Net Social Expenditure, 3rd edition", Social, Employment and Migration Working Paper, OECD, Paris.

Albrecht, J., A. Björklund and S. Vroman (2001), "Is There a Glass Ceiling in Sweden?", IZA Discussion Paper, No. 282, Forschungsinstitut zur Zukunft der Arbeit (Institute for the Study of Labour), Bonn.

Albrecht, J., P. Edin, M. Sundström and S. Vroman (1999), "Career Interruptions and Subsequent Earnings: A Reexamination Using Swedish Data", The Journal of Human Resources, Vol. 34, No. 2, University of Wisconsin Press, Madison, pp. 294- 311.

Alewell, D. and K. Pull (2001), "An International Comparison and Assessment of Maternity Leave Legislation", Comparative Labor Law and Policy Journal, Vol. 22, pp. 297-326, Champaign, IL.

Antecol, H. (2000), "An Examination of Cross-Country Differences in the Gender Gap in Labour Force Participation Rates", Labour Economics, Vol. 7, pp. 409-426, Amsterdam.

Anxo, D., L. Flood and Y. Kocoglu (2002), "Offre de travail et répartition des activités domestiques et parentales au sein du couple: Une comparaison entre la France et la Suède", Economie et Statistiques, Institut National de la Statistique et des Études Économiques, No. 352-353, Paris, pp. 127-150.

Apps, P. and R. Rees (2004), "Fertility, Taxation and Family Policy", Scandinavian Journal of Economics, Vol. 106, No. 4, Oxford, pp. 745-763.

Bargain, O. and K. Orsini (2004), "In-Work Policies in Europe: Killing Two Birds with One Stone?", IZA Discussion Paper, No. 1445, Forschungsinstitut zur Zukunft der Arbeit (Institute for the Study of Labour), Bonn.

Barker, J., J. Ireland, V. Morrow, F. Smith, and V. Hey (2004), "Evaluation of the Childcare Partnership Manager Role", Department for Work and Pensions, London.

Barnes, M. and M. Willits (2004), "Families and Children in Britain. Findings from the 2002 Families and Children Study (FACS)", Department for Work and Pensions Research Report, No. 206, London.

Batljan, I. (2001), "Focus on Fertility: From a Population Policy to a Child-Friendly Society", Ds, Vol. 57, Fritzes public publications, Stockholm.

Bennett, F. and J. Millar (2005), "Making Work Pay", Benefits, Vol. 13, No. 1, Colchester, UK, pp. 28-33.

Berg, A. (2004), "Report Examines Gender Pay Gap", for European Industrial Relations Observatory (EIRO), www.eiro.eurofound.eu.int/2004/02/feature/se0402103f.html.

Bertram, T. and C. Pascal (2000), Thematic Review of Early Childhood Education and Care: Background Report for the United-Kingdom, Centre for Research in Early Childhood, University College, Worcester.

Bevan, S, S. Dench, H. Harper and S. Hayday (2004), *How Employers Manage Absence*, Employment Relations Research Series, No. 25, Department of Trade and Industry, London.

Bevan, S, S. Dench, P. Tamkin and J. Cummings (1999), "Family-Friendly Employment: The Business Case", Research Brief, No. 136, Institute for Employment Studies, Department for Education and Employment, London.

Bielenski, H., G. Bosch and A. Wagner (2002), *Working Time Preferences in Sixteen European Countries*, European Foundation for the Improvement of Living and Working Conditions, Dublin.

Bingley, P. and I. Walker (2001), "Rents and Work: the Implications of Housing Costs and Housing Benefits for Work Incentives in the UK", *The Economic Journal*, Vol. 111, No. 471, The Royal Economic Society, Oxford, pp. 86-103.

Blau, F. and J. Currie (2004), "Preschool, Daycare, and Afterschool Care: Who is Minding the Kids", National Bureau of Economic Research Working Paper, No. 10670, Cambridge, MA.

Bonjour, D. and R. Dorsett (2002), "New Deal for Partners: Characteristics and Labour Market Transitions of Eligible Couples", Department for Work and Pensions, London.

Bonjour, D. and S. Lissenburg (2004), *Maternity Rights in Britain 2002: Survey of Employers*, Department for Work and Pensions, London.

Bradshaw, J. and N. Finch (2002), "A Comparison of Child Benefit Packages in 22 Countries", Department for Work and Pensions Research Report, No. 174, Leeds.

Brewer, M. and A. Shephard (2004), *Has Labour Made Work Pay?*, Joseph Rowntree Foundation, York.

Brewer, M., A. Duncan, A. Shephard and M.J. Suarrez (2003), "Did Working Families' Tax Credit Work? Analysing the Impact of In-Work Support on Labour Supply and Programme Participation", Inland Revenue Working Paper, No. 2, London.

Brooker, S. (2002), *Parents' Perceptions of and Attitudes towards Government Work-Life Balance Initiatives: A Survey of Parents*, Women's Equality Unit, Department of Trade and Industry and Department for Education and Employment, London.

Burgess, S., P. Gregg, C. Propper, and E. Washbrook (2002), "Maternity Rights and Mothers' Return to Work", The Centre for Market and Public Organisation (CMPO) Working Paper Series, No. 02/055, University of Bristol, Bristol.

CAALL (2002), *Work-Life Balance in Canada: A Report to Ministers Responsible for Labour in Canada*, Canadian Association of Administrators of Labour Legislation Ad Hoc Committee on Work-Life Balance, Ottawa.

Carvel, J. (2004), "Employers Failing Pregnant Workers", *The Guardian*, 6 September 2004, *http://money.guardian.co.uk/work/story/0,1456,1297878,00.html*.

Castles, F. (2003), "The World Turned Upside Down: Below Replacement Fertility, Changing Preferences and Family-Friendly Public Policy in 21 OECD Countries", *Journal of European Social Policy*, Vol. 13, No. 3, Sage Publications, London, pp. 209-227.

Catalyst (2004), *The Bottom Line: Connecting Corporate Performance and Gender Diversity*, *www.catalystwomen.org/knowledge/titles/files/full/financialperformancereport.pdf*.

CCSD (2003), "Statistics – Estimated 2002 Annual Basic Social Assistance Income by Type of Household", Canadian Council on Social Development, *www.ccsd.ca/factheets*.

CEIC (2004), *Employment Insurance 2003 Monitoring and Assessment Report*, submitted to the Minister of HRSDC on 31 March 2004 and prepared by HRSDC Strategic Policy (Labour Market Policy Directorate), Canada Employment Insurance Commission, Gatineau, Québec.

CIPD (2004), *Employee Absence 2004: A Survey of Management Policy and Practice*, Chartered Institute of Personnel and Development, London.

Clark, W. (2001), "Economic Gender Equality Indicators 2000", *Canadian Social Trends*, March 2001, Statistics Canada, Ottawa.

Cleveland, G., and M. Krashinsky (1998), *The Benefits and Costs of Good Child Care*, Childcare Resource and Research Unit, University of Toronto, Toronto.

Cleveland, G. and M. Krashinsky (2003), *Fact and Fantasy : Eight Myths about Early Childhood Education and Care*, Childcare Resource and Research Unit, University of Toronto, Toronto.

Comfort, D., K. Johnson and D. Wallace (2003), *Part-Time Work and Family-Friendly Practices in Canadian Workplaces*, The Evolving Workplace Series, Human Resources Development Canada and Statistics Canada, *www11.sdc.gc.ca/en/cs/sp/arb/publications/research/2003-000183/page01*.

Cummings C., A. Dyson and L. Todd (2004), "Evaluation of the Extended Schools Pathfinder Projects", Research Report No. 530, Department for Education and Skills (DfES) and University of Newcastle upon Tyne, *www.dfes.gov.uk/research/data/uploadfiles/RR530.pdf*.

Currie, J. (2004), "Viewpoint : Child Research Comes of Age", *Canadian Journal of Economics*, Canadian Economics Association, Vol. 37, No. 3, Montreal, pp. 509-527.

D'Addio, A-C. and M. Mira D'Ercole (2005), "Fertility Trends and Determinants in OECD Countries", Social, Employment and Migration Working Paper, OECD, Paris.

Datta Gupta, N. and Smith, N. (2000), "Children and Career Interruptions: The Family Gap in Denmark", Working Paper, No. 00-03, Centre for Labour Market and Social Research, Aarhus, Denmark.

Datta Gupta, N, R. Oaxaca and N. Smith (2001), "Swimming Upstream, Floating Downstream – Trends in the US and Danish Gender Wage Gaps", Working Paper, No. 01-06, Centre for Labour Market and Social Research, Aarhus.

Daycare Trust (2004), *Childcare Cost Survey*, Daycare Trust/TUC Conference, *www.daycaretrust.org.uk/article.php?sid=194*.

Department of Finance Canada (2004), *Federal Transfers to Provinces and Territories*, October, Ottawa.

Dex, S. (2003), *Families and Work in the 21st Century*, Joseph Rowntree Foundation, York.

DfES (2002), *Inter-departmental Childcare Review: Delivering for Children and Families*, Department for Education and Skills, November, London.

DfES (2004), *Departmental Annual Report*, Department for Education and Skills, London, *www.dfes.gov.uk/deptreport2004/uploads/DfES-Annual%20Report.pdf*.

DfES (2004a), *Every Child Matters: Next Steps*, Department for Education and Skills, London.

Dingeldey, I. (2001), "European Tax Systems and Their Impact on Family Employment Patterns", *Journal of Social Policy*, Vol. 30, Cambridge University Press, Cambridge, pp. 653-672.

Doherty, G., M. Friendly and J. Beach (2003), *Thematic Review of Early Childhood Education and Care: Canadian Background Report*, OECD, Paris.

Drolet, M. (2002), "The "Who, What, When and Where' of Gender Pay Differentials,", *The Evolving Workplace Series*, No. 4, Business and Labour Market Analysis Division, Statistics Canada, Ottawa.

DTI (2000), *Work and Parents: Competitiveness and Choice*, A Green Paper presented to Parliament, December 2000, Department of Trade and Industry, London.

DTI (2001), "A Simplified Framework of Maternity Pay and Leave", public consultation document, Department of Trade and Industry, London, *www.dti.gov.uk/er/simp8.pdf*.

DTI (2004), "Achieving Best Practice in Your Business: Maximising Potential through Work-Life Balance. Case Studies from the IT, Electronics and Communications Industries", Department of Trade and Industry, London.

Duxbury, L. and C. Higgins (1998), *Work-Life Balance in Saskatchewan: Realities and Challenges*, Government of Saskatchewan Department of Labour, Saskatoon, *www.business.carleton.ca/sask.98*.

Duxbury, L. and C. Higgins (2003), *Work – Life Conflict in Canada in the New Millennium: A Status Report*, prepared for Health Canada, *www.hc-sc.gc.ca/pphb-dgspsp/publicat/work-travail/pdf/rprt_2_e.pdf*.

Duxbury, L., C. Higgins and K. Johnson (1999), *An Examination of the Implications and Costs of Work-Life Conflict in Canada*, submitted to Health Canada, *www.hc-sc.gc.ca/dca-dea/publications/pdf/ duxbury_e.pdf*.

Eaton, F., S. Hamel and S. Tétrault (2000), "L'impact net du programme aide aux parents pour leurs revenues de travail (Apport), et sommaire des autres résultats", Ministère de la Solidarité Sociale du Québec.

Edwards, P., M. Ram and J. Black (2003), "The Impact of Employment Legislation on Small Firms: A Case Study Analysis", Employment Research Series, No. 20, Department of Trade and Industry, London.

EFILWC (2000), *Third Survey on European Working Conditions (2000)*, European Foundation for the Improvement of Living and Working Conditions, Dublin, *www.eurofound.eu.int/working/3wc/ 3wcindex.htm*.

EFILWC (2002), *Reconciliation of Work and Family Life and Collective Bargaining: An Analysis of EIRO Articles*, European Foundation for the Improvement of Living and Working Conditions, Dublin, *www.eiro.eurofound.eu.int/other_reports/work_family_life.pdf*.

Einarsdóttir, Þ. with G.M. Pétursdóttir (2004), *Culture, Custom and Caring: Men's and Women's Possibilities to Parental Leave*, Centre for Gender Equality, Centre for Women's and Gender Studies, Akureyri, Iceland.

EIRO (2004), "Working Time – Developments in EU and National Regulation (29.04.2004)", European Commission, European Industrial Relations Observatory (EIRO), Dublin, *www.eiro.eurofound.eu.int/2004/03/feature/ tn0403108f.html*.

Eklind, B., T. Nilsson and I. Batljan (2003), "Efter skatt – om sanningen skall fram" (After Tax – The Truth of the Matter), Ds, Vol. 12, Fritzes public publications, Stockholm.

Engelhardt, H., T. Kögel, and A. Prskawetz (2001), "Fertility and Women's Employment Reconsidered: A Macro-level Time Series Analysis for Developed Countries, 1960-2000", MPIDR Working Paper WP 2001-021, Max Planck Institute for Demographic Research (MPIDR), Rostock.

EOC (2004), *Tip of the Iceberg: Interim Report of the EOC's Investigation into Discrimination Against New and Expectant Mothers in the Workplace*, Equal Opportunities Commission, London, *www.eoc.org.uk/cseng/policyandcampaigns/p_interimreport.pdf*.

Ermish J. and M. Francesconi (2001), *The Effects of Parents' Employment on Children Lives*, Joseph Rowntree Foundation, Family Policy Studies Center, York.

ESO (2002), "Den svenska sjukan – sjukfrånvaron i åtta länder" (The Swedish Disease – Absenteeism Due to Sickness in Eight Countries), Ds, Vol. 49, Fritzes public publications, Stockholm.

Evans, M., J. Eyre, J. Millar and S. Sarre (2003), "New Deal for Lone Parents: Second Synthesis Report of the National Evaluation", Department for Work and Pensions Working Age Research and Analysis Report, No. 163, HMSO, London.

Flexecutive with the Chartered Institute of Marketing and People Management (2002), "Work-Life Balance or Career Death: Issues and Paradoxes Facing Marketing and Human Resource Professionals", London.

Flood, L., J. Hansen, and R. Wahlberg (2004), "Household Labor Supply and Welfare Participation in Sweden", *The Journal of Human Resources*, University of Wisconsin Press, Madison, Vol. 39, No. 4, pp. 1008-1032.

Flood, L., E. Pylkkänen, and R. Wahlberg (2003), "From Welfare to Work: Evaluating a Proposed Tax and Benefit Reform Targeted at Single Mothers in Sweden", IZA Discussion Paper, No. 891, Forschungsinstitut zur Zukunft der Arbeit (Institute for the Study of Labour), Bonn.

Ford, R., D. Gyarmati, K. Foley, D. Tattrie and L. Jimenez (2003), *Can Work Incentives Pay for Themselves? Final Report on the Self-Sufficiency Project for Applicants*, Social Research and Demonstration Corporation, Ottawa.

Forssén, K., A-M. Laukkanen and V-M. Ritakalliofrom (2003), "Labour Supply: The Case of Finland", Report prepared for SPRU and NOVA project on Welfare Policy and Employment in the Context of Family Change, *www.york.ac.uk/inst/spru/research/nordic/finlandlabo.pdf*.

Förster, M. and M. Mira d'Ercole (2005), "Income Distribution and Poverty in OECD Countries in the Second Half of the 1990s", Social, Employment and Migration Working Paper, OECD, Paris.

Fortin, S. (2004), "Work/Life Balance Programs: A Key to Attracting, Satisfying and Keeping Employees", Watson/Wyatt, Bristol Myers Squibb Canada, Presentation at meeting of provincial and territorial labour market and social services Ministers, 22 August 2004, La Malbaie, Canada.

Francesconi, M. and W. van der Klaauw (2004), "The Consequences of "In-Work' Benefit Reform in Britain: New Evidence from Panel Data?", IZA Discussion Paper, No. 1248, Forschungsinstitut zur Zukunft der Arbeit (Institute for the Study of Labour), Bonn.

Friendly, M., J. Beach and M. Turiano (2003), *Early Childhood Education and Care in Canada 2001*, Childcare Resource and Research Unit, University of Toronto, Toronto.

GESIS (2004), *Codebook ZA Study 3880 ISSP 2002: Family and Gender Roles III*, Zentralarchiv für Empirische Sozialforschung (Central Archive for Empirical Social Research), German Social Science Infrastructure Services, *www.za.uni-koeln.de/data/en/issp/codebooks/s3880cdb.pdf*.

Gibbons, S. and A. Manning (2003), *The Incidence of UK Housing Benefit: Evidence from the 1990s Reforms*, Centre for Economic Performance, London School of Economics and Political Science, London.

Gornick, J. and M. Meyers (2003), *Families that Work: Policies for Reconciling Parenthood and Employment*, Russell Sage Foundation, New York.

Government of Canada (2003), *The National Child Benefit, Progress Report: 2002*, Her Majesty the Queen in Right of Canada, Ottawa.

Gray, H. (2002), "Family-Friendly Working: What a Performance! An Analysis of the Relationship between the Availability of Family-Friendly Policies and Establishment Performance", Centre for Economic Performance, Discussion Paper, No. 529, London School of Economics and Political Science, London.

Gregg, P. and L. Washbrook (2003), "The Effects of Early Maternal Employment on Child Development in the UK", CMPO Discussion paper, No. 03/70, Leverhulme Centre for Market and Public Organisation, University of Bristol.

Gregg, P., M. Gutiérrez-Domènech and J. Waldfogel (2003), "The Employment of Married Mothers in Great-Britain 1974-2000", Centre for Economic Performance, Working Paper, London School of Economics, December 2003, London.

Haataja, A. (2001), "Family Leave and Employment Rates in the EU, Transition of Working Mothers in and Out of Employment – the Case of Finland", Gender Group Working Paper, University of Aalborg, Aalborg.

Harkness, S. (1996), "The Gender Earnings Gap: Evidence from the UK", *Fiscal Studies*, Vol. 17, No. 2, Institute for Fiscal Studies, London, pp. 1-36.

Herrington, A. and E. Cattell (2004), "Childcare as a Barrier to Work: Evidence on Lone Parents in Britain", Department for Work and Pensions, London.

Hewitt, P. (2004), *Unfinished Business: The New Agenda for the Workplace*, Institute for Public Policy Research (IPPR), London.

Hiilamo, H. (2004), "Changing Family Policy in Sweden and Finland during the 1990s", *Social Policy and Administration*, Vol. 38, No. 1, pp. 21-40.

HM Treasury (2004), *Choice for Parents, The Best Start for Children: A Ten Year Strategy for Childcare*, Her Majesty's Treasury, London.

Hofferth, S. and S. Curtin (2003), "The Impact of Parental Leave on Maternal Return to Work after Childbirth in the United States", Social, Employment and Migration Working Paper, No. 7, OECD, Paris.

Howes, C., and E. W. Smith (1995), "Relations among Child Care Quality, Teacher Behaviour, Children's Play Activities, Emotional Security, and Cognitive Activity in Child Care", *Early Childhood Research Quarterly*, Vol. 10, No. 4, Elsevier Science, Amsterdam, pp. 381-404.

HRDC (2000), *Work and Family Provisions in Canadian Collective Agreements*, Labour Program, Human Resources Development Canada, Ottawa/Hull.

HSE (1999), *The Costs to Britain of Work Place Accidents and Work-Related Ill-Health in 1995/96*, Health and Safety Executive, Norwich.

Hudson, M., S. Lissenburgh and M. Sahin-Dikmen (2004), *Maternity and Paternity Rights in Britain 2002: Survey of Parents*, report for the Department for Work and Pensions and the Department of Trade and Industry, Policy Studies Institute, London.

ILO (2004), *Sources and Methods: Labour Statistics, Volume 3: Economically Active Population, Employment, Unemployment and Hours of Work*, International Labour Office, Geneva, http://laborsta.ilo.org.

Inland Revenue (2004), "Child and Working Tax Credit, Summary Statistics", London, *www.inlandrevenue.gov.uk/stats/personal-tax-credits/child-workingtc-july04.pdf*.

ISQ (2001), *Rapport d'enquête sur les besoins des familles en matière de services de garde éducatifs*, Institut de la Statistique, Québec.

ISQ (2004), *Les services de garde éducatifs: nouveaux besoins et préférences des familles, Enquête sur les besoins des familles en matière de services de garde éducatifs*, Institut de la Statistique, Québec.

Jansson, F., E. Pylkkänen and L. Valck (2003), *En jämställd föräldraförsäkring?* (An Equal Parental Insurance?), Statens Offentliga Utredningar series, Vol. 36, Stockholm.

Jaumotte, F. (2003), "Female Labour Force Participation: Past Trends and Main Determinants in OECD Countries", Economics Department Working Paper, No. 376, OECD, Paris.

Jenson, J. (2003), *Redesigning the welfare mix for families : Policy Challenges*, Discussion paper F 30, Canadian Policy Research Network, Ontario.

Jeon, S.-H. (2004), "The Impacts of the 1988 Tax Reform on Married Women's Labour Supply in Canada", Department of Economics Working Paper, Vol. 19, McMaster University, Hamilton, Ontario.

Johnson, A. (1995), "The Business Case for Work-Family Programs", *Journal of Accountancy*, Vol. 180, No. 2, The American Institute of Certified Public Accountants, New York, pp. 53-59.

Joshi, H. and P. Paci (1998), *Unequal Pay for Women and Men: Evidence from the British Birth Cohort Series*, Massachusetts Institute of Technology Press, Cambridge, MA.

Kamerman, S., M. Neuman, J. Waldfogel and J. Brooks-Gunn (2003), "Social Policies, Family Types and Child Outcomes in Selected OECD Countries", Social, Employment and Migration Working Paper, No. 6, OECD, Paris.

Kaplan, G., A. Goodman and I. Walker (2004), "Understanding the Effects of Early Motherhood in Britain: the Effects on Mothers", IZA Discussion Paper, No. 1131, Forschungsinstitute zur Zukunft der Arbeit (Institute for the Study of Labour), Bonn.

Karasek, R. (1979), "Job Demands, Job Decision Latitude and Mental Strain: Implications for Job Redesign", *Administrative Science Quarterly*, Vol. 24, No. 2, Johnson Graduate School of Management, Ithaca, pp. 285-308.

Kingsmill, D. (2001), *Review of Women's Employment and Pay*, prepared at the request of UK government ministers, *www.kingsmillreview.gov.uk/docs/Kingsmillreviewreport.pdf*.

Knight, G. and S. Lissenburgh (2004), "Evaluation of Lone Parent Work Focused Interviews: Final Findings from Administrative Data Analysis", Department for Work and Pensions Working Age Research and Analysis Report, No. 182, HMSO, London.

Kögel, T. (2002), "Did the Association between Fertility and Female Employment within OECD Countries Really Change its Sign?", Max Planck Institute for Demographic Research, Rostock.

Kurjenoja, J. (2004), *Veronmaksajien Keskusliitto, Kenelle työ kannattaa? Kannustinloukut 2004*, Verotietoa 39, Veronmaksajat, Helsinki.

Kuusisto, A. (2004), "Measures to Narrow Gender Wage Gap Evaluated", for European Industrial Relations Observatory (EIRO), *www.eiro.eurofound.eu.int/2004/09/feature/ fi0409203f.html*.

La Valle, I. *et al.* (2002), "The Influence of Atypical Working Hours on Family Life", *Findings*, No. 982, Joseph Rowntree Foundation, York.

Laferrière, C. (2003), "Les garderies à cinq dollars sont-elles une aubaine? Edition 2003", Université de Québec à Montréal, *www.er.uqam.ca/nobel/r14154/ Doc_PDF/Fge2003/garderie2003tx.PDF*.

Lefebvre, P. (2004), "Québec's Innovative Early Childhood Education and Care Policy and its Weaknesses", *Policy Options*, Vol. 25, No. 03, Institute for Research on Public Policy, Montreal, pp. 52-57.

Lefebvre, P. and P. Merrigan (2002), "The Effect of Childcare and Early Education Arrangements on Developmental Outcomes of Young Children", *Canadian Public Policy*, Vol. 28, No. 2, University of Toronto Press, Downsview, Ontario, pp. 159-186.

Lefebvre, P. and P. Merrigan (2003), "Assessing family Policy in Canada, A new deal for Families and Children", *Choices*, Vol. 9, No. 5, IRPP, June, *www.irpp.org*.

Lei, Y. and C. Michalopoulos (2001), *SSP Plus at 36 Months: Effects of Adding Employment Services to Financial Work Incentives*, Social Research and Demonstration Corporation, Ottawa.

Leighton, P. and R. Evans (2004), *Pregnant Women at Work: A Survey of Small Business Employers in Wales*, Equal Opportunities Commission, Cardiff.

Lessof, C., M. Miller, M. Phillips, K. Pickering, S. Purdon and J. Hales (2003), "New Deal for Lone Parents Evaluation: Findings from the Quantitative Survey", Department for Work and Pensions Working Age Research and Analysis Report, No. 147, HMSO, London.

Lilja, R. (2003), "Over a Third of Employees Would Like to Change Weekly Working Time", for EIRO, *www.eiro.eurofound.eu.int/2003/05/feature/fi0305202f.html*.

Lochhead, C. (2000), *Factors Associated with Time Stress among Mothers and Fathers in Two-parent Families*, DataQuest Consulting, Ottawa.

Lommerud, K.E. and S. Vagstad (2000), "Mommy Tracks and Public Policy: On Self-Fulfilling Prophecies and Gender Gaps in Promotion", Discussion Paper, No. 2378, Centre for Economic Policy Research, London.

Manning, A. and B. Petrongolo (2004), *The Part-Time Pay Penalty*, Department of Trade and Industry, London.

Marshall, K. (1998), "Couples Working Shift", *Perspectives on Labour and Income*, Catalogue No. 75-001 XPE, Statistics Canada, Ottawa, Autumn, pp. 9-14.

MESSF (2002), *Le Programme d'assistance-emploi et l'aide à l emploi*, Ministère de l'Emploi, de la Solidarité Sociale et de la Famille, Québec.

MESSF (2003), *Soutenir les familles:vers une conciliation famille-travail plus harmonieuse*, Ministère de l'Emploi, de la Solidarité Sociale et de la Famille, Québec.

MESSF (2004), *Scénarios de développement et de financement pour assurer la pérennité, l'accessibilité et la qualité des services de garde*, consultation 2003, Ministère de l'Emploi, de la Solidarité Sociale et de la Famille, Québec.

MESSF (2004a), *Concilier liberté et justice sociale : un défi pour l'avenir ; plan d'action gouvernemental en matière de lutte contre la pauvreté et l'exclusion sociale*, Ministère de l'Emploi, de la Solidarité Sociale et de la Famille, Québec.

MESSF (2004b), *La volonté d'agir, la force de réussir : Stratégie nationale de lutte contre la pauvreté et l'exclusion sociale*, Ministère de l'Emploi, de la Solidarité Sociale et de la Famille, Québec.

MESSF (2005), "Services à la famille, Consultation sur le financement et le développement des services de garde", Ministère de l'Emploi, de la Solidarité Sociale et de la Famille, Québec *www.messf.gouv.qc.ca/services-a-la-famille/ consultation-services-garde/document/services-garde.asp#2*.

MESSF (2005), "Entente Canada-Québec sur le régime québécois d'assurance parentale – Un gain pour les familles, un gain pour le Québec", Communiqués, Ministère de l'Emploi, de la Solidarité Sociale et de la Famille, Québec *www.communiques.gouv.qc.ca*.

Meyer, C.S., S. Mukerjee and A. Sestero (2001), "Work-Family Benefits: Which Ones Maximize Profits?", *Journal of Managerial Issues*, Pittsburgh State University, Vol. 13, No. 1, Pittsburgh, pp. 28-44.

Meyerson, E.M. and T. Petersen (1997), "Är kvinnor utsatta för lönediskriminering", *Ekonomisk Debatt*, No. 25, pp. 17-23.

Michalopoulos, C., D. Tattrie, C. Miller, P.K. Robbins, P. Morris, D. Gyarmati, C. Redcross, K. Foley, and R. Ford (2002), *Making Work Pay: Final Report on Long-Term Welfare Recipients in the Self-sufficiency Project*, Social Research and Demonstration Corporation, Ottawa.

Michalski, J. (1999), *Values and preferences for the "Best Policy Mix" for Canadian Children*, Canadian Policy Research Networks, Research Paper No. F05, Ottawa.

Millar, J. and K. Gardiner (2004), *Low Pay, Household Resources and Poverty*, Joseph Rowntree Foundation, York.

Milligan, K. (2002), "Québec's Baby Bonus, Can Public Policy Raise Fertility?", *Backgrounder*, 24 January 2002, C.D. Howe Institute, Toronto.

Milligan, K. and M. Stabile (2004), "The Integration of Child Tax Credits and Welfare: Evidence from the National Child Benefit Program", NBER Working Paper 10968, National Bureau of Economic Research, Cambridge, Massachusetts, United States, *www.nber.org/papers/w10968*.

Ministère du Travail, Québec (2003), *Rapport annuel de gestion de la Commission des normes du travail Année fiscale 2002-2003*, Québec.

Morris, P. and C. Michalopoulos (2000), *The Self-Sufficiency Project at 36 Months: Effects on Children of a Program that Increased Parental Employment and Income*, Social Research and Demonstration Corporations, Ottawa.

MSAH (2000), Early Childhood Education and Care Policy in Finland, Ministry of Social Affairs and Health, Vol. 21, Helsinki.

MSAH (2003), *Trends in Social Protection in Finland 2003*, Ministry of Social Affairs and Health, Helsinki.

Mumford K. and P. Smith (2004), "The Gender Earnings Gap in Britain," IZA Discussion Paper, No. 1109, Forschungsinstitut zur Zukunft der Arbeit (Institute for the Study of Labour), Bonn.

Myerson, E.M. and T. Petersen (1997), "Lika Lön för lika arbete", in I. Persson and E. Wedensjö (eds.), *Kvinnors och mäns löner – varför så olika?*, SOU, Vol. 136.

NAER (2004), *Descriptive Data on Childcare, Schools and Adult Education in Sweden 2003*, National Agency for Education Research, Stockholm.

NAO (2004), "Omnibus Survey of Parents of 0 to 4 Year Old Children", National Audit Office, London, *www.nao.org.uk/publications/nao_reports/034/268_omnibus_surveys.pdf*.

NAO (2004a), *Early Years: Progress in Developing High Quality Childcare and Early Education Accessible to All*, National Audit Office, London.

Nelson, A. K. Nemec, P. Solvik and C. Ramsden (The Tavistock Institute) (2004), *The Evaluation of the Work-Life Balance Challenge Fund*, Employment Relations Research Series, No. 32, Department of Trade and Industry, London.

Nielsen, H., M. Simonsen and M. Verner (2004), "Does the Gap in Family-Friendly Policies Drive the Family Gap?", *Scandinavian Journal of Economics*, Vol. 106, No. 4, Oxford, pp. 721-744.

Nyberg, A. (2000), "European Consolidated Report on Actual and Preferred Working Hours, Sweden", commissioned by European Foundation for the Improvement of Living and Working Conditions, *www.eurofound.eu.int/working/balance/worklife/options/sweden.rtf*.

O'Driscoll, M. et al. (2003), "Family-Responsive Interventions, Perceived Organizational and Supervisor Support, Work-Family Conflict and Psychological Strain", *International Journal of Stress Management*, Vol. 10, No. 4, Educational Publishing Foundation, New Zealand, pp. 326-344.

OECD (1999), *Early Childhood Education and Care Policy in Sweden*, Background report prepared for the OECD Thematic Review on Early Childhood Education and Care, OECD, Paris.

OECD (1999a), *The Battle Against Exclusion, Vol. 3, Social Assistance in Canada and Switzerland*, OECD, Paris.

OECD (2000), *Early Childhood Education and Care Policy in the United Kingdom: Country Note*, OECD, Paris.

OECD (2000a), *Early Childhood Education and Care Policy in Finland*, Background report prepared for the OECD Thematic Review on Early Childhood Education and Care, OECD, Paris.

OECD (2001), *Employment Outlook*, OECD, Paris.

OECD (2001a), *Starting Strong: Early Childhood Education and Care*, OECD, Paris.

OECD (2002), *Babies and Bosses: Reconciling Work and Family Life, Vol. 1, Australia, Denmark and the Netherlands*, OECD, Paris.

OECD (2002a), *Employment Outlook*, OECD, Paris.

OECD (2003), *Babies and Bosses, Reconciling Work and Family Life, Vol. 2, Austria, Ireland and Japan*, OECD, Paris.

OECD (2003a), *The Sources of Economic Growth in OECD Countries*, OECD, Paris.

OECD (2003b), *Trends in International Migration*, Paris.

OECD (2003c), *OECD Economic Survey: Iceland*, Paris.

OECD (2004), *Babies and Bosses: Reconciling Work and Family Life, Vol. 3, New Zealand, Portugal and Switzerland*, OECD, Paris.

OECD (2004a), *Economic Surveys: Finland*, OECD, Paris.

OECD (2004b), *Economic Surveys: Canada*, OECD, Paris.

OECD (2004c), *Economic Outlook*, No. 75, June, OECD, Paris.

OECD (2004d), *Economic Outlook*, No. 76, November, OECD, Paris.

OECD (2004e), *Economic Surveys: United Kingdom*, OECD, Paris.

OECD (2004f), *Learning for Tomorrow's World, First Results from PISA 2003*, OECD, Paris.

OECD (2004g), *Employment Outlook*, OECD, Paris.

OECD (2004h), *Labour Force Statistics*, OECD, Paris.

OECD (2004i), *OECD Social Expenditure Database, 1980-2001*, OECD, Paris, *www.oecd.org/ els/social policy/social expenditure*.

OECD (2004j), *OECD Revenue Statistics, 1965-2003*, OECD, Paris.

OECD (2004k), *Education at a Glance*, OECD, Paris.

OECD (2004l), *Economic Surveys, Sweden*, OECD, Paris.

OECD (2004m), *Early Childhood Education and Care Policy: Canada Country Note*, OECD, Paris.

OECD (2004n), *Benefits and Wages*, OECD, Paris.

OECD (2004o), *Main Economic Indicators*, OECD, Paris.

OECD (2005), *Extending Opportunities: How Active Social Policies Can Benefit Us All*, OECD, Paris.

OECD (2005a), *Society at a Glance – OECD Social Indicators*, OECD, Paris.

OECD (2005b), *Taxing Wages 2004-2005*, OECD, Paris.

Oreopoulos, P. (2003), "The Long-run Consequences of Living in a Poor Neighbourhood", *The Quarterly Journal of Economics*, Vol. 118, MIT Press, Cambridge, MA, pp. 1533-1575.

Palmer, T. (2004), *Results of the First Flexible Working Employee Survey*, Employment Relations Occasional Papers, Department of Trade and Industry, London.

Paull, G. and J. Taylor with A. Duncan (2002), *Mothers' Employment and Childcare Use in Britain*, Institute for Fiscal Studies, London.

Pearson M. and S. Scarpetta (2000), "An Overview: What do we Know about Policies to Make Work Pay?", *Economic Studies*, No. 31, 2000/2, pp. 12-23, OECD, Paris.

Phipps, S., P. Burton and L. Lethbridge (2001), "In and Out of the Labour Market: Long-Term Income Consequences of Child-Related Interruptions to Women's Paid Work", *Canadian Journal of Economics*, Vol. 34, No. 2, Canadian Economics Association, Montreal, pp. 411-429.

PricewaterhouseCoopers (2003), "Universal Childcare Provision in the UK – Towards a Cost-Benefit Analysis", discussion paper, *www.pwcglobal.com/uk/eng/ about/ind/ gov/PwC_UCC_Report-Aug_03.pdf*.

Pylkkänen, E. and N. Smith (2003), "Career Interruptions Due to Parental Leave-A Comparative Study of Denmark and Sweden", Social, Employment and Migration Working Paper, No. 1, OECD, Paris.

Queisser, M. and E. Whitehouse (2005), "The Effects of Partial Careers on Pension Entitlements", Social, Employment and Migration Working Paper, OECD, Paris, forthcoming.

Reynolds, T., C. Callender and R. Edwards (2003), "The Impact of Mothers' Employment on Family Relationships", Findings, No. 773, Joseph Rowntree Foundation, York.

RFV (2003), Social Insurance in Sweden 2003: Family Assets – Time and Money, Riksforsäkringsverket (The National Social Insurance Board), Stockholm.

RFV (2004), "Skilda världar, världar", en kartläggning av särlevande föräldrar, ombildade familjer och deras barn inom bidragssystemen, Riksforsäkringsverket (The National Social Insurance Board), Analyserar, Vol. 4, Elanders Gotab, Mölnlycke, Sweden..

Rochette, M. (2002), La conciliation travail-famillle dans les conventions collectives québécoise : secteurs public, de l'éducation, de la santé et des services sociaux, secteurs universitaires et municipal, Ministère de l'Emploi, de la Solidarité Sociale et de la Famille, Montréal.

Rochette M. and J. Deslauriers (2003), "Standard and Non-Standard Parental Work Schedules and Childcare Arrangements", Québec Longitudinal Study of Child Development (1998-2002), From Birth to 29 Months, Vol. 2, No. 10, Institut de la Statistique du Québec, Québec.

Roy, L. (2002), Les allocations à la naissance et leurs effets présumés, Ministère de la Famille et de l'Enfance, Québec.

Roy. F. (2004), "Social Assistance by Province, 1993 – 2003", Canadian Economic Observer, Vol. 17, No. 11, November, Statistics Canada, Ottawa.

Ruhm, C.J. (2004), "How Well do Parents with Young Children Combine Work and Family Life", NBER Working Paper, No. 10247, National Bureau of Economic Research, Cambridge, MA.

Salmi, M. (2000), "Analysing the Finnish Homecare Allowance System: Challenges to Research and Problems of Interpretation", in L. Kalliomaa-Puha (ed.), Perspectives of Equality – Work, Women and Family in the Nordic Countries and EU, Nord 2000, Vol. 5, Nordic Council of Ministers, Copenhagen 2000, pp. 187-207.

Salmi, M., J. Lammi-Taskula and A. Karttunen (2000), "Actual and Preferred Working Hours, National Report, Finland", commissioned by European Foundation for the Improvement of Living and Working Conditions, www.eurofound.eu.int/working/balance/worklife/options/finland.doc.

Sceviour, R. and R. Finnie (2004), "Social Assistance Use: Trends in Incidence, Entry and Exit Rates", Canadian Economic Observer, August, Statistics Canada, Ottawa.

SDC (2005), "Governments of Canada and Quebec sign Final Agreement on Quebec's Parental Insurance Plan", news release, Social Development Canada, Ottawa, 1 March (www.hrsdc.gc.ca)

Shannon, M. and M. Kidd (2001), "Projecting the Trend in the Canadian Gender Wage Gap 2001-2031: Will an Increase in Female Education Acquisition and Commitment be Enough?", Canadian Public Policy, Vol. 27, No. 4, University of Toronto Press, Downsview, Ontario, pp. 447-467.

Sigle-Rushton, W. and J. Waldfogel (2004), "Motherhood and Women's Earnings in Anglo-American, Continental European and Nordic Countries", paper presented for the Conference on Cross-national Comparisons of Expenditures on Children, Princeton University, 7-9 January, Princeton.

Sleebos, J. (2003), "Low Fertility Rates in OECD Countries: Facts and Policy Responses", Social, Employment and Migration Working Paper, No. 15, OECD, Paris.

Smith, A. (2004), "Who Cares? Fathers and the Time They Spend Looking After Children", Department of Sociology Working Paper, No. 2004-05, Nuffield College University of Oxford, www.sociology.ox. ac.uk/swps/2004-05.pdf.

SOM Recherche et Sondages (2003), "Sondage sur la conciliation entre la famille et le travail", www.mfe.gouv.qc.ca/Publications/sendFile.asp?fn=/publications/pdf/sondage_SOM_conciliation_famille_travail.pdf.

SOU (2004), Vem tjänar på att arbeta?, Bilaga 14 till LU 2003/04, Statens Offentliga Utredningar (SOU), SOU Government Studies, Stockholm.

Sparks, K., B. Faragher and C. Cooper (2001), "Well-Being and Occupational Health in the 21st Century Workplace", Journal of Occupational and Organizational Psychology, Vol. 74, The British Psychological Society, pp. 489-509.

Spence, M. (1973), "Job Market Signalling", The Quarterly Journal of Economics, Vol. 87, No. 3, MIT Press, Cambridge, MA, pp. 355-374.

Statistics Canada (1996), Vital Statistics Compendium, Ottawa.

Statistics Canada (2004), Annual Demographic Statistics 2003, Catalogue No. 91-213-XPB, Ottawa.

Statistics Canada (2004a), "Employment Insurance Coverage Survey 2002", The Daily, 14 January, Ottawa.

Statistics Sweden (2003), Tid for vardagsliv (Time for everyday life: Women and Men's Time Use 1990/91 and 2000/01), No. 99, Örebro, Sweden.

Statistics Sweden (2004), Statistical Yearbook of Sweden, Stockholm.

Stevens, J., J. Brown and C. Lee (2004), The Second Work-Life Balance Study: Results from the Employees' Survey, Department of Trade and Industry, Employment Relations Research Report, No. 27, London.

STM (2003), "Developing Sectoral Strategies to Address Gender Pay Gaps," Publications 2003:1, Ministry of Social Affairs and Health, Helsinki.

Sutherland, H., T. Sefton and D. Piachaud (2003), Poverty in Britain: The impact of government policy since 1997, Joseph Rowntree Foundation, York.

Sylva, K., E. Melhuish, P. Sammons, I. Sirja-Blatchford and B. Taggart (2004), "The Effective Provision of Pre-School Education Project: Final Report Results", DfES, www.ioe.ac.uk/projects/eppe, November, London.

Thomas, A. and R. Griffiths (2004), "Integrated Findings from the Evaluation of the First 18 Months of Lone Parent Work Focused Interviews", Department for Work and Pensions Working Age Research and Analysis Report, No. 184, HMSO, London.

Tougas, J. (2002), "Reforming Quebec's Early Childhood Care and Education : the First Five Years", Centre for Urban and Community Studies Occasional Paper, No. 17, University of Toronto, Toronto.

Tremblay, S. (2003), Enquête Grandir en qualité. Cadre de référence de l'évaluation de la qualité des services de garde éducatifs au moyen de l'enquête, Direction de la recherche, de l'évaluation et de la statistique, Ministère de la Famille et de l'Enfance, Québec.

TUC (2003), Working Time Directive Review 2003: The Use and Abuse of the "Opt-out" in the UK, Trades Union Congress, London.

Turner, D., L. Boone, C. Giorno, M. Meacci, D. Rae and P. Richardson (2002), "Estimating the Structural Rate of Unemployment for the OECD Countries", *Economic Studies*, No. 33, 2001/II, OECD, Paris, pp. 171-216.

United Nations (2003), *World Population Prospects: The 2002 Revisions*, New York *www.un.org/esa/population/unpop.htm*.

Vartiainen, J. (2001), "The Measurement and Statistics of the Gender Wage Differential", Office of the Ombudsman for Equality, December, Ministry of Social Affairs and Health, Helsinki.

Vartiainen, J. (2003), "Gender Wage Differentials in the Finnish Labour Market", Palkansaajien Tutkimuslaitos (Labour Institute for Economic Research) Discussion Paper, No. 1791, Helsinki.

Viitanen, T. (2004), "The Impact of Children on Female Earnings in Britain", German Institute for Economic Research Discussion Paper, No. 415, Berlin.

Walby, S. and W. Olsen (2002), *The Impact of Women's Position in the Labour Market on Pay and Implications for UK Productivity*, Report to the Women and Equality Unit, Department of Trade and Industry, London.

Womack, S. (2004), "Inquiry to Help Parents who Want to Work Flexible Hours,"*Telegraph*, 16 July 2004, London.

Woodland, S., M. Miller and S. Tipping (2002), "Repeat Study of Parents' Demand for Childcare", Department for Education and Skills Research Report, No. RR348, London.

Woodland, S., N. Simmonds, M. Thornby, R. Fitzgerald and A. McGee (2003), *The Second Work-Life Balance Study: Results from the Employers' Survey*, National Centre for Social Research, Department of Trade and Industry, Employment Relations Research Report, No. 22, London.

World Values Survey Association (2004), *World Values Survey*, Stockholm.

Worrall, L. and C. Cooper (1999), "Working Patterns and Working Hours: Their Impact on UK Managers", *Leadership and Organization Development Journal*, Vol. 20, No. 1, MCB University Press, Bradford, United Kingdom, pp. 6-10.

Wortsman, A. and C. Lochhead (2002), *Full-Time Equivalents and Financial Costs Associated with Absenteeism, Overtime and Involuntary Part-time Employment in the Nursing Profession*, Canadian Labour and Business Centre (CLBC), report commissioned for the Nursing Advisory Committee, Ottawa.

Zuzanek, J. (2001), "Parenting Time: Enough or too Little?", ISUMA *Canadian Journal of Policy Research*, Université de Montréal, pp. 125-133, Montréal.

Background Annex to the Review

This annex gives a more detailed description of the main family benefit programmes and child-related leave schemes in the four countries under review.

A1. Average earnings, exchange rates and purchasing power parities

Throughout, "average earnings" refer to the annual earnings of an average production worker. This concept refers to the average gross wage earnings of adult, full-time workers in the manufacturing sector in each country. In 2004, these amounted to CAD 41 574 (USD 29 696) in Canada, EUR 29 779 (USD 33 649) in Finland, SEK 254 544 (USD 31 511) in Sweden and GBP 21 359 (USD 35 015) in the United Kingdom (Table A.1).

Table A.1. **Average earnings and GDP per capita**[a]

	Canada	Finland	Sweden	United Kingdom
Average earnings in national currency	41 574	29 779	254 544	21 359
Exchange rate (towards 1 USD)	1.400	0.885	8.078	0.610
Purchasing power parities (USD = 1.00)	1.210	0.994	9.670	0.643
Average earnings (USD)	29 696	33 649	31 511	35 015
Average earnings (USD adjusted for PPP)	34 359	29 959	26 323	33 218
GDP per capita (USD PPP)	31 400	27 500	28 200	29 100
APW earnings relative to GDP per capita (%)[b]	109%	109%	93%	114%

a) Data as used in this review, most recent year available.
b) Average earnings as a proportion of GDP per capita, both in USD PPP.

Source: OECD, Main Economic Indicators; OECD (2005), Taxing Wages 2004 2005, OECD, Paris.

The exchange rate used is the average of the daily rates in 2003, with 1 USD equivalent to CAD 1.400, EUR 0.885, SEK 8.078 and GBP 0.610 (OECD, 2004o). Purchasing power parities (PPP) account for the difference in price levels between countries: in this context 1 USD is equal to CAD 1.210, EUR 0.993, SEK 9.670 and GBP 0.637 (OECD, 2004o).

A2. Characteristics of family cash benefits

Canada

Canada provides support to families with children through the tax system and the province of Québec has tax/benefit programs that provide additional support to families with children (Table A.2) Furthermore, the province of Québec pays a family allowance ("allocation familiale") based on a family's income for residents in Québec with children under age 18. The benefit increases with additional children and provides a supplement to sole families. To further support low-income workers with children in Québec, the parental wage assistance program ("l'aide aux parents pour leurs revenus de travail" or APPORT) provides monthly assistance and childcare assistance for each child attending a low-cost day care centre (annual family income less than CAD 15 000 for sole parents and CAD 22 000 for couples. A new child assistance programme replaced the family allowance and APPORT was replaced with a new refundable tax credit for child assistance on 1 January 2005 (Box 5.1).[1]

In the 2004-05 budget, the province of Québec announced a CAD 2.5 billion five-year plan to reduce poverty among low-income families (Table A.3). The measures include, for example, increasing employment assistance with work-based incentives, creating a new child allowance for low-income families, building new 16 000 new units of social housing and increasing the minimum wage by 4% by May 2005.

Finland

The family allowance is a tax-free benefit for all families residing in Finland with a child below age 17. The monthly allowance is paid with an increasing rate for additional children, while a monthly supplement for sole parents is also available. In 2004, the benefits were EUR 100 for the first child, EUR 111 for the second, EUR 131 for the third, EUR 152 for the fourth and EUR 172 for the fifth and subsequent children. These amounts are increased by EUR 37 per child for sole parents. Sole parents are guaranteed a maintenance payment of EUR 118 per child in case the absent parent defaults on his/her obligations.

Sweden

All families with dependent children in Sweden are eligible to receive child allowances. The flat-rate basic benefit increases when there are at least three children in the family. In 2004, the monthly benefit was SEK 950 per child and the monthly supplement for families was SEK 254 for the 3rd child,

Table A.2. **Main family support programmes delivered through the tax system in Canada, the province of Québec and the United Kingdom, 2004**

Programme name	Target group	Features
Canada (federal)		
Canada Child Tax Benefit (CCTB)	Low and middle income families with dependent children under age 18.	Maximum annual amount for basic benefit: CAD 1 208 per child. Reduced at a 2% rate on income for income exceeding CAD 35 000 when there is one child per family and at a 4% rate for families with two or more children. A *CCTB supplement* (flat rate CAD 239), which is granted for children less than 7 years old, can be reduced by 25% (see CCED below) and a *large family supplement* (flat rate of CAD 84) is paid to families with three or more children.
National Child Benefit (NCB) Supplement	Low and middle income families with dependent children under age 18.	Annual benefit: CAD 1 511 for the first child, CAD 1 295 for the second child and CAD 1 215 for each additional child. Allowance reduced at a rate of 12.2% (1 child), 22.7% (two children) and 32.5% (additional children) for family net income exceeding CAD 22 615.
Child Care Expense Deduction (CCED)	Working families with dependent children under age 16. Parents can also be self-employed or students.	Deduction of childcare expenses from federal taxation. Yearly maximum deduction: CAD 7 000 for a child ages 0-6; CAD 4 000 for a child ages 7-16; CAD 10 000 for a mentally or physically disabled child of any age. Claiming CCED reduces the CCTB supplement for children under 7 by 25% of childcare cost claimed.
Province of Québec		
Child Care Expense Tax Credit	Working families with dependent children under age 17 using non subsidised day care centres.	The refundable credit covers 75% to 26% of child care expenses (excluding subsidised fees) based on family income. Maximum annual expense claimed is CAD 7 000 per child less than 7 years old (equivalent to about CAD 26 per day of care) and CAD 4 000 per child ages 7 to 16.
Non-refundable Tax Credit	Families with dependent children.	Tax credit value: CAD 553 for the first child plus CAD 510 for each additional child. Additional credit for sole parents, CAD 276.
Tax Reduction for Families	Low and middle income families with dependent children.	Income-tested non-refundable tax reduction: maximum value is CAD 1 195 for one-parent family and CAD 1 500 for two-parent family. Reduced by 3% of taxable income exceeding CAD 27 635. The base reduction is phased out at CAD 66 929 for sole parents and CAD 77 095 for couple families.
United Kingdom		
Child Tax Credit (CTC)	Low and middle income families with dependent children under 16, or aged 16 to 18 and in full-time non-advanced education.	CTC has four components: *family element* (GBP 545 per year); *baby element (GBP 545 per year)* for a child under age 1; *child element* (GBP 1 445 per child); and *disabled child element* (GBP 2 155 per year). CTC is paid in full to families with an annual joint income of less than GBP 50 000; above this, the credit is reduced and discontinued at GBP 58 000 (GBP 66 000 for families with a child under age 1).
Working Tax Credit (WTC)	All low-income working families with one adult employed or self-employed for at least 16 hours per week. Household-based credit.	Basic element: GBP 1 525 per year. Additional GBP 1 500 for couples and sole parents and GBP 620 for working at least 30 hours per week (total, if couple). Full credit granted for income up to GBP 5 060 and reduced at a marginal rate of 37% for additional income thereafter. Childcare credit: For parents with at least 16 hours of work, credit for 70% of weekly parental fees for registered childcare up to a maximum cost of GBP 135 for 1 child and GBP 200 for 2 or more children. Can be claimed during first 26 weeks of maternity or adoption leave and 2 weeks of paternity leave if the job on which leave is based meets the 16-hours condition. Full credit granted for income up to GBP 50 000 and reduced by GBP 1 for every GBP 15 thereafter.

Source: National authorities.

Table A.3. **Investments by the government of the province of Québec in the fight against poverty and social exclusion as announced in the 2004-05 budget**

Over the next five years, in millions of CAD

	2004-2005	2005-2006	2006-2007	2007-2008	2008-2009	Five-year total
Increase the income of low-income individuals and families						
Indexing of social assistance benefits:						
Significant employment limitations: full indexing	4	21	45	71	99	240
No severely limited capacity for employment						
– Indexing	3	14	28	43	58	146
– Participation premium	2	6	21	43	58	129
Subtotal	9	41	94	157	215	515
Work premium[a]	10	68	144	144	144	510
Child assistance[a]	112	359	201	201	201	1 074
Subtotal	131	468	439	502	560	2 099
Investment in social housing						
Build 16 000 low-cost, affordable housing units	75	91	91			256
Adapt the dwellings of 6 010 people with disabilities	13	14	13			39
Grant rent supplements to 5 276 households to ease the effects of the housing shortage	17	7	4	6		34
Subtotal	104	112	107	6		329
Other significant measures for employment assistance recipients						
Offer all families a partial exemption on child support income under the Employment – Assistance Program	0	4	14	14	14	46
Establish a low-income cutoff for welfare	0	10	10	10	10	38
Encourage savings by low-income households	0	2	7	7	7	23
Invest in the Réseau québécois du crédit communautaire	1	1	1	1	1	5
Subtotal	1	17	32	32	32	112
Total	236	596	577	540	592	2 540

Note: Amounts have been rounded.
a) Includes only the portion intended for low-income households according to the low-income measure (before taxes).
Source: Ministry of Finance in the province of Québec.

SEK 760 for the 4th and SEK 950 for the 5th and subsequent child. The insurance schemes for families with children are income-related parental and temporary parental cash benefits, child pension, pregnancy cash benefits and pension rights for childcare years (Table A.6).

United Kingdom

The United Kingdom has pursued multiple policies since the late 1990s to assist working families (Table A.4). Most recently, in April 2003, the United Kingdom introduced two new tax credits: Child Tax Credit (CTC) and Working Tax Credit (WTC) which are income-tested and based on family circumstances (Table A.2). They both are refundable credits, meaning that the entitlement is payable if it exceeds a family's tax liabilities. CTC and WTC replace various tax reliefs, payments and child-related elements which were incorporated in other income support measures (e.g. Working Families' Tax Credit, Disabled Person's Tax Credit, Children's Tax Credit, Income Support, Job Seeker's

Table A.4. **"Making Work Pay" in the United Kingdom**

Public policy measures developed since the late 1990s to target low-paid individual workers or working families

		Measure	Target
1998-2000		Earnings top up (means-tested in-work benefit) piloted	Household
1998	April-June	Subsidised jobs for young under New Deal for Young People; subsidised jobs for adult long-term unemployed under New Deal 25+	Individual
	1998 (budget)	Maximum childcare costs disregard in family credit increased	Household
	June	National minimum wage becomes law: GBP 3 per hour for 18 to 21 year olds, GBP 3.60 per hour for adults	Individual
1999	April	Introduction of 10% lower income tax rate, replacing 20% lower band	Individual
		Abolition of National Insurance 'entry fee' for employees	Individual
		Working Families Tax Credit (with child support disregarded) and Childcare Tax Credit	Household
	October	Disabled persons tax credit	Household
		Increases in child benefit	Household
2000	April	Increases in Working Families Tax Credit rates for children under age 16	Household
	June	National minimum wage raised from GBP 3 per hour to GBP 3.20 for 18 to 21 year olds	Individual
	October	National minimum wage increased from GBP 3.60 per hour to GBP 3.70 for adults	Individual
		Campaign to encourage take-up of Working Families Tax Credit	Household
2001	April	Introduction of 'primary threshold' (at tax threshold level) for employees with National Insurance contributions above lower earnings limit	Individual
	2001 (budget)	Increase in 10% income tax band	Individual
	June	Higher Working Families Tax Credit and Childcare Tax Credit	Household
	October	Adult hourly minimum wage increased 10.8% to GBP 4.10 from GBP 3.70 and equivalent youth rate rises from GBP 3.20 to GBP 3.50	Individual
2002	April	Independent Living Funds payment rules allow severely disabled people with job to keep more of their pay	Individual
	June	Increases in basic credits in tax credits	Household
	October	Adult minimum hourly wage increased to GBP 4.20 and youth rate to GBP 3.60	Individual
2003	April	Working Tax Credit: based on 2001/02 income levels initially, but current working circumstances	Household
		Childcare element of Working Tax Credit	Household
	October	Adult minimum hourly wage increased to GBP 4.50 and youth rate to GBP 3.80	Individual

Source: Bennett, F. and J. Millar (2005), "Making Work Pay", *Benefits*, Vol. 13, No. 1, Colchester, United Kingdom, pp. 28-33.

Allowance). About 90% of British families receive the CTC family element. The WTC provides in-work support for low-paid working adults as well as a childcare credit for working parents (Chapter 4). In addition, all families can receive a child benefit of GBP 16.50 a week for the first child (GBP 17.55 for sole parents) and GBP 11.05 per week for subsequent children.

A3. Characteristics of child-related leave programmes (as per mid-2004)

Canada

While the job-protected leave duration is determined by provincial employment legislation, eligibility for and duration of leave payments are governed by the Federal Employment Insurance (EI) Act:

- *Maternity leave payments* of up to 15 weeks for the mother, beginning up to eight weeks before the expected birth or during the week the mother gives birth. Unused payments expire within 17 weeks of the actual or expected week of birth, whichever is later.

- *Parental leave payments* can be claimed by one parent or shared, but cannot exceed a combined maximum of 35 weeks. The payment rate is the same as for the maternity benefit. Parents may choose to take leave periods simultaneously. If both parents are sharing parental leave payments, only one parent will have to serve the two-week waiting period. Leave must be taken within the first 52 weeks after birth.

- *Sickness leave payments* of up to 15 weeks extend the total combined leave period to a maximum of 50 weeks. In addition, some mothers who need sickness leave before or after the child's birth can be eligible for a combined 65 weeks of combined maternity, parental and sickness benefits instead. Eligibility conditions for the benefit extension are threefold: 1) parents have not received regular unemployment or fishing benefits; 2) parents have already received less than 15 weeks of sickness payments, less than 35 weeks of parental payments and all maternity payments; 3) the additional 15 weeks are composed of unused parental leave payments only. That is, if a parent qualifying for the full sickness leave has already benefited from the entire maternity leave, 15 weeks of sick leave and 25 weeks of parental leave, the remaining 10 weeks of parental leave are the basis for the leave extension.

- *Job protected leave* depends on the type of employment. For federal employees, job protection is extended for a maximum 52 weeks in combined maternity, parental and sickness leave. Federal jurisdiction allows job protection for 17 weeks during maternity leave and 37 weeks during parental leave (the waiting period accounts for the discrepancy between the length of job-protected leave for federal employees and of EI receipt). In the province of Québec, mothers are eligible for 18 weeks of maternity leave and parents can share 52 weeks of parental leave.

An individual needs to work 600 contributable hours in the year preceding the leave period or since the last claim to be eligible for all EI payments (including the special EI payment categories, such as parental leave). Self-employed workers, student interns and occasional workers are not eligible for benefits under the federal provision. Eligibility for job protection during child-related leave is based on one day of work (prior to taking leave) in the province of Québec and six months of continuous service for federal employees.

The basic EI benefit rate for eligible recipients is 55% of average insured earnings with a maximum of CAD 413 per week. Low-income parents with a net annual income below CAD 25 921 are entitled to a family supplement if the household is already in receipt of the Canada Child Tax Benefit. For families earning less than CAD 55 000 (gross annual household income), the Québec Maternity Allowance Program (Programme d'allocation de maternité du Québec or PRALMA) fills the two-week gap between the duration of job-protected leave and EI payments. In 2004, the PRALMA lump sum allowance was CAD 360.

Since 1956, Canadian employers can top up EI payments using Supplementary Unemployment Benefits (SUB), a non-insurable supplement to employee's revenues. Until 1993, employers had to submit a plan to the government for topping up EI for the purposes of maternity, paternity or compassionate care benefits. The plan verified that employers were not considering top-up payments as EI-related earnings or deductible from EI benefits because SUB payments are exempt from withholdings for EI premiums and pension payments.

In 2006, the Québec maternity and parental insurance arrangements will come into force that are likely to be different from the existing EI-benefit rules on payment rates, time periods and coverage (MESSF, 2005a).

Finland

Finland has four primary leave policies, some of which can be taken part-time.

- *Maternity leave* of up to 105 weekdays[2] (17.5 weeks), starting 30 to 50 weekdays (5 to 8 weeks) before expected birth and can be used until 55 to 75 weekdays (9 to 12.5 weeks) after birth. Mothers qualify for the maternity allowance from the 154th day of pregnancy and must have been insured by National Health Insurance for at least 180 days preceding the birth date.

- *Paternity leave* of up to 18 weekdays (3 weeks) can be taken in up to four segments during the maternity or mother's parental allowance period. The paternity leave can be extended by 12 weekdays if the father takes the last

12 weekdays of the parental leave. The bonus must be taken in a single period immediately following the parental leave and when the mother is not receiving any family-related allowance. Eligibility for paternity or parental allowance is based on residency in Finland for at least 180 days before the due date and cohabitation with the child's mother.

- *Parental leave* of up to 158 weekdays (26 weeks), extended by 10 weeks for each additional child in the case of multiple births. Full-time parental allowance is paid alternatively to the mother or father for 158 weekdays and has the same value as maternal allowance. Parents can share the full-time leave if each parent takes a maximum of two block periods (lasting at least 12 weekdays apiece). Partial parental leave is of the same duration but allows parents to work part-time in alternation for a minimum stretch of two months. Its payment rate is half that of the full allowance.

- *Child home care leave* until the child is 3 years old. Employees are on job-protected leave during this time, but employers are not required to compensate employees. Each parent can take two periods of leave of at least one-month duration. Although home care leave cannot be taken by both parents simultaneously, it can be combined when another parent is on maternity or parental leave. Parents can also use partial home care leave based on mutual agreement with the employer for either part-time work (up to 30 hours per week) until the child is 3 years old and during the child's first two years in school.

Allowances for maternity, paternity and parental leave are based on the previous year's income for working parents. In 2004, earnings less than EUR 26 720 receive payments at about 70% of gross salary; an additional 40% is added for earners between EUR 26 720 and EUR 41 110 and a further 25% of salary for higher earners. Minimum leave for non-working parents is EUR 11.45 per day.

The child home care allowance (HCA) compensates parents who do not place their children in municipal childcare centres, even if the parents are not eligible for home care *leave*. The child can be looked after by either of the parents or some other relative or by a private childcare provider. HCA payments, which are taxable income, can be received immediately following the end of parental allowances until the youngest child in the household reaches the age of three or transfers to municipal day care. In 2004, the basic allowance is EUR 252 per month, equivalent to 9% of average earnings. For additional child cared for at home, parents receive a supplement of EUR 84 when the child is under age 3 or EUR 50 when under school age (less than 7 years old). There is also an income-tested supplement, which is capped at EUR 168 (and ceases when the monthly family income exceeds EUR 3 829 for two-adult families or EUR 3 219 for sole parent families with two children). The partial home care allowance is worth EUR 70 per month. Many municipalities also grant a special municipal supplement: Helsinki's supplement, for example, is EUR 219. All municipal supplements in 2001 totalled EUR 41 million.

Sweden

All parents are entitled to take full leave with a job guarantee until their child is 18 months old, irrespective of receiving a leave payment during that time. After that, parents must come to an agreement with their employer as to how to take the remaining leave period. Parental leave and the right to shortening working hours are conditional upon the parent having worked six months prior to the birth or a combined period of at least 12 months during the two years preceding the birth.

- *Maternity leave* of seven continuous weeks both prior and following birth. This entitlement is guaranteed to all working women regardless of their employment history.
- *Parental leave* of no more than 480 days (16 months) for the birth of a child. All days are transferable between parents except for pappa månad (daddy month) and mamma månad (mommy month), which are each 60 days long. Sole parents receive all 480 days. The parental leave benefit can be used from before birth (in the case of the mother) until the child is 8 years old and can be taken as a five-, six- or seven-day – week. The leave can also be taken for different portions of the day, that is as a whole, three-quarter, half, quarter or eighth of a day.
- *Temporary parental leave* of up to 10 days for fathers during the first 60 days of the child's return to the house. This leave is paid at the same rate as the highest parental benefit (see below).

Expecting mothers can receive a special pregnancy benefit (at 80% of qualifying income) if she is unfit to work or a sickness or parental benefit. Parents who are eligible for the income-based parental benefit must have been insured for sickness benefits for at least 240 consecutive days prior to the birth or expected birth of the child. In 2004, during the first 390 days of the parental leave, eligible parents receive the highest allowance level which is equal to 80% of their salary, subject to a maximum of 7.5 base amounts (SEK 294 750). All other parents receive the basic benefit level, which is SEK 180 per day. The benefit for the remaining 90 leave days is the same for all parents, at SEK 60 per day. Parents can receive this benefit only after having taken 180 days at the highest compensation rate.

United Kingdom

Child-related leaves in the United Kingdom are primarily awarded to the mother.

- *Pregnant workers* are entitled to paid time off for antenatal care, which includes doctor visits and relaxation classes.

- *Ordinary maternity leave* of up to 26 weeks. All employed or self-employed mothers are entitled to this job-protected leave period, which can be taken no earlier than 11 weeks before birth or at birth.

- *Additional maternity leave* of 26 weeks. Eligibility for this additional unpaid job-protected leave is based on 26 weeks of continuous service with the mother's employer completed 14 weeks before the expected week of birth.

- *Paternity leave* of up to two weeks to be taken within 56 weeks after birth. Eligible fathers must have worked for 26 weeks with the same employer as of 14 weeks before the expected week of birth. Fathers must sign a declaration of family commitment and also continue to work for the same employer until the childbirth.

Eligibility for maternity and paternity benefits is based on levels of National Insurance contributions as well as length of service with current employer. To receive statutory maternity pay (SMP) or statutory paternity pay (SPP), parents must be employed by their employer for a continuous period of at least 26 weeks ending with the 15th week before the expected week of childbirth. Average earnings must be at least equal to the lower earnings limit for National Insurance contributions. In addition, if mothers are not eligible for SMP but satisfy National Insurance contribution conditions (must be been employed or self-employed for 26 weeks out of the 66 weeks before the expected week of childbirth and have average weekly earnings of at least GBP 30), then they are eligible to receive Maternity Allowance, which is the smaller of 90% of earnings or GBP 102.80 per week.

Employers are reimbursed either 92% of the SMP or SPP they have paid out or, in the case of small employers, 104.5% (100% plus additional costs). Small employers are defined those with a total National Insurance liability in the previous tax year of no more than GBP 40 000.

Notice for leave periods

Employees are bound to provide their employer with reasonable notice of the duration of the leave from work. This enables employers to manage and prepare for the temporary absence. Yet, requirements to provide notice to the employer regarding the beginning and end dates of a child-related leave differ among the countries in this review (Table A.5).

Pension credit for child care

Career interruptions for child care is a concern for working parents when retirement-income entitlements are based on earnings-related contributions. In these types of national pension systems, most provide some credit to compensate specifically for a temporary absence due to child care (Table A.6). The credit effectively takes into account the time spent outside the labour market

Table A.5. **Employee-employer notice provisions for child-related leaves**
Legal notice provisions in Canada, Finland, Sweden and the United Kingdom, 2004

	Notice to start leave	Notice to return to work	Type of employment position upon return from leave[a]
Canada[b]			
Maternity leave	Four weeks written notice before start and should include estimated date of return to work	Requires four weeks notice before return only if change of date requested	Same or similar
Parental leave	If taken directly after maternity leave, provide 4 weeks written notice before the end of the maternity leave; if taken separately, provide four weeks before leave begins	Requires four weeks notice before return only if change of date requested	Same or similar
Sickness leave	No notice required, but medical certificate indicating pre- and post-birth illness and length of inability to work is mandatory	Requires two weeks notice if there is a change in the length of inability to work	same or similar
Finland			
Maternity and paternity leaves	Two months notice before intention to leave; changes with one month's notice, although starting date may begin earlier without advance notice	Two months notice if change of date requested	Same or similar
Full time and partial parental leave; fulltime home care leave	Two months notice, although can be reduced to 1 month notice and with a valid reason	Two months notice if change of date requested	Same or similar
Partial child care leave	Two months notice, changeable by mutual agreement; or, if employer and employee have agreed to the right to interruption for a valid reason with one month advance notice	Two months notice if change of date requested	Same or similar
Sweden			
Parental leave	Two months notice prior to beginning of leave, indicating expected duration of leave; if unpractical, as quickly as possible	Return date already provided with notice to start leave. If early return is more than 1 month in advance, employer can postpone resumption by no more than one month.	Same or similar
United Kingdom			
Maternity leave	By the end of the 15th week before the expected due date; date can be changed at least 28 days in advance[c]	For full leave, none (employer responsibility); for early return to work, provide 28 days notice of new date of return	Same for ordinary maternity leave; same or similar for additional maternity leave
Paternity leave	Provide notice by the end of the 15th week before the partner's expected due date; date can be changed at least 28 days in advance	Return date already provided with notice to start in which father must state length of leave expected	Same
Parental leave	Provide notice at least 21 days start date and include expected start and finish dates	Provide notice at least 21 days start date and include expected start and finish dates	If less than 4 weeks, same; for more than 4 weeks, same or similar.

a) Leaves are associated with a guaranteed protection of the type of position (with the same employer) to which an employee returns following family leave. Although legal standards and definitions of protection vary across the countries, generally, employees are entitled to return to their same former duties at work or, if such work is no longer available, employees should be offered work of a similar kind.

b) The amount of notice described for Canada refers to the Canada Labour Code, which covers federal employees. Notice period in provinces depend on provincial regulation.

c) Claim to maternity-related benefits: to qualify for Standard Maternity Pay (SMP), women must state to their employer at least 28 days in advance the date on which they want SMP to start and provide medical evidence of pregnancy. Women who fail to give the required notifications within the specified time limits may lose their rights to SMP.

Source: National authorities.

Table A.6. **Pension credits for childcare**

	Characteristics of credit
Canada	Years spent caring for children under age 7 are excluded from the averaging period in pension calculation.
Province of Québec	Employer (and, in some cases, employees) required to continue contributions, allowing regular accrual to Québec Pension Plan. Months during which the family receives or is eligible for a Québec family allowance or a Canada Child Tax Benefit for a child under the age of 7 are excluded from the contributory period and deducted from the averaging period for retirement income calculation.
Finland	Employment pension: years of parental leave with no or low pay are left out of the calculation of the average wage for pensions, but counted as working time. Non-salaried maternity leave up to a year is considered as employment; caring work under a contractual agreement is credited according to income (about EUR 230 per month); from 2005 onwards, pension accrual during parental leave is considered fictitious income of EUR 500 per month (for a maximum of three years, if carer is not working).
Sweden	Years caring for children under age 4 are credited as years with income for notional pension accounts.
United Kingdom	State Pension: credit for non-working carers of their children under age 16 and receiving child benefits. Only time, not income is credited. State Second Pension: credit if receiving child benefits for child under age 6 and having low earnings. Credit of fictitious income is set at GBP 10 800.

Source: Queisser, M. and E. Whitehouse (2005), "The Effects of Partial Careers on Pension Entitlements", Social, Employment and Migration Working Paper, OECD, Paris, forthcoming; and provincial authorities.

and adds it to the existing history. In some countries, such as Finland and Sweden, the credit also includes fictitious earnings in the retirement-income calculations.

A3. Characteristics of compassionate care policies (as per mid-2004)

Table A.7. **Compassionate care and other allowances beyond the child's first year**

	Purpose	Duration of job-protected period	Average benefit (% average earnings)
Canada			
Compassionate care leave	Care of dying family relative	6 weeks	52%
Finland			
Temporary child care leave	Care of sick child until age 10	1 to 4 days per child per illness	Unpaid
Special care allowance	Treatment or rehabilitation of sick child between ages 7 and 16	60 workdays per child per year	12%
Sweden			
Temporary parental leave	Care of sick child under age 12	120 days per child per year	80%
United Kingdom			
Parental leave	Flexible care of child under age 5	13 weeks	Unpaid

Source: National authorities, OECD Secretariat calculations.

Canada

Federal and provincial employment standards in Canada incorporate generally unpaid leave provisions for a serious family illness ranging from 8 to 12 weeks. Furthermore, in 2004, Canada introduced payments for family members taking time off from work to care for gravely ill family members (*e.g.* spouse, common law partner, parent, spouse or common law partner of a parent, child, child of the spouse or common law partner) at risk of dying within 26 weeks. EI payments can be claimed for six weeks during a 26 week period as long as employees reduce their earnings by at least 40% and produce a medical note indicating the gravity of the health condition. Similar to other EI programmes, there is a two-week waiting period. Employees can claim subsequent compassionate care payments as long as they have fulfilled the necessary 600 hours of insurable employment to qualify for the benefit. The basic benefit rate is 55% of average insured earnings or a maximum of CAD 413 per week.

Finland

Working parents are entitled to a temporary childcare leave to care for their sick child below age 10. The temporary leave is for four workdays per illness and is usually unpaid. Parents may divide the leave as desired, but cannot take it simultaneously.

Parents also have the right to be temporarily absent from work for a compelling family reason, which includes illness or accident of a family member or a close relative as well as accidents in the home.

Sweden

The temporary parental cash benefit enables parents to stay at home with their sick child under age 12. The paid leave can be transferred to another person beside the parent staying at the home to care for the child. The benefit period is paid at 80% of qualifying income (same conditions as for parental leave) for 120 days per child per year and can be taken as whole, three-quarters, half, one-quarter or one-eighth days.

United Kingdom

As of December 1999, employees who have one year of service with their employers have a legal entitlement to up to 13 weeks of a "parental leave" to care for a child under age 5. The leave is unpaid, but remains flexible in terms of its use (e.g. first day of school, child sickness, arranging childcare). This non-transferable right is applicable to both parents. Parents and employers usually attempt to find a mutually agreeable solution, but, if that fails, the default parental leave can be taken in one-week units up to a maximum of four weeks per year per child with 21 days notice.

Parents also have the right to unpaid leave for emergencies regarding a dependent family member. While the length of this right is undetermined, it is usually expected to be of short duration to arrange for longer term care or leave, if necessary.

Notes

1. See *www.rrq.gouv.qc.ca/fr/famille/10_01_03.htm.*

2. In the Finnish system, weeks are defined as six "weekdays".

OECD PUBLICATIONS, 2, rue André-Pascal, 75775 PARIS CEDEX 16
PRINTED IN FRANCE
(81 2005 09 1 P) ISBN 92-64-00928-0 – No. 53973 2005